The
PASTORAL EPISTLES

The
PASTORAL EPISTLES

Studies in 1 and 2 Timothy and Titus

By

HOMER A. KENT, JR.

BMH Books
P.O. Box 544
Winona Lake, Indiana 46590

Library of Congress Cataloging in Publication Data

Kent, Homer Austin, 1926-
  The Pastoral Epistles.

  Bibliography: p.
  1. Bible. N.T. Pastoral Epistles—Commentaries.
I. Title.
BS2735.3.K43   1982   227'.83077   81-18873
ISBN 0-8024-6357-6   AACR2

3 4 5 6 7 Printing/LC/Year 87 86 85 84

Printed in the United States of America

To my father,
HOMER AUSTIN KENT
whose pastoral ministry and paternal
counsel have been in the best traditions
of the Pastoral Epistles,
and to my mother,
ALICE WOGAMAN KENT
whose unfeigned faith and loving
labors enriched our Christian home

Contents

PREFACE

THE EPISTLES OF PAUL to Timothy and Titus have gripped my interest and imagination for many years. Not only is the content rich in doctrinal and practical discussion, so pertinent to the Christian life, but the historical, geographical, and personal notices also make the letters colorful and intensely human. Furthermore, these epistles are the only part of the New Testament that deals with church problems from an administrative rather than a theological viewpoint.

During the years in which I taught the course, "The Pastoral Epistles," in Grace Theological Seminary, I have seen the need of a text that will deal adequately with the problems of these letters, and yet be sufficiently readable for every Christian. References to the Greek text are, of course, basic to the study of problem passages. However, the reader limited to English can profit from the exegesis. The extremely literal translation of the epistles has been made by the writer with this twofold audience in mind. If the English rendering seems somewhat rough in places, the Greek student will recognize the original construction that lies behind, and the English reader will be made aware of the actual wording of Paul, not what an Americanized Paul is made to say by the freedom of the translator. Much gratitude is due the students in my classes who have through class discussion and research aided in my labors.

I am indebted to the many scholarly and godly writers both past and present whose efforts have assisted in the molding of opinion. Sincere gratitude is due my colleagues at Grace Theological Seminary, Doctors Herman A. Hoyt, James L. Boyer, and John C. Whitcomb, for their study of the manuscript, and their valuable suggestions regarding the material in chapters 1-4. A special note of appreciation is here expressed to my wife, Beverly, whose patience and encouragement have been beyond measure during the many months of writing.

My studies, conducted with the assistance of those cited above, have given me an even greater admiration for the intrepid apostle. His versatility, his energy and courage, his wise and fatherly counsel in many realms, and his fervent devotion to Christ and His ministry, combine to convince me of the grace of God in granting such a one as a gift to the church (Eph. 4:11).

INTRODUCTION

A LL CHRISTIANS may find in the epistles to Timothy and Titus a practical approach to the Christian life, especially as it relates to their local church. These short letters also have a special appeal for the Christian minister or ministerial student. Many of the practical problems that he faces as a leader of God's people are discussed by the author from the administrator's viewpoint. In some instances, the only scriptural discussion of those problems occurs in these valuable letters.

Yet the attacks leveled against the Pastoral Epistles demand an investigation into the matters of authorship, text, and content. It certainly makes a great difference to a Christian whether these letters were actually written by the apostle Paul to his proteges Timothy and Titus, or whether they were the work of a forger (regardless of his motives) who fabricated them from Pauline fragments, liberally sprinkled with his own ideas. It means the difference between a properly attested portion of Scripture from the pen of Christ's apostle, and an intriguing piece of literature, not quite as trustworthy as the works of Ignatius, Polycarp, Irenaeus, and other second-century writers.

This volume is the outgrowth of extended study into the text and message of the Pastoral Epistles. The views presented have undergone the rigorous test of classroom discussion in Grace Theological Seminary over a period of many years. Chapters 1, 2, 3, and 4, and the appendixes are adapted from my doctoral dissertation, with some of the more technical data simplified, shortened, or eliminated. Most teachers of courses covering the Pastoral Epistles concentrate on 1 Timothy, inasmuch as it provides the bulk of the pastoral material. Also the pressure of time, and the fact that Titus offers some repetition and 2 Timothy more personal references, make this a logical procedure. Therefore, the discussion of 1 Timothy in this volume is more extended, and the shorter treatment of Titus and 2 Timothy may be expanded by the teacher to suit his purpose.

I have made all translations of the Fathers, unless otherwise noted. In chapters 4, 5, and 6, my original translation is in indented paragraphs at the beginning of each discussion. These translations of the text are purposely rough and extremely literal. Only by such a method can the student be provided with the means of properly understanding Paul's thought. The problems of translation being what they are, there is always the danger of undue interpretation infiltrating what purports to be simple translation. Those dangers increase as hopes of providing idiomatic and flowing English are indulged. Thus I have contented myself with extreme literalness, adhering as closely as possible to the Greek word order and mode of expression. The use of transliteration in the exegesis is necessitated by economic factors in publication.

It is my sincere hope that this volume will clarify the issues involved in evaluating the Pastoral Epistles, and that the reader will come to appreciate more intelligently the value of these priceless letters.

1

GENERAL BACKGROUND OF 1 TIMOTHY

AUTHOR

THIS LETTER to a young co-worker claims to have been written by the apostle Paul (1:1), as do 2 Timothy (1:1) and Titus (1:1). From the letter itself several bits of information concerning the whereabouts and plans of the writer are indicated.

Paul must have been at liberty and not imprisoned at the time of writing, since he describes a recent journey and prospects for a visit to Timothy in the near future. Paul had recently made a trip to Macedonia (1:3), instructing his colleague Timothy to care for the work at Ephesus, capital of the province of Asia in Asia Minor. It has been inferred (1:3) that Paul himself had been at Ephesus and had left Timothy there while he went on. However, that is not a necessary inference, since Paul could have given the instruction referred to by letter from any place along the way. But the reference to Paul's action regarding Hymenaeus and Alexander seems to demand that he had been at Ephesus (1:20).

Paul's hope was to make a personal visit to Timothy in

Ephesus very soon (3:14). That plan may still have been in the tentative stage at the time of writing, for he recognized the distinct possibility of a delay in accomplishing his purpose (3:15).

Any delineation of the author of 1 Timothy must take into account the pertinent information contained in 2 Timothy and Titus. It is commonly agreed that all three, which claim to be the work of Paul, are the product of one writer and come from approximately the same period of time. First Timothy and Titus were first, with only a brief interval of time between their composition. It is not absolutely proved that 1 Timothy preceded Titus, but most students feel that such did occur, for the facts can be readily reconstructed if that were the case. Second Timothy was written from a Roman prison with Paul facing imminent death.

In the book of Titus (1:5) Paul reveals a recent visit to the island of Crete, where, upon departing, he had left Titus to guide the church. He also informs Titus of his plan to spend the winter in Nicopolis, probably the city of that name in Epirus, which was in the Roman province of Achaia (3:12).

In 2 Timothy, Paul was writing as a bound prisoner in Rome (1:16, 17; 2:9). He had recently visited Miletus (4:20), Troas (4:13), and perhaps Corinth (4:20).

When the data from all three epistles are collected, one is able to reconstruct several possible itineraries. (See chapter 3, page 50, for a full itinerary compiled from additional sources.) There is not sufficient and compelling data to prove any one itinerary to be the proper one. Many of the stopping points on Paul's program could be reversed in order. To take a dogmatic position regarding his route is obviously unrealistic. It is not a problem of conflicting data, but of insufficient data. The recipients of these epistles had more knowledge of contemporary events and the plans of Paul, which undoubtedly enabled them to fill in any gaps in the history.

The following itinerary is suggested as reasonable and in accord with the facts of 1 and 2 Timothy, and Titus. Other suggestions may be equally reasonable (see map 1, page 21). A full itinerary based on additional sources is constructed in chapter 3.

1. Trip to Crete, leaving Titus to carry on the work (Titus 1:5).
2. Trip into Macedonia, with Timothy instructed to minister at Ephesus (1 Tim. 1:3).
3. A possible visit to Ephesus, fulfilling Paul's intention (1 Tim. 3:14).
4. Winter spent at Nicopolos (Titus 3:12). This is the primary reason for believing 1 Timothy to have preceded Titus, since a visit to Ephesus could hardly have been the next item on Paul's agenda ("shortly") if he planned to winter in Nicopolis. Probably, if the proposed visit to Ephesus did occur it was made just before the letter to Titus was written.
5. Visit to Miletus where Trophimus was left sick (2 Tim. 4:20).
6. Visit to Troas where a cloak and parchments were left (2 Tim. 4:13).
7. Perhaps a visit to Corinth (2 Tim. 4:20).
8. Imprisonment at Rome (2 Tim. 1:16-17).
   The cities Miletus, Troas, Corinth, and Rome suggest the order one would follow en route to Rome. Since we know Rome was the final point reached, the others can be arranged in their geographical order.

DESTINATION

The addressee of the letter was a young man named Timothy, who was described in the greeting as a "genuine child in faith," and in the second letter as a "beloved child." His name appears twenty-four times in the New Testament, and from those occurrences we glean the only reliable information extant concerning him.

Timothy was a native of the Lycaonian city of Lystra (Acts 16:1-2) in Asia Minor. Acts 16:1 does not indicate whether he was from Derbe or Lystra, but the naming of Lystra and Iconium (v. 2) as places where his good reputation was known has led most interpreters to choose Lystra, because it is the city common to both verses. Another reason lending support to Lystra is based on Acts 20:4, where Paul's companions are listed according to their places of residence. In this geographical grouping, Timothy is distinguished from Gaius of Derbe. If he were from Derbe, one would have expected the statement to read "Gaius and Timotheus of Derbe" or "of Derbe, Gaius and Timotheus" in conformity to the other groupings in the list.

His mother Eunice and grandmother Lois were devout Jewesses (Acts 16:1; 2 Tim. 1:5). His father, however, was a Greek, and there is nothing to indicate that he was a Jewish proselyte (Acts 16:1, 3). One would rather suppose that he was not a believer in any sense, since his son had not been circumcised.

Timothy was probably converted on Paul's first journey, since on Paul's second visit he was chosen as his traveling companion. Paul on his first missionary journey preached in Lystra (Acts 14:6-7). Because of the childhood training which Timothy had received in the Scriptures (2 Tim. 3:14, 15), in addition to the example of "unfeigned faith" exhibited in his grandmother and mother, he was prepared for a receptive hearing of the gospel message. Timothy also had opportunity to witness Paul's sufferings for the cause of Christ, since at Lystra occurred the stoning and extraordinary recovery of the apostle (Acts 14). Doubtless those factors all had a part in convincing young Timothy that Jesus was truly his Messiah. Paul claims a spiritual relationship to Timothy, calling him "my child" (1 Cor. 4:17; 2 Tim. 2:1), which may indicate him as the one humanly responsible for his spiritual life, that is, the one who brought about his conversion.

The good reputation in the community of this young convert led Paul to select him as a traveling companion and assistant (Acts 16:1-3). On this second journey Silas had been chosen to take the place of Barnabas, and now Timothy was perhaps to fill the place that John Mark had formerly occupied (see Acts 13:5). Timothy first submitted to circumcision at the hands of Paul to avoid unnecessarily antagonizing the Jews who knew of his pagan father. It should be noted that his circumcision was not for salvation. Timothy was already saved when Paul arrived this time. But his mixed nationality would cause problems. Since he was uncircumcised, Jews regarded him as a gentile, but the gentiles classed him as a Jew because of his religion and his mother. The operation would regularize his status. Furthermore, the writer of Acts explains that that rite was performed as an aid to the work in Jewish areas (Acts 16:3). Otherwise Jewish synagogues would have been closed to him wherever his family background was known. Now he would be able to enter with Paul into the synagogues and take part in the services, bearing his testimony and expounding the Scriptures as they pointed to Christ. It should be clearly understood that circumcision was not performed to make him more acceptable to Christians, but to make him acceptable to Jewish audiences. It was an instance of Paul's principle of expediency (1 Cor. 9:20).

Being set apart for the work of ministry by the laying on of the hands of Paul and the presbytery (1 Tim. 4:14; 2 Tim. 1:6), Timothy joined Paul on the second missionary journey (Acts 16:2-4; 17:14-15; 18:5; 1 Thess. 1:1; 3:2, 6; 2 Thess. 1:1). On this journey he was sent back to Thessalonica to assist the church.

Timothy also was a companion of Paul on the third missionary journey (Acts 19:22; 20:4; 2 Cor. 1:1, 19). At that time he was sent by the apostle on a mission to the church at Corinth to give special instruction (1 Cor. 4:17; 16:10). Later he rejoined Paul and accompanied him back to Corinth, for he sends greetings along with Paul in the epistle to the Romans written from Corinth (Rom. 16:21).

During Paul's first imprisonment at Rome, Timothy was his close companion (Phil. 1:1; Col. 1:1; Philem. 1). Paul purposed to send him on a special mission to Philippi (Phil. 2:19-23). Sometime in his career Timothy was imprisoned, but the time and place are not recorded (Heb. 13:23).

After Paul's release, he sent Timothy to guide the church at Ephesus, and that task seems to have involved a considerable amount of time and responsibility. Timothy was at Ephesus when the first epistle was written to him, and was probably there at the writing of the second epistle also (1 Tim. 1:3; 2 Tim. 1:16-18; 4:19). The church at Ephesus must have been dear to the apostle's heart, for he had stayed longer at Ephesus than at any other center on his journeys (Acts 20:31). Yet the city itself was a focal point of wickedness and thus was greatly in need of the gospel. Archaeologists have unearthed the great temple of Artemis (Latin: Diana) in Ephesus. The temple itself was one of the wonders of the ancient world. The building was 163 feet by 342 feet, and had 117 columns. The roof was covered with large white marble tiles. Brilliant colors, as well as gold, were used to decorate the stonework of the temple. The sacred object within was an image of Artemis. The top part of the image was a woman, carved grotesquely to emphasize the fertility of nature. The lower part was left uncarved, and was merely a rough block of wood. It was reputed to be so ancient, that the tradition arose that it had fallen from heaven (Acts 19:35). Silversmiths in Ephesus had developed a lucrative business by selling small replicas of the shrine as images and souvenirs. The characterization of Ephesus by Shakespeare in his *Comedy of Errors* shows its reputation:

They say this town is full of cozenage,
  As, nimble jugglers that deceive the eye,
Dark-working sorcerers that change the mind,
  Soul-killing witches that deform the body,
Disguised cheaters, prating mountebanks,
  And many such-like libertines of sin.[1]

Thus Timothy's field of labor was not an easy one.

The relationship of the apostle Paul to the younger Timothy is one both beautiful and challenging. That an older man should selflessly love, instruct, and repose confidence in a youth and then continue to exhibit such close companionship for approximately twenty years is surely admirable. For a young man to respond with similar respect, confidence, and heartfelt admiration without jealousy, impatience, or resentment is equally commendable. The relationship of the two men is a remarkable display of Christian virtues at their best.

The function Timothy fulfilled in the early church should not be confused with the present-day pastor. Rather, in those formative days of the church he seems to have been one of several who helped to carry out the transition from the times of the apostles to the post-Apostolic era of the church. In the beginnings of the church, the authority of the apostles brought into being the church, and served to guide and instruct it. Although it seems clear that from the beginning local churches were congregationally controlled, still the influence of the apostles was strong. Timothy, therefore, was an apostolic representative. He exercised the guidance and counseling ministry that Paul would have performed had he been present. Titus occupied a similar position (Titus 1:5). Thus it is probably not correct to visualize Timothy as the pastor of the local Christian church at Ephesus. Rather, he was Paul's official delegate to assist the Ephesian church with its officials in conducting affairs in the proper manner.

OCCASION

The designation "Pastoral Epistles" is appropriate for

the letters to Timothy and Titus because they contain instruction for pastoral work in churches.

First Timothy was written to the young minister at Ephesus because of a possible delay in Paul's arrival (3:14). During his absence, which might be prolonged, Timothy needed the instructions only the apostle Paul, with his great experience and revelations from the Lord, could give. Thus 1 Timothy contains advice on specific matters of church polity. Timothy is urged to enforce the teaching of sound doctrine, to see that meetings are conducted orderly and scripturally. He is to insure that church officers are sufficiently qualified, and that they be motivated by spiritual considerations rather than a desire for worldly prestige or gain. The letter also took occasion to warn of the danger presented by false teachers, who in spite of claims of wisdom and learning in the Mosaic Law were actually hypocrites, motivated by demonic powers.

Although 1 Timothy is a personal letter addressed to one individual, it is also official rather than private. The contents were not meant for Timothy alone, but were for the edification of all the church. Thus we find such expressions in the letter as, "These things command and teach" (4:11). The epistle deals with church matters, not just personal matters. Hence 1 Timothy and the other pastorals were included in the canon from the start.

It is possible that the young minister Timothy was of a timid, retiring disposition, and frail health, who needed encouragement. Several passages may indicate this.

> Let no man despise thy youth, but be thou an example of the believers, in word, in conversation, in charity, in spirit, in faith, in purity (4:12).

> Neglect not the gift that is in thee (4:14).

> Meditate upon these things; give thyself wholly to them; that thy profiting may appear to all. Take heed unto thyself, and unto the doctrine; continue in them: for in doing this thou shalt both save thyself, and them that hear thee (4:15, 16).

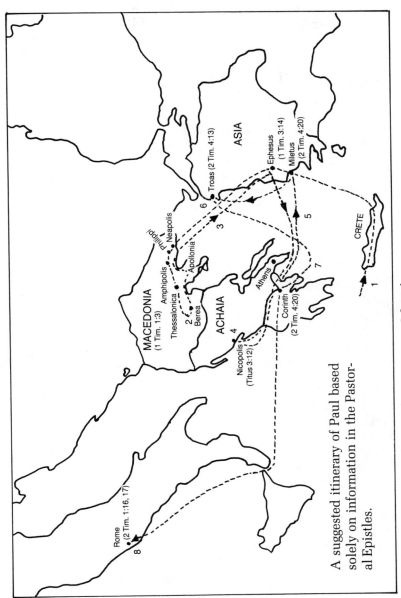

MACEDONIA
(1 Tim. 1:3)

Philippi
Neapolis
Amphipolis
Thessalonica
Apollonia
Berea

ACHAIA

Athens

Corinth
(2 Tim. 4:20)

Nicopolis
(Titus 3:12)

ASIA

Troas (2 Tim. 4:13)

Ephesus
(1 Tim. 3:14)
Miletus
(2 Tim. 4:20)

CRETE

Rome
(2 Tim. 1:16, 17)

A suggested itinerary of Paul based
solely on information in the Pastoral Epistles.

Map 1

Drink no longer water, but use a little wine for thy stomach's sake and thine often infirmities (5:23).

However, this is in no way to be understood as a disparagement of Timothy, and may be an unwarranted inference. All ministers need encouragement from time to time. Every servant of God needs constantly to exercise his gifts, to meditate on the Word, and to concern himself with setting a proper example before the believers entrusted to his care. The more I have studied these Pastoral Epistles, the less convinced I have become of Timothy's timidity. The tremendous confidence Paul reposed in Timothy, sending him to this most important field, reveals him to have been worthy to some degree at least of the title "man of God" that Paul uses of him (1 Tim. 6:11).

DATE

The dating of 1 Timothy depends on the solution of the great chronological problem of the Pastoral Epistles. Must we find room for these epistles somewhere in the period covered by the book of Acts, on the assumption that Paul died as a result of the first Roman imprisonment? Or may we safely assume a release and then a second imprisonment? This problem is dealt with fully in chapter 3. At this point, however, it can be said that the Pastoral Epistles cannot be fitted into the framework of Acts without making some of the historical references impossible of harmonization. On the other hand, assuming the release of Paul in A.D. 62 after the two years of the first imprisonment, and a trip to the East, particularly Macedonia (1 Tim. 1:3), it is likely that 1 Timothy was written during the years A.D. 62 or 63. Other chronologies may differ slightly because of variation in dating the release from A.D. 60 to 63.

NOTES

[1]J. Payne Collier, *The Complete Works of William Shakespeare* (New York: World Syndicate, 1925), p. 89.

2

HISTORICAL TESTIMONY TO THE AUTHORSHIP OF 1 TIMOTHY

IN STUDYING ANY ITEM from the past, whether it be an ancient city, a battle, or a piece of literature, it is always pertinent to consider the opinions and observations of those who lived contemporaneously, or in proximity to the object under study. To assess 1 Timothy with its proper value, the student must listen to the voice of history, especially that segment of history from the opening centuries of the Christian era. From such sources, emanating from years so close to the purported time of writing of 1 Timothy, it should be possible to ascertain the conclusions of men who were in a much better position than we today to know the facts. Following is the more obvious external evidence to the existence and authorship of 1 Timothy. This writer has not endeavored to include all possible allusions that conceivably show an acquaintance with this epistle, but has proceeded on the basis that a few clear and undeniable evidences are worth more than a multiplicity of questionable ones. Of course, the similarity of the quotations to the text of 1 Timothy is more clearly seen when the Greek texts of both are compared. The writer has endeavored to demonstrate the similarity by a very literal translation of each.

A. EVIDENCE OF ACQUAINTANCE WITH AND ACCEPTANCE OF 1 TIMOTHY

CLEMENT OF ROME

First Epistle to the Corinthians (A.D. 95)

Section xxxvii.

Let us wage war therefore, men brethren, with all earnestness in his blameless command.[1]

To this should be compared 1 Timothy 1:18:

... in accord with the prophecies which led forward upon you, in order that you wage war in them the good warfare.

Clement is not making an attempt to quote 1 Timothy, but he does seem indebted to the literary figure and vocabulary employed there. The same verb is used to create the figure of warfare, and in both cases the warfare is to be conducted in accordance with divine orders or prophecy. In view of the fact that Clement of Rome makes such allusions repeatedly, it is not rash to suggest that he had a thorough acquaintance with the Pastoral Epistles.

Section xxix.

Let us therefore come to him in holiness of life, lifting up to him pure and undefiled hands.[2]

Compare 1 Timothy 2:8:

I wish therefore the men to pray in every place, lifting up holy hands.

Other instances in Clement's epistle showing literary acquaintance with 1 Timothy make allusions to the following passages, listed by White:[3] 1 Timothy 6:1; 5:17; 2:9, 11; 6:8; 6:12; 2:3-4; 3:10; 1:17.

IGNATIUS

Epistle to Polycarp (c. A.D. 110)

Section iv.

Men slaves and female slaves not proud: but neither let them be puffed up, let them serve more unto God's glory.[4]

Compare the text of 1 Timothy 6:1, 2:

As many as are slaves under yoke . . . in order that the name of God and the teaching be not blasphemed . . . let them not despise . . . but let them serve more.

Section iii.

The ones seeming to be trustworthy and teaching that which is different, let them not browbeat you.[5]

Compare 1 Timothy 1:3; 6:3:

. . . that you charge some not to teach that which is different. . . . If anyone teaches that which is different and does not come to the healthful words of our Lord Jesus Christ. . . .

Ignatius reflects familiarity with 2 Timothy and Titus also. In the *Epistle to Polycarp* he employs the method of 1 Timothy in giving advice to the church in general, as well as addressing much of its contents to Polycarp personally.

POLYCARP

Epistle to the Philippians (c. A.D. 110)

Section iv.

But the beginning of all troublesome things is the love of money. Knowing therefore that we brought nothing into the world, but neither have we anything to carry out, let us arm ourselves with the arms of righteousness.[6]

Compare 1 Timothy 6:7, 10:

For we brought nothing into the world because neither

are we able to carry anything out . . . for a root of all the
evil things is the love of money.

Section viii.

Unceasingly therefore let us adhere constantly to our
hope . . . which is Christ Jesus.[7]

Compare 1 Timothy 1:1:

Paul, apostle of Christ Jesus according to command of
God our Saviour and Christ Jesus our hope.

Section xii.

Pray ye also in behalf of kings and authorities and rulers and in behalf of the ones persecuting and hating
you, and in behalf of the enemies of the cross, in order
that your fruit may be manifest among all, in order that
ye may be perfect in him.[8]

Compare 1 Timothy 2:2; 4:15:

Prayers . . . in behalf of kings and all who are in
authority. . . . In order that thy progress may be manifest to all.

The testimony of Polycarp's letter is probably the
strongest and clearest evidence that the Pastoral Epistles
were extant in his day, and were familiar to him. If there
had been any question of forgery or other fraud in their
composition, it is exceedingly doubtful that Polycarp
would have cited them so clearly without apology or explanation. The comment of Newport J. D. White is pertinent:

> There can be no question that in the Letter of Poly-
> carp to the Philippians we have express citations from I
> and II Timothy. It is, to say the least, difficult to believe
> that a man like Polycarp, who had been a disciple of the
> Apostle John, and who, when he wrote this letter, was
> bishop of Smyrna and in full vigor of life, would have
> made such honourable use of letters which had been
> compiled by an unknown Paulinist a few years before.
> We regard the evidence of Polycarp as a fact of capital
> importance; for it removes any possible doubt that may

hang over inferences drawn from Ignatius; and it supports us in our belief that the Pastoral Epistles were also known to Clement of Rome.[9]

The Acts of the Martyrdom of Polycarp
(A.D. 115 or 156)

Section x.

For we have been taught to render honor to rulers and authorities appointed by God, according to that which is fitting, which is not hurting us.[10]

Compare 1 Timothy 2:2:

Prayers . . . in behalf of kings and all who are in authority.

It may be objected that this allusion is too general and could be an allusion to ideas found in other epistles. The writer readily admits this, but in view of the unmistakable evidence in Polycarp's "Letter to the Philippians" showing the existence of I Timothy, it may at least be suggested that the allusion is to 1 Timothy.

THE SO-CALLED Second Epistle of Clement of Rome to the Corinthians (c. A.D. 120-140)

Section viii.

Keep ye the flesh pure and the seal spotless, in order that we may receive the life.[11]

Compare 1 Timothy 6:14, 12, 19:

That you keep the commandment spotless, irreproachable. . . .
Take hold upon the eternal life.
That they might take hold of the real life.

Section xx.

To the only God invisible . . . to him the glory forever and ever. Amen.[12]

Compare 1 Timothy 1:17:

But to the king of the ages, incorruptible, invisible, only God, honor and glory forever and ever. Amen.

Though it seems assured that this epistle was not written by Clement of Rome, its early date is not generally disputed. And it is as a witness to the text of 1 Timothy that it claims our attention. The allusions to the phrases of the Pastorals seem very clear. The same value is seen in the other epistles whose actual authors are still unknown.

THE SO-CALLED *Epistle of Barnabas*
(A.D. 70-132)

Section xii.

The transgression came in Eve through the serpent.[13]

Compare 1 Timothy 2:14:

And Adam was not deceived, but the woman having been completely deceived has become in transgression.

Section xii.

The Son of God . . . manifested in flesh.[14]

Compare 1 Timothy 3:16:

He who was manifested in flesh.

The Epistle to Diognetus (c. A.D. 150.)

Section iv.

But the mystery of their own godliness do not expect to be able to learn from man.[15]

Compare 1 Timothy 3:16:

And confessedly, great is the mystery of godliness.

JUSTIN MARTYR
Dialogue with Trypho, a Jew (c. A.D. 140)

Section vii.

They glorify the spirits and demons of error.[16]

Compare 1 Timothy 4:1:

Giving heed to deceiving spirits and teachings of demons.

Section xxxv.

Out of such are men, confessing themselves to be Christians and . . . to confess Jesus . . . Christ, and not teaching the doctrines of that one but those from the spirits of error.[17]

Compare also 1 Timothy 4:1, as above.

ATHENAGORAS, *A Plea for the Christians*
(*c.* A.D. 176)

Section xvi.

For God is himself all things to himself, light unapproachable.[18]

Compare 1 Timothy 6:16:

The only one having immortality, dwelling in light unapproachable.

Section xxxvii.

But this is also to us, that we may lead a peaceable and quiet life.[19]

Compare 1 Timothy 2:2:

That we may lead a peaceable and quiet life.

The Epistles of the Churches of Vienne and Lyons
(*c.* A.D. 180)

The wrath fell . . . on Attalus, of Pergamus by race, one having been always a pillar and support of the ones there.[20]

Compare 1 Timothy 3:15:

Which is the church of the living God, the pillar and support of the truth.

But Pothinus . . . was being dragged before the judgment seat . . . as himself being Christ, he was giving the good testimony.[21]

Compare 1 Timothy 6:13:

Christ Jesus who testified before Pontius Pilate the good confession.

Alcibiades, not using the creatures of God . . . but Alcibiades having been persuaded of all things was freely partaking and giving thanks to God.[22]

Compare 1 Timothy 4:3-4:

Forbidding to marry, to abstain from foods, which things God created for partaking with thanksgiving by those who believe and have full knowledge of the truth. Because every created thing of God is good and nothing to be cast away, being received with thanksgiving.

THEOPHILUS OF ANTIOCH TO AUTOLYCUS (c. A.D. 181)

Book III, Chapter xiv.

Moreover concerning being subject to rulers and authorities and praying on behalf of them, the divine word commands us, in order that we may lead a peaceable and quiet life.[23]

Compare 1 Timothy 2:2:

Prayers . . . in behalf of kings and all those who are in authority, in order that we may lead a peaceable and quiet life.

In this citation the reference is unmistakable. There is no question of mere coincidence, for Theophilus clearly and consciously makes reference to a portion of recognized Scripture.

HEGESIPPUS (A.D. 170)

Memoirs: Concerning the Martyrdom of Symeon

But when the sacred band of apostles had in various ways closed their lives, and that generation of men to whom it had been vouchsafed to listen to the Godlike Wisdom with their own ears had passed away, then did the confederacy of godless error take its rise through the treachery of false teachers, who seeing that none of the apostles any longer survived, at length attempted with bare and uplifted head to oppose the preaching of the truth by preaching "knowledge falsely so-called."[24]

Compare 1 Timothy 6:3, 20:

> If anyone teaches that which is different and does not come to healthful words of our Lord Jesus Christ and the teaching which is according to godliness . . . oppositions of the falsely-named knowledge.

CLEMENT OF ALEXANDRIA (ca. A.D. 155-215)

Stromata

Book II, Chapter vi.

> As the apostle also says . . . "This charge," he says, "I commit to thee, son Timothy, according to the prophecies which went before on thee, that thou mightest war the good warfare; holding faith, and a good conscience; which some having put away concerning faith have made shipwreck."[25]

It will be readily recognized that this is a direct quotation of 1 Timothy 1:18-19, which he attributes to "the apostle." Clement of Alexandria makes numerous other citations of this nature from 1 Timothy, showing his ready acceptance of it as the work of Paul, and revealing his readers' similar knowledge.

TERTULLIAN (c. A.D. 150-222)

On Prescription Against Heretics. Chapter xxv.

> Paul addressed even this expression to Timothy: "O Timothy, guard that which is entrusted to thee"; and again: "That good thing which was committed unto thee keep." What is this deposit? Is it so secret as to be supposed to characterize a new doctrine? Or is it a part of that charge of which he says, "This charge I commit unto thee, son Timothy"? and also of that precept of which he says, "I charge thee in the sight of God, who quickeneth all things, and before Jesus Christ, who witnessed a good confession under Pontius Pilate, that thou keep this commandment"?[26]

The direct citing of 1 Timothy 6:20; 1:18, and 6:13 is obvious, and the attributing of them to Paul is the significant fact for our purpose. Numerous other references in the writings of Tertullian could be mentioned.

Irenaeus (ca. a.d. 140-203)

Against Heresies

Preface, Section i.

> Inasmuch as certain men have set the truth aside, and bring in lying words and vain genealogies, which, as the apostle, says, "minister questions rather than godly edifying which is in faith" . . .[27]

Here Irenaeus has quoted 1 Timothy 1:4.

Book II, Chapter xiv, Section vii.

> And Paul well says (of them, that they make use of) "novelties of words of false knowledge."[28]

There is an obscurity in the text here, but the citation from Paul is obviously from 1 Timothy 6:20: "the profane, empty talk and oppositions of the falsely-named knowledge."

There are many other citations from 1 Timothy and the other Pastorals in the writings of Irenaeus.

Muratorian Canon (c. a.d. 170)

This fragment, discovered in the Ambrosian Library at Milan (in 1740) contains a list of accepted New Testament books, and the following statement is included:

> An Epistle to Titus, and two to Timothy, which, though written only from personal feeling and affection are still hallowed in the respect of the Catholic Church, and in the arrangement of ecclesiastical discipline.[29]

Old Latin Version (before a.d. 170)

This early translation of the Greek Testament into Latin contained thirteen epistles of Paul, including the Pastorals.

EUSEBIUS (A.D. 265-340)

This early historian divided the New Testament books into acknowledged ones (homologoumena) and disputed ones (antilegomena). Here is his statement:

> But now that we have reached this point, it is reasonable to sum up the writings of the New Testament already mentioned. Well then, we must set in the first place the holy quaternion of the Gospels; which are followed by the book of the Acts of the Apostles. After this we must reckon the epistles of Paul; following which we must pronounce genuine the extant former epistle of John, and likewise the epistle of Peter. After these we must place, if it really seem right, the Apocalypse of John, the views that have been held as to which we shall set forth at the proper time. These, then (are to be placed) among the acknowledged writings. But of those which are disputed, nevertheless familiar to the majority, there is extant the epistle of James, as it is called; and that of Jude; and the second epistle of Peter; and the second and third of John, so named, whether they belong to the evangelist or perhaps to some other of the same name as he.[30]

Eusebius thus places the Pastorals among the accepted epistles of Paul, rather than among the disputed books.

PESHITTA-SYRIAC VERSION (A.D. 411-435)

Formerly this version was dated around 170, but today it is not generally believed that the present form of the Peshitta came into being before the fifth century. This version contains the Pastoral Epistles.

More names could be listed almost without end showing approval of the Pastoral Epistles. They appear in all the great manuscripts and versions. The foregoing are merely the earliest and thus the most significant.

B. EVIDENCE OF THE REJECTION OF 1 TIMOTHY

In the early centuries the only writers known to us who

rejected some or all of the Pastoral Epistles were certain Gnostic heretics. In most cases we are indebted to orthodox church writers for a description of these heretics' opinions.

BASILIDES (A.D. 130)

This Gnostic heretic came under attack by many of the early Christian writers. Jerome accused him of rejecting the Pastoral Epistles as Pauline.[31] Clement of Alexandria, in a treatise in *The Stromata* refuting Basilides and other Gnostics by name, makes this statement:

> As then philosophy has been brought into evil repute by pride and self-conceit, so also gnosis by false gnosis called by the same name; of which the apostle writing says, "O Timothy, keep that which is committed to thy trust, avoiding the profane and vain babblings and oppositions of science (*gnōsis*) falsely so-called; which some professing, have erred concerning the faith." Convicted by this utterance, the heretics reject the Epistles to Timothy.[32]

Thus Clement explains the Gnostic attitude to have been provoked by their dislike of 1 Timothy 6:20.

MARCION (A.D. 140)

This Gnostic writer produced a canon of New Testament books composed of the Gospel of Luke and ten of Paul's epistles, omitting all three of the Pastorals. Tertullian states in Book V of his work *Against Marcion:*

> I wonder, however, when he received (into his Apostolicon) this letter which was written but to one man (i.e., Philemon), that he rejected the two epistles to Timothy and the one to Titus, which all treat of ecclesiastical discipline.[33]

Another comment of Tertullian is most enlightening, showing that the purpose of Marcion dictated his rejection of the pastorals, and not any intellectual doubt as to their genuineness.

One man perverts the Scriptures with his hand, another their meaning by his exposition. For although Valentinus seems to use the entire volume, he has none the less laid violent hands on the truth only with a more cunning mind and skill than Marcion. Marcion expressly and openly used the knife, not the pen, since he made such an exposition of the Scriptures as suited his own subject matter.[34]

TATIAN (A.D. 170)

This disciple of Justin produced the *Diatessaron*, or first harmony of the gospels. In his later years he joined a monastic group and became heretical. Some of the New Testament books he rejected, although he did not go as far as Marcion. We are indebted to the statement of Jerome (*ca.* A.D. 340-420) that Tatian rejected 1 and 2 Timothy but retained Titus.

Tatian, the patriarch of the Encratites, who himself rejected some of Paul's Epistles, believed this especially, that is (addressed) to Titus, ought to be declared to be the apostle's, thinking little of the assertion of Marcion and others who agree with him on this point.[35]

It was the firm opinion of the early church that the rejection by heretics of the various portions of the New Testament was due to the nature of the subject matter, rather than to any critical arguments concerning authorship, date, and style. The Gnostics rejected those books that did not fit their system. Therefore, the rejection by these men does not constitute an argument against their genuineness as Pauline letters. Rather, it indicates that the orthodox opinion of the church was not one maintained without study, but was held in spite of attack by heretics.

MODERN CRITICAL REJECTION

The term "modern" is used because of the comparatively recent appearance of this viewpoint in relation to the Gnostic heretics of the early church. Only the earliest and outstanding writers will be mentioned, as they are largely responsible for shaping modern thought.

J. E. C. Schmidt (1804) and Schliermacher (1807) began the attack by rejecting 1 Timothy, suggesting that it had been fabricated out of the previously existing 2 Timothy and Titus which were genuine. The basis of criticism was the internal evidence, especially the peculiarities of 1 Timothy.

Eichhorn (1752-1826) and DeWette (1780-1849) took the arguments that had been directed against 1 Timothy and applied them to all three of the Pastoral Epistles, arguing that none of them was the work of Paul.

F. C. Baur (1792-1860), founder of the Tübingen School, held that the Pastorals were written after the middle of the second century, during the Marcionite heresy. The unknown author thought he could accomplish more for the cause of Paul's epistles by putting his attack on the Gnostics into the mouth of Paul. This view of Baur has met much opposition, even among liberal scholars.

The foregoing scholars established the trend, and many follow their leading today. The specific items of criticism are discussed in chapter 3.

C. Summary and Conclusion of the Historical Evidence

The foregoing material has shown abundant evidence for the existence and acceptance of 1 Timothy. To the reader of the writings of the early Fathers, it is obvious that 1 Timothy is referred to by allusion or direct citation with as much frequency as the other New Testament books. The earliest clear reference is probably Polycarp's *Epistle to the Philippians*, but it is not an isolated case. The frequent allusions to 1 Timothy by other contemporaries of Polycarp indicate the widespread recognition of 1 Timothy by the church, there being no need to argue for its inclusion in the canon.

Furthermore, the unanimity of the early historical testimony is significant. First Timothy was never classed among the disputed books (antilegomena) in the days of the canon's formation. The only dissenting voices were the Gnostic heretics whose heresy was on other grounds. Those men, particularly Basilides, Marcion, and Tatian, having taken their doctrinal position, proceeded to discount any portions of Scripture that did violence to their teaching. For this reason, said Clement of Alexandria and Tertullian, 1 Timothy was rejected by them. However, this circumstance does not injure the historicity of 1 Timothy, for the problems created by those heretics focused attention on all the Pastoral Epistles and caused them to be studied carefully in order to be defended. Thus the unanimity of orthodox opinion was the result of scholarly investigation. This opinion prevailed from the first century until the beginning of the nineteenth century.

Finally, the modern critical rejection of 1 Timothy, dating from the year 1804, is based not on information gained externally, but upon internal considerations. The testimony of the early church remains unshaken. No support for rejection of the genuineness of the epistle can be obtained from any orthodox writer of Ante-Nicene days. All modern attacks, therefore, have been based upon internal grounds. The epistle itself has been analyzed, and from such analysis the contents have been thought to preclude Pauline authorship. An investigation into these internal objections constitutes the subject of chapter 3.

NOTES

[1]Translated by the writer from J. B. Lightfoot, *The Apostolic Fathers* (London: Macmillan, 1890), 2:113.
[2]*Ibid.*, p. 93.
[3]N. J. D. White, "The First and Second Epistles to Timothy." *The Expositor's Greek Testament*, ed. W. Robertson Nicoll (Grand Rapids: Eerdmans, n.d.), 4:76-77.
[4]Lightfoot, 3:230.
[5]*Ibid.*, p. 229.
[6]*Ibid.*, p. 328.
[7]*Ibid.*, p. 336.

[8]*Ibid.*, pp. 346-47.
[9]White, *op. cit.*, p. 79.
[10]Lightfoot, 3:381.
[11]*Ibid.*, 2:228.
[12]*Ibid.*, pp. 260-61.
[13]White, p. 79.
[14]*Ibid.*
[15]*Ibid.*, p. 80.
[16]*Ibid.*
[17]*Ibid.*
[18]*Ibid.*
[19]*Ibid.*
[20]*Ibid.*
[21]*Ibid.*, p. 81.
[22]*Ibid.*
[23]*Ibid.*
[24]English translation given in Hegesippus *Commentaries on the Acts of the Church*, *The Ante-Nicene Fathers*, ed. by Alexander Roberts and James Donaldson (reprint ed., Grand Rapids: Eerdmans, 1951), 8:764.
[25]English translation given in Clement *The Stromata*, *The Ante-Nicene Fathers*, ed. by Alexander Roberts and James Donaldson (Grand Rapids: Eerdmans, reprinted 1951), 2:354.
[26]English translation given in Tertullian *On Prescription against Heretics*, *The Ante-Nicene Fathers*, ed. by Alexander Roberts and James Donaldson (Grand Rapids: Eerdmans, 1951), 3:255.
[27]English translation given in Irenaeus *Against Heresies*, *The Ante-Nicene Fathers*, ed. by Alexander Roberts and James Donaldson (Grand Rapids: Eerdmans, 1951), 1:315.
[28]*Ibid.*, p. 378.
[29]Quoted by H. D. M. Spence, "The Pastoral Epistles of St. Paul," *Ellicott's Commentary on the Whole Bible* (Grand Rapids: Zondervan, n.d.), 8:171.
[30]Eusebius *The Ecclesiastical History and the Martyrs of Palestine*, trans. Hugh J. Lawlor and John E. L. Oulton (London: Society for Promoting Christian Knowledge, 1927), 1:86-87. Used with permission of the Macmillan Company, New York, which handles this volume in U.S.A.
[31]Alexander Roberts and James Donaldson (eds.), *The Ante-Nicene Fathers* (Grand Rapids: Eerdmans, 1951), 2:380.
[32]English translation given in Clement, *The Stromata*, *op. cit.*, p. 359.
[33]English translation given in Tertullian, *Against Marcion*, *The Ante-Nicene Fathers*, ed. by Alexander Roberts and James Donaldson (Grand Rapids: Eerdmans, 1951), 3:473.
[34]English translation given in Tertullian, *On Prescription against Heretics*, *The Ante-Nicene Fathers*, ed. by Alexander Roberts and James Donaldson (Grand Rapids: Eerdmans, 1951), 3:262.
[35]English translation given in Jerome, *Prolegomena ad Titum*, *The Ante-Nicene Fathers*, ed. by Alexander Roberts and James Donaldson (Grand Rapids: Eerdmans, 1951), 2:83.

3

PROBLEMS OF PAULINE AUTHORSHIP
OF 1 TIMOTHY

THOUGH ORTHODOX CHRISTIANITY held unwaveringly for eighteen centuries to the Pauline authorship of the Pastoral Epistles, subsequent investigation has raised problems which must be studied. All modern doubt or outright rejection of these letters as Pauline is based upon one or more of five problems. These problems are stated and answered. In the light of overwhelming historical testimony to the genuineness of 1 Timothy (and all the Pastorals), the investigator has upon himself the burden of proof if he wishes to disprove Pauline authorship. If it can be shown that there is a reasonable explanation for the problems, which will allow Pauline authorship and thus be in agreement with the centuries-old testimony of the early church, then the genuineness of 1 Timothy is vindicated. Merely to raise questions and suggest other possibilities, meanwhile disregarding the significant voice of history, is too subjective a basis for rejecting the historicity of a document.

The five problems are:

1. Chronological Setting.
2. Ecclesiastical Complexity.
3. Doctrinal Viewpoint.
4. Heretical Opposition.
5. Linguistic Peculiarities

These problems are considered in the order listed.

CHRONOLOGICAL SETTING

The Statement of the Problem

It is impossible to fit the writing of the epistles to Timothy and Titus in the chronological framework provided by the book of Acts. If we must assume, as rejecters of Pauline authorship of the Pastorals do, that the closing lines of Acts mark the end of Paul's life, then we are at a loss to fit these letters into Acts without causing violent contradictions between some of the historical data mentioned. If the imprisonment with its impending death, which Paul was experiencing while writing 2 Timothy (1:16-17; 2:9; 4:6), was the Roman imprisonment of Acts 28, then 1 Timothy and Titus must have been written at some earlier time in Paul's ministry, while he was still at liberty. Yet careful study reveals that to be impossible.

The Examination of the Evidence

Evidence is gleaned from four sources, which must be considered individually before a final solution is attempted.

The Pastoral Epistles. Paul was in prison at the time of writing 2 Timothy, and was in imminent danger of execution (4:6). First Timothy and Titus, however, were written in happier circumstances. Paul was at liberty, traveling in Macedonia and Crete, and had visited such places as Troas and Miletus before being imprisoned. Is it possible to fit all of this information into the structure of Acts? If the liberty demanded for the writing of 1 Timothy and Titus be prior to the two-year Roman imprisonment of

Acts 28, then it must also be prior to the arrest and cap-
ture in Jerusalem and the two-year detention in Caesarea
(Acts 21-27), for there were no intervals between. Paul's
relationship to Timothy began on his second journey and
was also maintained on his third journey. On his second
journey Paul stayed very briefly in Ephesus at his first
visit (Acts 18:19-22), and departed for Jerusalem and
Antioch, not to Macedonia (*contra.* 1 Tim. 1:3).

On Paul's third journey, he stayed at Ephesus for three
years (Acts 20:31), and then departed for Macedonia
(Acts 20:1). Timothy was one of his companions on this
journey, at least the latter stages of it (Acts 20:4). This
would make the statement: "These things write I unto
thee, hoping to come unto thee shortly" (1 Tim. 3:14), a
curious one indeed, since Timothy would be rejoining
Paul before he ever reached Ephesus again. Furthermore,
the tasks Paul enjoined upon Timothy in the first epistle
are ones that would demand or at least assume a ministry
of considerable duration. Timothy could not quickly fulfill them and then join Paul in Macedonia.

The Book of Acts. Some material in Acts has been considered in the previous section, merely however as a
check against the statements of 1 Timothy. Now it is necessary to discover what positive evidence Acts can provide.

The closing words of the book are more significant:

> And Paul dwelt two whole years in his own hired
> house, and received all that came in unto him, preach-
> ing the kingdom of God, and teaching those things
> which concern the Lord Jesus Christ, with all confi-
> dence, no man forbidding him (Acts 28:30-31).

What can be concluded from this statement? Some
assume that at the end of the two years, Paul died. Others
assert that he was set free. It should be clearly understood
that both viewpoints are hypothetical. Acts states neither
one. Hence we must conclude that the book of Acts is
incomplete regarding the life of Paul. The author

apparently wished to cover Paul's life up to the Roman imprisonment. Having fulfilled his purpose, and also having now produced a lengthy scroll, he concluded his work. (The opinion of Sir William Ramsay, based on the use of the superlative *ton prōton logon*, "the first account" in 1:1, that Luke contemplated a third volume on the later life of Paul, is interesting but is based on what is probably a too specific inference from the grammar.)[1]

Since whatever inference is drawn must remain hypothetical, as far as Acts is concerned, is either one of the hypotheses more likely than the other? Two factors relating to Acts make the weight of probability rest on the side of a release from imprisonment. First, the book of Acts contains no charge against Paul which would cause his continued imprisonment when the case finally came up for disposal. When Paul was under detention in Caesarea, with no charge filed against him, the governor Festus said of him to Agrippa:

> Of whom I have no certain thing to write unto my lord. Wherefore I have brought him forth before you, and specially before thee, O king Agrippa, that, after examination had, I might have somewhat to write. For it seemeth to me unreasonable to send a prisoner, and not withal to signify the crimes laid against him (Acts 25:26-27).

At the conclusion of this hearing before Agrippa, the innocence of Paul was restated:

> And when they were gone aside, they talked between themselves, saying, This man doeth nothing worthy of death or of bonds. Then said Agrippa unto Festus, This man might have been set at liberty if he had not appealed unto Caesar (Acts 26:31-32).

That was followed by the voyage to Rome and the awaiting of the hearing before Caesar's tribunal. Paul had appealed to Caesar in order to obtain justice, and since there was no charge against him worthy of death or imprisonment, he must have expected release. That is the impression left by the book of Acts.

The second factor lending weight to the probability of Paul's release is the unlikelihood of Acts' ending as it does if Paul had been executed. If Paul, the main character in the last half of the book, had died after the two-year imprisonment in Rome, then the failure of Luke to correct the impression of impending release he had fostered is unexplainable. Thus although Acts does not state release or execution, the testimony of the book itself lends more weight to the hypothesis of release than to that of execution.

A problem appears in Acts 20:25, where at the conclusion of Paul's third journey, he tearfully bids farewell to the Ephesian elders at Miletus, with this statement: "I know that ye all, among whom I have gone preaching the kingdom of God, shall see my face no more." Does that preclude any future visits to Ephesus? The question is whether or not the statement is a prophecy or a reflection of Paul's feelings at that time. I believe that the latter is the case. In view of the Spirit's revelation as to the sufferings to befall him, he held out no hope of seeing them all again. Two other plausible explanations may be given to this verse. The use of *pantes* (all) emphasizes the fact that the whole group would not see him again. This was probably true, even if Paul did visit Ephesus five or six years later. Some of that group of elders may have died by that time. The probability of the group remaining exactly intact is small. Many a pastor, on leaving a pastorate, has stated his regret that he would not see them all again, even though he might return at a later time. The composition of the group at a later date would not be exactly the same. Another explanation of the verse is that Paul never did visit Ephesus again, even though assuming the genuineness of 1 Timothy. There is no evidence that absolutely demands a personal visit. It is possible that his intention (1 Tim. 3:14) went unrealized, and the delivery unto

Satan of Hymenaeus and Alexander does not necessarily demand Paul's personal presence in Ephesus.

Paul's Epistles. Four of Paul's epistles are acknowledged to have been written during the Roman imprisonment of Acts 28—Ephesians, Philippians, Colossians, and Philemon. In two of those there are statements pertinent to the problem.

> For I am in a strait betwixt two, having a desire to depart, and to be with Christ, which is far better; nevertheless to abide in the flesh is more needful for you. And having this confidence, I know that I shall abide and continue with you all for your furtherance and joy of faith (Phil. 1:23-25).

> But I trust in the Lord that I also myself shall come shortly (Phil 2:24).

> But withal prepare me also a lodging; for I trust that through your prayers I shall be given unto you (Philem. 22).

In each of those statements Paul indicates a confidence of release, a confidence that is totally lacking in 2 Timothy. Those expectations of Paul, coupled with the historical antecedents to Paul's case already seen in Acts, lend their weight on the side of a release from the first Roman imprisonment.

One further reference in another epistle must be mentioned.

> Whensoever I take my journey into Spain, I will come to you: for I trust to see you in my journey, and to be brought on my way thitherward by you, if first I be somewhat filled with your company (Rom. 15:24).

The epistle to the Romans was written on Paul's third journey before he had ever visited Rome. At that time he planned a trip to Spain. An examination of the record in Acts shows that the trip to Spain did not materialize as Paul planned, since he was arrested at the end of this journey and ultimately was sent to Rome as a prisoner.

From this one Scripture reference we cannot know how strong Paul's intention was to visit Spain. If it was extremely important to him, then it is difficult to see how he could write, "I have finished the course" (*ton dromon teteleka*, 2 Tim. 4:7), unless the trip to Spain had at some time been realized. That would call for a release from imprisonment in order for the westward journey to be accomplished. I am aware of the precarious nature of such an argument, and do not attach too much significance to it per se. However, in the light of the evidence from early historical notices, Paul's statement should at least be mentioned at this point.

Early historical notices. Among the earliest Christian writers outside the New Testament we find several pertinent statements.

Clement of Rome (A.D. 95), in his *First Epistle to the Corinthians*, chapter V, wrote:

> Peter, through unrighteous envy, endured not one or two, but numerous labours; and when he had at length suffered martyrdom, departed to the place of glory due to him. Owing to envy, Paul also obtained the reward of patient endurance, after being seven times thrown into captivity, compelled to flee, and stoned. After preaching both in the east and west, he gained the illustrious reputation due to his faith, having taught righteousness to the whole world, and come to the extreme limit of the west, and suffered martyrdom under the prefects.[2]

Clement states that before Paul was martyred, he had gone to the extreme limit of the West. It has been suggested that by that expression was meant Rome. However, it is difficult to see how a person writing from Rome would think of himself as at the extreme limit of the West. E. K. Simpson has answered this argument forcefully:

> Now all authorities are agreed that Paul suffered in Rome; yet Clement of Rome, writing on the spot only thirty years later, treats it as an accepted fact that he had sealed his testimony with his blood after preaching

the gospel in both east and west, *epi to terma tēs duseōs elthōn.* Moffatt and others have sought to identify this limit of the west with the imperial city itself. But that notion flies in the face of current usage. Clement's phrase can bear only one construction. Rome was not a point on the circumference of her own empire, but its proud centre, *Roma domina rerum.* The phrase *to terma tēs duseōs* denotes either the whole or a specific portion of the Spanish Peninsula, entitled by Strabo *termones tēs oikoumenēs* and by Philostratus *to terma tēs Eurōpēs.* That distinguished classical scholar, J. E. B. Mayor, cites Clement's phrase in his notes on Juvenal as clear proof of Paul's visit to Spain, pointing out how Gades, the modern Cadiz, was reckoned the frontier-line of western civilization; in the words of Velleius Paterculus, *extremus nostri orbis terminus.* Both Seneca and Pliny call Spain *terrarum fines;* and this conception reaches back as far as Pindar, and becomes a commonplace with the latter-day Roman poets. So Ramsay and Mayor and Zahn confidently, and Harnack with more hesitation, infer from Clement's phraseology a personal visit of the apostle paid to Spain.[3]

Another notice appears in the Muratorian Canon (A.D. 170) in the account of the book of Acts:

> Luke relates to Theophilus events of which he was an eyewitness, as also in a separate place [Luke 22:31-33] he evidently declares the martyrdom of Peter, but omits the journey of St. Paul to Spain.[4]

Although a journey to Spain is not necessary to the genuineness of the Pastoral Epistles, if such a journey did occur, then there must have been a release from the first Roman imprisonment. The foregoing evidence calls for such a journey and hence a release.

A third witness is Eusebius, who in book II, chapter *xxii* records the following:

> And Luke, the same who delivered in writing the Acts of the Apostles, brought his history to a close at that point of time, after indicating that Paul spent two

whole years at Rome without restraint, and preached
the word of God, none forbidding him. Having therefore made his defence at that time, it is recorded that
the apostle again journeyed on the ministry of preaching, and, having set foot for the second time in the same
city, was perfected in his martyrdom. While still in
bonds he composed his second epistle to Timothy,
mentioning both his former defence and also his imminent perfecting. . . . Probably it was for this reason that
Luke used that point of time as a terminus for the Acts
of the Apostles, having traced the course of the history
so long as he was present with Paul. . . . Now we have
made these statements in proof of the fact that Paul's
martyrdom was not accomplished during that stay at
Rome which Luke has recorded. In fact it is probable
that Nero received Paul's defence of the faith more gra-
ciously, since at first he was of a milder disposition, but
that, when he proceeded to unhallowed crimes, he coupled with his other deeds his attacks upon the
apostles.[5]

In the "Chronicles of Eusebius," the martyrdom of Paul
is listed as the thirteenth year of Nero (the year 2083,
commencing October, A.D. 67).[6]

Thus early historical notices are very specific in their
reference to a release of Paul and a visit to Spain. Furthermore, there is no contrary tradition. All the positive evidence points to such a release and western journey.

A Proposed Solution

On the basis of the evidence, I propose without hesitation the theory of two imprisonments as the most reasonable solution to the chronological difficulties. The following itinerary of Paul is suggested as being in accord with
the facts we have. This is not to say that another arrangement of order could not be made. It could. But this
arrangement is logical and reasonable.

1. Paul reached Rome in A.D. 60 (Acts 28:16).
2. He was under detention two full years, with no

apparent charge filed against him (Acts 28:30; cf. 25:26-27; 26:31-32). During this time he wrote the epistles to the Ephesians, Philippians, Colossians, and Philemon. As he wrote he expected his soon release (Phil. 1:25; 2:24; Philem. 22).

3. Released in A.D. 62, he visited in the East and West, probably including Spain. His release could not have been earlier than A.D. 62 because of Luke's mention of "two whole years" in Rome. Nor could it have been any later than July 19, A.D. 64, the date of the burning of Rome and subsequent persecution of Christians. I have chosen A.D. 62 on the basis of Luke's mention. During this release Paul first traveled eastward. He visited Colosse (Philem. 22) and perhaps Ephesus, where he dealt with Hymenaeus and Alexander (1 Tim. 1:20). Then he journeyed into Macedonia (1 Tim. 1:3) where he visited Philippi (Phil. 1:25; 2:24). First Timothy was probably written from Macedonia. I have placed this eastern trip before the journey to Spain, since in writing from prison to the Philippians Paul hoped to see them shortly (2:24). He would not have said this had he planned on making the long journey to Spain first. After the trip into Macedonia, Paul may have fulfilled his wish to reach Ephesus again (1 Tim. 3:14). During that eastern trip there was also a visit to the island of Crete (Titus 1:5), with Titus left behind to carry on the work. This visit may have been on the apostle's journey toward Colosse, or on his return. Sometime after this, he wrote the epistle to Titus, and urged Titus to join him for the winter at Nicopolis (Titus 3:12).

Must all of these events be pressed into one summer? If so, it was probably the summer of A.D. 62. I believe, however, that such would be a most strenuous tour for one just released from a two-year incarceration, and suggest A.D. 62-63 as the time taken for

this journeying. The intervening winter may have
been spent at Ephesus or Colosse. There is no
scriptural hint.

In the summer of A.D. 64 (or 63, if only one year is
allowed for the previous labors), Paul made his
long-planned trip to Spain. He may have stayed a
year. Then he apparently returned to Greece and
Asia Minor before going to Rome. There occurred a
visit to Miletus, where Trophimus was left sick (2
Tim. 4:20); a visit to Troas, where a cloak and parchments were left (2 Tim. 4:13), and perhaps a visit to
Corinth (4:20). Those cities form a natural route to
Rome. (The reason I believe those cities came after
the visit to Spain is because of the mention of the
cloak [2 Tim. 4:13]. If the leaving of the cloak occurred before the trip to Spain, then Paul had
already been without it for a winter).

4. A second imprisonment occurred in Rome (2 Tim.
1:16-17). Since Nero had placed the blame for the
burning of Rome upon the Christians, Christianity
was now an illegal religion. To evangelize was a
crime. Probably on that charge Paul the apostle was
apprehended and after the initial hearing (2 Tim.
4:16), he expected soon execution (2 Tim. 4:6). During the last stages of that imprisonment, 2 Timothy
was written.

The date of execution is uncertain. It must have
been between A.D. 64 and 68. Eusebius, in the passage previously referred to, places it in the year A.D.
67. Since there is no contrary evidence, that date is
as likely as any.

This suggested itinerary of the last journeys of Paul has
been delineated in map 2. As already stated, this is not
the only possible arrangement of events. However, it is a
reasonable solution of the chronological problem, and
thus the contention that 1 Timothy is not Pauline because
of the chronological difficulties must be rejected.

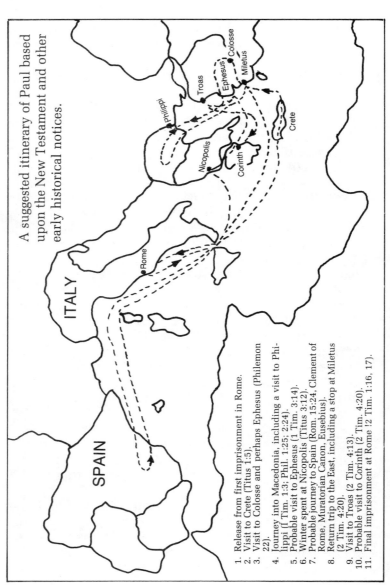

A suggested itinerary of Paul based upon the New Testament and other early historical notices.

1. Release from first imprisonment in Rome.
2. Visit to Crete (Titus 1:5).
3. Visit to Colosse and perhaps Ephesus (Philemon 22).
4. Journey into Macedonia, including a visit to Philippi (I Tim. 1:3; Phil. 1:25; 2:24).
5. Probable visit to Ephesus (1 Tim. 3:14).
6. Winter spent at Nicopolis (Titus 3:12).
7. Probable journey to Spain (Rom. 15:24. Clement of Rome, Muratorian Canon, Eusebius).
8. Return trip to the East, including a stop at Miletus (2 Tim. 4:20).
9. Visit to Troas (2 Tim. 4:13).
10. Probable visit to Corinth (2 Tim. 4:20).
11. Final imprisonment at Rome (2 Tim. 1:16, 17).

Map 2

ECCLESIASTICAL COMPLEXITY

The Statement of the Problem

It is objected by some that the Pastoral Epistles, especially 1 Timothy, reflect a state of ecclesiastical organization far too advanced for the days of Paul. It is averred that such organizational complexity did not occur until the second century. The specific items objected to will be considered.

The Examination of the Evidence

Various grades of clergy. First Timothy contains qualifications for bishops and deacons. Some conclude that deacons could attain the higher grade of presbyter (1 Tim. 3:13). The presbyters were salaried, liable to discipline, and new converts could not receive such an office.

A study of the passages involved does not, however, show an unusually high state of ecclesiastical development regarding elders (that is, presbyters). The two officers mentioned, bishops (another designation for elders) and deacons (1 Tim. 3:1-13) are mentioned elsewhere in the undisputed letters of Paul. (Phil. 1:1 mentions both groups.) Likewise the Jerusalem church had deacons (at least the functions of the seven chosen in Acts 6 resemble closely the qualifications expected in a deacon, 1 Tim. 3:8-10) and elders (Acts 15:2-6).

Furthermore, there is no evidence in 1 Timothy to cause us to see the rise of episcopacy. Rather, the Pastorals use the terms *elder* and *bishop* interchangeably (see especially Titus 1:5-7 for a clear instance). This is an unmistakable first-century usage. It is incorrect to suppose that Timothy was the bishop who appointed elders for the various churches in Asia Minor. On the contrary, he is shown to be at Ephesus and to him are given the qualifications for bishops (*episkopoi*), not elders (*presbuteroi*) (1 Tim. 3:1). If there were a distinction between those terms at that time, we should have expected the latter to have been used. But the synonymous use in the first century is generally agreed upon.

The plurality of elders indicated in 1 Timothy (5:17) agrees with Paul's policy. On the first missionary journey, he ordained "elders in every church" (Acts 14:23; cf. Phil. 1:1). The remuneration of elders is also Pauline teaching (1 Cor. 9:7-14). The liability of guilty elders to be punished is not a particularly complicated idea, nor is the prohibiting of new converts from the office unusually advanced. Both are reasonable, and it is unwarranted to affirm the passing of a century before such practice began. To insist that the "good degree" (1 Tim. 3:13) deacons might obtain is a promotion to the eldership and thus an indication of advanced administrative procedure, and then to reject the epistle on such grounds, is to beg the question. I view the passage in a different light (see the exegetical comments *in loco*).

Female deacons. The matter of identifying these persons (mentioned in 1 Tim. 3:11) is discussed in the exegetical section. Assuming, however, that the reference is to women whose function is closely connected to that of the deacons, does that demand second-century organization? I think not. Paul mentions a deaconess (*diakonos*) named Phoebe from the church at Cenchrea (Rom. 16:1). It does not take much effort to see how the need for women deacons would quickly arise. Ministration regarding other women or orphans, which the male deacons might in some situations be unsuited for, would make the need for women most necessary. There are reflections from even earlier days in the church of the ministry of godly women. Consider the cases of Dorcas (Acts 9:36-39) and Lydia (Acts 16:14-15).

Enrollment of widows. 1 Timothy 5:3-16 discusses widows at some length, and indicates an enrolled group of widows past the age of sixty who met certain qualifications. Some objectors say this indicates second-century organization, during which time even virgins and ascetics were classed as widows. (Baur advanced this view.)

The passage does not indicate anything different from ordinary widows, however. There is absolutely no indication that the word was used in the second-century sacerdotal sense. Furthermore, the Jerusalem church many years before had a serious problem concerning the support of widows, which brought forth emergency measures. Is it supposing too much to suggest that similar problems throughout the church in those early days caused the enrolling of widows with no other means of support? This charge is rejected on the grounds of an even earlier instance of widow-care in Acts.

Worship services. The regulation of worship services in 1 Timothy 2 is said to be too detailed for the first century. Prayers are urged on behalf of all men and especially for kings. Men are to do the praying. Women are not to do the teaching, but are to dress becomingly and learn in silence. (Titus shows that women could teach other women, however.)

I see in this description and regulatory passage no warrant for objecting to Pauline authorship. The same principles of women's subjection to men is taught by him with more detail elsewhere (1 Cor. 11:1-16). The recognition of civil authority is also Pauline (Rom. 13:1-7). Certainly the regulations in 1 Timothy 2 are of the simplest kind. All the reader need do is consult the letters of Ignatius to see what complexity the second-century church had assumed.

The Conclusion to the Problem

On the basis of the specific passages in 1 Timothy (each of which will be more fully developed in the exegesis of chapter 4), it is my conclusion that there is no unusual complexity of organization demanded by this epistle. Each item in question can be explained on the basis of other first-century information. Only by expanding the simple references in 1 Timothy into unwarranted dimensions can one find great complexity. Such is not legitimate exegesis.

Doctrinal Viewpoint
The Statement of the Problem

It is alleged that the Pastoral Epistles represent a lowered theology than that of Paul. James Moffatt writes:

> It is not easy to suppose that in three epistles the apostle, for example, would ignore such fundamental truths of his gospel as the fatherhood of God, the union of the believing man with Jesus Christ, and the power of the Holy Spirit in the Christian experience. The only explanation of this seems to be that the epistles were written by a disciple of St. Paul who, in the name of his master, and on the basis of some authentic fragments of Pauline correspondence, wrote against tendencies which threatened the later church, denouncing incipient forms of gnosticism, for example, roundly and indiscriminately.[7]

The accusation is made that the writer has descended from the high level of Pauline theology to a lower strata of mere piety.

Examination of the Evidence

It is difficult to agree with Moffatt that the "only explanation" is to predicate some unknown author. Consider the evidence. It is rather precarious to assert that the fatherhood of God is a fundamental Pauline doctrine, and then reject the Pastoral Epistles as Pauline because it cannot be found. It must be demonstrated first that the fatherhood of God is a fundamental Pauline doctrine. Certain modern theologians have become so enamored with the idea of the fatherhood of God that they assume its

teaching throughout Scripture. Yet does Scripture, especially Paul, teach this? Many fail to distinguish carefully
what the Scripture does teach. Although it is a biblical
truth that God is the creator of all men and thus their
father in that sense, the Bible does not teach that God is
the spiritual father of all men. Paul teaches that men apart
from the spiritual life in Christ will die in their sins (Rom.
8). Only true believers can call God "Father" (Rom. 8:15).

As far as 1 Timothy is concerned, God is the Savior of
men through the mediation of the God-Man, Christ Jesus
(1:1; 2:5-6). Certainly that is in agreement with Paul's
teaching (Gal. 4:4-5). The work of the Spirit is not exten-
sively dealt with in 1 Timothy, although the Spirit is
referred to as the one speaking warnings to the church
concerning dangers in the latter seasons (4:1), thus having
a part in guiding the daily walk of believers. In reference
to the charge that the pious and practical exhortations are
a far cry from the mystical theology of Paul, why must we
deny Paul a practical side to his theology? His epistles are
infused with exhortations to walk in the light of theological truths (e.g., Eph. 2:10; 4:1-3, 17-32; 5:1-4).

Furthermore, the student of any piece of literature must
take into account the type of work it is. First Timothy
does not propose to discuss the crucial questions of theology. It is a manual of practical instruction to Timothy, to
assist him in regulating the life of the church in an orderly and efficient way.

The writer agrees with the comment of Simpson:

> Occupied as he is with practicalities rather than prin-
> ciples, he does not wholly drop his old battle cries. Do
> they not ring in our ears when we read in Titus: "Not by
> works done in righteousness by us, but according to his
> mercy he saved us, by washing of regeneration and re-
> newing of the Holy Ghost, that being justified by his
> grace we might be made heirs according to the promise
> of eternal life (3:5, 6). . . ." If these passing reaffirma-
> tions of his gospel fail to satisfy critical censors, we

would remind them that a tract on church government differs from a body of divinity, and that one mark of a disciplined intellect consists in ability to keep to the subject in hand.[8]

Conclusion to the Problem

Careful study reveals that the charge fails to make sufficient allowance for the difference in subject matter between 1 Timothy and some of the other epistles of Paul. Any argument from silence is risky, and certainly Paul's comparative silence is accounted for by the nature of his letter. Furthermore, the charge is not altogether accurate. There are theological statements and viewpoints in 1 Timothy that are in complete harmony with Paul's doctrines elsewhere, and there is no proved variance.

HERETICAL OPPOSITION

The Statement of the Problem

It has been objected that heresy opposed in 1 Timothy is the Gnostic heresy of the second century. Various terms found in the epistle are made to refer to some of the technical aspects and terminology of Gnosticism. If that allegation is true, then 1 Timothy cannot be of Pauline authorship, for he had died more than thirty years before the second century began.

Examination of the Evidence

Probably the most frequently quoted passage in this connection is 1 Timothy 6:20. Here the reference to *antitheseis tēs pseudōnumou gnōseōs* (oppositions of the knowledge falsely named) is said to be a directly significant Gnostic reflection. Baur averred that the word *antithesis* indicated that the writer was issuing a polemic against Marcion's treatise, which bore that title. But the classical scholar, E. K. Simpson, states that that Aristotelian term was no novelty, and thus there is no compelling reason to suppose a reference to the second-century

Marcion.[9] As to the appearance of the term gnōsis, it is
true that later Gnostics made much use of this word,
claiming to possess a superior knowledge. However,
there is nothing unusual about the word gnōsis, nor is
there any reason to understand Paul's use in any other
than its ordinary sense. The fact that the term is applicable to Gnostics does not prove that it must refer to them.
Reynolds expresses well the thought on this point:

> The absurd position is involved that "Gnosis" must
> have meant in the year 65 A.D. precisely what it meant
> in 180 A.D.; that no more technical signification could
> have grown up about it in the course of a century. In the
> same way, a multitude of expressions in both the Old
> and New Testaments, from their singular applicability
> to modern controversy, might be supposed to have
> been forged in the eighteenth century.[10]

A second passage is 1 Timothy 1:4, where reference is
made to muthois kai genealogiais aperantois (myths and
endless genealogies). Some have attempted to identify the
myths and genealogies with the fantastic speculations of
Gnosticism. The series of aeons emanating from the Supreme Being are supposed to be in the author's mind as he
wrote this description. However, it is not at all certain
that this must be Paul's object. In Titus 1:14 the myths
(muthois) are characterized as Jewish (Ioudaikois). Since
that definitely fixes the reference, it is more reasonable to
understand the genealogies as Jewish also, since Philo
and others had previously developed the Mosaic genealogies into all sorts of traditions. This viewpoint is confirmed by the context of 1 Timothy 1, where the teachers
of these false doctrines are called nomodidaskaloi
(teachers of the law). Obviously, those false teachers had
a Jewish slant to their teaching, in contrast to second-
century Gnosticism, which was violently anti-Jewish.

A third passage, 1 Timothy 4, is supposed to be a refutation of Gnosticism. The warnings against the teachings of celibacy and asceticism are claimed to be a

reflection of Gnostic dualism. Of course, it is true that Gnostics taught such things, as have scores of other groups throughout human history. Yet the passage itself, if honestly handled, cannot be made to refute any group at the exact time of writing. The opening lines of the chapter state when these doctrines would appear: "Now the Spirit speaketh expressly that in the latter times some shall depart from the faith. . . ." Although the author may have seen the beginnings of these things, and may have detected dangerous tendencies toward them, it is hardly fair to demand that the text presupposes full-blown Gnosticism. This passage is a prophetic warning.

Those are the principal passages in 1 Timothy. The other Pastoral Epistles contain similar passages, although 1 Timothy is usually considered to present the more obvious ones. From the passages considered, it has been shown that there is not sufficient reason to demand our seeing full-flowered Gnosticism being attacked in 1 Timothy. Such Gnosticism was radically anti-Jewish, and yet these opponents are Jewish law teachers. However, the evidence also shows that these opponents were not the same type of Judaizers as those whom Paul had met earlier (Acts 15; Gal. 2; etc.). In those instances the Judaizers attempted to cause Christians to keep the whole law. There was no indication of profane myths or additional and superior knowledge. Alford sums up the evidence on this point:

> The false teachers then of our Epistles seem to hold a position intermediate to the Apostle's former Judaizing adversaries and the subsequent Gnostic heretics, distinct from both, and just at that point in the progress from the one form of error to the other, which would suit the period subsequent to the Epistle to the Philippians, and prior to the destruction of Jerusalem. There is therefore nothing in them and their characteristics, which can cast a doubt upon the genuineness of the Epistles.[11]

Solution of the Problem

The evidence as seen in the epistle itself shows that the opposition being faced was mainly Jewish. The differences between these Jewish teachers and the earlier Judaizers may be accounted for on the basis of heathen speculations joined to Jewish legalism. If one wishes to call this incipient Gnosticism, let him do so. But certainly it is not Gnosticism fully developed. The reader need only consult the second-century writings of Irenaeus, Clement of Alexandria, and Tertullian to see what a refutation of true Gnosticism is like. Further indication that Paul's opposition could not be more than the initial stages of Gnosticism is the fact that the adversaries were still within the church. They were not yet anathematized. Zahn states the argument in a masterful way, and the passage though somewhat long is reproduced here:

> The persons, the opposing of whose harmful activity is Timothy's chief business in Ephesus . . . are members of the Church, subject to its confession and discipline; for Timothy is not directed to warn the churches under his care against them, but is to command them to refrain from teaching. What Paul says in describing their work as teachers is manifestly designed not only to open Timothy's eyes and convince him of the peril to which the church is exposed through them, but to furnish him with the truths by the presentation of which he is to influence them to leave off their harmful activity. These persons are not yet *hairetikoi*, i.e., they have not yet separated themselves from the worship and fellowship of the church; persons of this character are to be left to their fate (Titus 3:10; cf. 1 Cor. 11:19). Only in the case of persistence in their work, in spite of the reprimand of Timothy or Titus, is it expected that they will continue outside the organized Church what they are forbidden to carry on within the same. This conclusion, namely, that until now these persons had remained in the Church, follows not only from the fact that Timothy is to command them to cease teaching,

but also from the fact that individuals belonging to this party who had gone farther than the rest had been subjected to Church discipline by Paul (1 Tim. 1:20).[12]

Thus the writer concludes that the heretical opposition being faced in 1 Timothy is no argument against Pauline authorship. The opponents are most reasonably understood as Judaizing teachers within the church, who were also becoming contaminated with pagan philosophical ideas, which may have developed into Gnosticism during the next hundred years.

Linguistic Peculiarities
Statement of the Problem

It is urged by many scholars that vocabulary and style of the Pastoral Epistles must preclude Pauline authorship. Many words appear in these short letters which do not occur in the other letters of Paul. Furthermore, certain common expressions of the apostle are missing in the Pastorals. The most exhaustive attempt to refute Pauline authorship of the Pastorals on the basis of linguistics is the work of P. N. Harrison, whose work, *The Problem of the Pastoral Epistles,* is referred to in this discussion. To be persuaded by those linguistic peculiarities, and yet to acknowledge the many obvious Paulinisms, has called forth a most imaginative hypothesis. This hypothesis, widely held by liberal critics, is stated in the words of Harrison:

> The positive conclusion, then, which forms the main thesis of the present work is that the real author of the Pastorals was a devout, sincere, and earnest Paulinist, who lived at Rome or Ephesus, and wrote during the later years of Trajan or (? and) the earlier years of Hadrian's reign. He knew and had studied deeply every one of our ten Paulines. In addition to these he had access to several brief personal notes written by the apostle on various occasions (to be specified in due course) to his friends Timothy and Titus, preserved by them till their

death, and then bequeathed as a priceless heirloom either to the church or to some trusted friend.[13]

The problem is to ascertain whether such an explanation of authorship is necessary. Is the linguistic evidence of such a nature as to compel the abandonment of early church opinion and the prima-facie evidence of the book itself? Let us look at the evidence from 1 Timothy.

Examination of the Evidence

There are 175 words used in 1 Timothy which do not appear in the ten generally acknowledged epistles of Paul, although some of them are used in the other Pastorals. (The number 175 may vary slightly by other computations, since in the case of some adverbs, adjectives, and particles, it is somewhat arbitrary whether they be counted separately or traced to the root.) Since there are 538 different words used in 1 Timothy, which is 1468 words in length, it is clear that more than 30 percent of the vocabulary is not used by Paul in the ten other epistles. Harrison compares the vocabulary of the various epistles by computing the number of *hapax legomena* (words used only once, not found elsewhere in Paul) per page of the Westcott and Hort Greek Testament. He shows by a diagram that 1 Timothy has 15.2 *hapax legomena* per page, whereas the ten epistles show a variation from the 3.3 of 2 Thessalonians to the 6.2 of Philippians.[14] Thus the proportion of new words per page in 1 Timothy is more than twice that of Philippians. The unique words of 1 Timothy must be examined, in order to assess their significance. A close study of those 175 words reveals some pertinent facts.

Proper names (3). The occurrence of new proper names cannot be held against Pauline authorship. Otherwise we are in the position of denying to Paul the widening of his acquaintance. This fact is admitted by all. A complete listing of these words and those in the following groups is found in Appendix A.

Words used by Paul in Acts (11). The history of Paul in the book of Acts contains many of his speeches and conversations. Here are found eleven words which are not found in the ten epistles, but do appear in 1 Timothy.

Cognates used by Paul in the Epistles or Acts (55). If Paul uses a cognate of the word under suspicion, then it is certainly reasonable to conclude that the highly educated and brilliant Paul was familiar with other words of the same root.

By removing proper names, words used by Paul in Acts, and cognates of words used by Paul, the number of unusual terms is reduced from 175 to 106, or less than 20 percent.

Words used in Hebrews (23). It is not the purpose of this volume to settle the authorship of Hebrews. However, if Paul is the author, as many others and I believe him to be, then the vocabulary of Hebrews must be examined for significant words. This group of words is listed separately, so as not to confuse the argument for those who are not assured of Paul's authorship of Hebrews. Those words used in Hebrews reduce the list of unusual words in 1 Timothy to 83, or 15 percent.

Words or cognates used by Luke (29). It is agreed by all that the vocabulary of all three Pastoral Epistles is similar. All were written by the same author during the space of just a few years. Furthermore, Paul states that Luke was his only companion during the imprisonment (2 Tim. 4:11), and could quite reasonably have served his friend as amanuensis. The close friendship of Paul and Luke for many years is indicated by the "we" sections of Acts as well as 2 Timothy. Therefore, in view of the similar vocabulary of all the Pastorals, it may be offered as a suggestion that Luke served as amanuensis for the writing of 1 Timothy as well. Although the letter is still Paul's, the hand of the educated Doctor Luke is reflected from time to time (see 2 Tim. 2:17, for an example). If this be true, then the remaining unusual words should be examined for evidence of Lukan usage. There are 29 such words, thus reducing the *hapax legomena* to 54, or 10 percent.

Words without other Pauline or Lukan usage (54). These constitute 10 percent of the total vocabulary of 1 Timothy.

Significant omissions. Examination reveals that a large number of words, particles, and expressions frequently used by Paul in the ten epistles are absent from the Pastorals. Of course, an argument from silence, especially one of this nature, is not too forceful, but since it is frequently advanced by a large group of critics, it demands our attention. The studies of Harrison of the liberal school are the most exhaustive in this respect. The reader is referred to many pages of diagrams and lists in that work if he desires specific illustrations.[15] White has discussed this problem by dividing Paul's other ten epistles into four groups, according to the time and circumstances of writing.[16] White then shows how 50 of the so-called Pauline words which are missing from the Pastorals are also missing from some of the previous groups of letters. By this method 27 of the missing words (more than half) are shown to be missing from several of those groups of letters, and thus need cause no special problem in the Pastorals.

As for the missing particles, White shows that the great majority of them are confined to Group Two of the epistles (Romans, 1 Corinthians, 2 Corinthians, Galatians). That is explained by the fact that those epistles are the most argumentative and controversial, and the subject matter demands inferential and similar particles.

Let the words of White sum up this discussion:

> It is difficult to treat seriously an argument which assumes that St. Paul was provided with only one set of words and terms; unalterable, no matter to whom, or on what subject, he was writing. It is not thus that non-Biblical compositions are critically examined. We do not demand that Shakespeare's *Sonnets* or *Cymbeline*

should exhibit a certain percentage of *Hamlet* words. And the argument becomes all the more unreasonable when one thinks how very small in extent is the extant literary work of St. Paul: less than 150 small octavo pages in Westcott and Hort's edition, and of these the Pastorals occupy only fifteen. . . . Antecedently, we should not expect that an author's favorite expressions would be distributed over the pages of his book like the spots on a wallpaper pattern.[17]

Strictly Pauline words (32). There are a number of words in 1 Timothy whose usage elsewhere occurs only in the writings of Paul. (See appendix B.)

Pauline phrases. A great number of these occur, sufficient to cause such critics as Harrison to postulate that the unknown author of 1 Timothy was deeply steeped in the genuine epistles and employed many Pauline phrases. Following are a few such expressions, compiled from Harrison and derived from the opening verses of 1 Timothy:[18]

"Paul apostle of Christ Jesus"
"According to command of God"
"Grace . . . peace from God the Father"
"Christ Jesus our Lord"
"We know that the law is good"
"According to the gospel of the glory of . . . God"
"But the grace of our Lord superabounded"

Other Pauline elements. E. K. Simpson calls our attention to certain stylistic mannerisms of the Pastoral Epistles that are clearly Pauline.[19]

1. Figures of speech which are drawn from the human, not the physical, realm.
2. Employment of meiosis or understatement.
3. Apposition.
4. Compendious compounds.
5. Enumerations.
6. Play on words.
7. Latinistic influences.

Those mannerisms are probably more indicative of authorship than vocabulary, since the subject matter would call for different words, but the style of writing would not be so likely to vary.

Conclusion to the Problem

With the above facts before us, we can attempt an answer to the linguistic problem.

First, the study of vocabulary is not a conclusive clue to the authorship of 1 Timothy, nor of any other piece of literature, unless in a negative way certain impossible anachronisms are employed in the writing. Such words do not appear in 1 Timothy, and thus there is no proof that Paul could not have employed each word that appears. It has been shown that the number of so-called un-Pauline words can be reduced from 30 percent to less than 20 percent, and if Hebrews is counted as Pauline, to 15 percent. If Lukan influence, as amanuensis, be admitted, the proportion of *hapax legomena* drops to 10 percent. Certainly no one can object to that proportion of different vocabulary.

To illustrate the precarious practice of rejecting authorship on the basis of new vocabulary, consider the vocabulary of Lincoln's "Gettysburg Address" as compared to his "Second Inaugural Address." The "Gettysburg Address" contains 68 words not appearing in the "Second Inaugural Address." This is 51 percent new words. Yet those two addresses were given only two years apart and both discussed the war. But some may object that that is too small an amount of literature to compare. And that is precisely our objection to attacks on the vocabulary of 1 Timothy. The total vocabulary of the ten epistles of Paul consists of 2177 words (apart from proper names). Are we to suppose that the vocabulary of the great apostle was no larger than this? Even as a working vocabulary, 2177 words is very meager for an educated scholar.

This is the height of capricious criticism: to object to the new words as non-Pauline, but to account for obvious Pauline expressions as original fragments. By this method any book or letter in which the writer employs some new words can be similarly dissected. But what does it prove? Merely the ingenuity of the dissector. Unless those new words are known to be outside the scope of the writer's experience (which the words in 1 Timothy are not), it does not prove one thing about the identity of the author. If a writer cannot employ new words as the occasion demands without having his identity challenged, then there has been placed upon writers a rigidity of expression which will utterly destroy any freshness and vitality of thought.

Second, the differences in vocabulary in 1 Timothy can be accounted for. The differences in subject matter call for a different vocabulary. The full discussion of widows, qualifications of bishop and deacon, and directions for worship are recognized by all students as new subjects in the Pastorals. Yet liberal critics have argued against genuineness on the basis of the change. Certainly the argument based on a so-called lowered theology or a too-complex organization or a later heresy (in other words, a different subject matter) ought to cancel the force of a peculiar language objection. If the different subject matter is admitted, then a different vocabulary should be expected. The evidence here presented has shown that the subject matter, while not at all impossible to Paul, is still of a type sufficient to necessitate some new words. The fact that the Pastoral Epistles were written to friends, not just churches, helps also to account for the vocabulary.

Changes in Paul could account for a less energetic style than his earlier epistles manifest. According to the two-imprisonment theory, Paul wrote the Pastoral Epistles after very trying circumstances. First Timothy and Titus appeared following approximately five years in prison. Second Timothy was written from a dungeon with death being an imminent prospect. Such factors would cause rapid physical aging, and would be reflected in his writings. White takes this view:

> The explanation of this may well be that before St. Paul wrote these letters he had ceased to be an elderly, and had, perhaps rapidly, become an old man. There is nothing impossible in this supposition. The surprising thing is that it has not been more generally recognized as a probable factor in the solution of the problem presented by the Pastorals. When we think of the intensity with which St. Paul had lived his life—always at high pressure—and what a hard life it had been, it would be a marvel indeed if old age with its diminished powers had not come suddenly upon him. We hold then that the author of the Pastorals was Paul; but "Paul the aged": much more aged, and more truly so, than when he penned his note to Philemon.[20]

The use of Luke as an amanuensis may possibly account for some of the words in 1 Timothy which are Lukan, but not in the ten epistles. The employment of Luke's services in 2 Timothy is entirely reasonable (see 2 Tim. 4:11), and it is certainly possible that he may have been with Paul at the writing of 1 Timothy also.

Third, the linguistic differences are not sufficient to account for the early historical acceptance of these letters. There is not one trace of suspicion in the early church. If this were a forgery (or even a "pious fraud"), it is certainly strange that it gained immediate approval, even by those who could have been personally acquainted with Paul, and there were no dissenters (apart from the heretics previously discussed) until the nineteenth century. The uniform testimony of early history must carry more weight than the variety of vocabulary.

NOTES

[1]William M. Ramsay, *St. Paul the Traveller and the Roman Citizen* (reprint ed., Grand Rapids: Baker Book House, 1949), pp. 27-28.

[2]English translation given in Clement, *First Epistle to the Corinthians, The*

Ante-Nicene Fathers, ed. by Alexander Roberts and James Donaldson (Grand Rapids: Wm. B. Eerdmans Pub. Co., reprinted 1951), 1:6.

[3]E. K. Simpson, *The Pastoral Epistles* (Grand Rapids: Eerdmans, 1954), pp. 4-5. The Greek in this quotation has been transliterated.

[4]Spence, p. 175.

[5]Eusebius, pp. 55-56. Used with permission of the Macmillan Company, New York, which handles this volume in U.S.A.

[6]Quoted by Henry Alford, *The New Testament for English Readers* (London: Rivingtons, 1872), 2:116.

[7]James Moffatt, *Encyclopaedia Britannica,* 1946 ed., s.v. "Pastoral Epistles."

[8]Simpson, p. 13.

[9]*Ibid.,* p. 11.

[10]H. R. Reynolds, "The Pastoral Epistles," *The Expositor,* 1:312.

[11]Henry Alford, *The New Testament for English Readers* (London: Rivingtons, 1872), 2:100.

[12]Theodor Zahn, *Introduction to the New Testament,* trans. John Moore Trout *et al* (reprint ed., Grand Rapids: Kregel, 1953), 2:99-100. Greek letters have been transliterated.

[13]P. N. Harrison, *The Problem of the Pastoral Epistles* (London: Oxford U. 1921), p. 8.

[14]*Ibid.*

[15]*Ibid.*

[16]White, pp. 67-72.

[17]*Ibid.,* p. 68.

[18]Harrison, Appendix IV.

[19]Simpson, pp. 18-21.

[20]White, pp. 59-60.

4

EXPOSITORY EXEGESIS AND TRANSLATION OF 1 TIMOTHY

OUTLINE

Introductory Matters (1:1-2)

I. CHARGE CONCERNING SOUND DOCTRINE (1:3-20).
   A. The danger to sound doctrine in Ephesus (vv. 3-11).
   B. The outstanding illustration of the results of sound doctrine (vv. 12-17).
   C. The responsibility of the minister toward sound doctrine (vv. 18-20).

II. CHARGE CONCERNING PUBLIC WORSHIP (2:1-15).
   A. Prayer in public worship (vv. 1-7).
   B. Men and women in public worship (vv. 8-15).

III. CHARGE CONCERNING CHURCH OFFICERS (3:1-16).
   A. The office of the overseer (vv. 1-7).
   B. The office of the deacon (vv. 8-13).
   C. The importance of this charge to the church (vv. 14-16).

IV. CHARGE CONCERNING FALSE TEACHERS (4:1-16).
   A. The appearance of false teachers (vv. 1-5).

Translation and Exegesis

Introductory Matters (1:1-2)

The writer.

> Paul, apostle of Christ Jesus according to command of God our Saviour and Christ Jesus our hope (v. 1).

In the usual manner of early writers, Paul names himself at the beginning of his letter, and then states his official position as "apostle of Christ Jesus." Although this greeting may seem somewhat formal for a personal letter to a close friend, it must be remembered that the contents of this letter were of an official nature and not merely private. Hence this letter was a written authorization that granted Timothy the right to act for Paul in this apostolic work, and gave written instructions for this work. Paul did not need to emphasize his authority to Timothy, but the mentioning of his position could conceivably prove very useful to Timothy as he endeavored to carry out the instructions of this letter in the face of false teachers.

The designation of Paul as "apostle of Christ Jesus" marks him as one of a select group. The word *apostle* (*apostolos*) means etymologically one who is equipped to fulfill his responsibility (from *stellō*, to equip, arrange, prepare), and then is sent off with a commission (*apo*, away from). "Apostle" became a technical term to denote one who was sent away with proper credentials to represent someone else. A papyrus fragment mentions a public official who sent to a delinquent a messenger (*apostolon*) bearing the orders he had disregarded.[1]

Other men in the New Testament are called apostles (e.g., Phil. 2:25; 2 Cor. 8:23; and others), but those are apostles of churches. The use of the subjective genitive "Christ Jesus" limits this title to those who belonged to Christ in some special way. In the strictest technical sense which this formal salutation implies, the title refers to those men who were specially chosen by Christ Himself. Thus it applies to the twelve (with the place of Judas being taken by Matthias), plus Paul. Those men were called to their mission by Jesus personally. No others were called in exactly the same way.

The order of the names *Christ Jesus* is significant. It is likely that whichever name occurs first indicates the idea that was prominent in the writer's mind at that moment. *Christ* is the title of national and theological function. It denotes our Lord in His Person as the Messiah and divine Savior of men. The name *Jesus* emphasized the historic human person. Inasmuch as Paul's experience with the Son of God began with his vision of the glorified Christ on the Damascus Road, it is to be expected that this impression would be the prominent one. From that vision Paul learned that the Christ in glory was the same historic Jesus. With the other disciples the process was reversed. They became acquainted with the historic Jesus of Nazareth and later learned to recognize Him as the Christ.

Consequently John, Peter, and James use the order "Jesus Christ" more frequently. But Paul, especially in his later epistles, shows a definite preference for the name "Christ Jesus."

The authority of the writer is next given. Paul is an apostle "according to command" (*kat' epitagēn*). Simpson states on the basis of inscriptional data that this phrase was a recognized formula, similar to our official notices: by order of.[2] Paul regarded himself as a messenger under orders, and he had no doubts of his authority. He traces this authority first to "God our Saviour." This expression in the New Testament is peculiar to the Pastoral Epistles, Jude 25, Luke 1:47. The term *sōtēr* appears in the Septuagint twenty times, and all but two refer to God. Hence there is no need to suggest any pagan allusions here. The fact that the ancients applied the title *Savior* to their heroes (e.g., Ptolemy Soter) is interesting but irrelevant. Paul had abundant scriptural warrant for his usage. Timothy, being reared on the Old Testament, would have understood the designation in that sense. God the Father is the fountain of our salvation in all its aspects. It was He who gave the Son (John 3:16). We who so often speak of Christ as Savior must not overlook the great part which the Father filled in planning and directing our spiritual deliverance. It is suggested by some that the reference to God as Savior points to the past aspect of salvation, whereas the mention of Christ as our hope looks to the future. That may be partly true, but the chronological aspect should not be unduly pressed. God is the Savior of men in all aspects of salvation, and there are certainly present and future aspects to be considered.

Paul's authority is also traced to the command of Christ Jesus, "our hope." As the Father is the fountain of our salvation, so Christ is the embodiment of our hope. We are looking for Him to return (Titus 2:13). In Him are all our expectations. Our basis for eternal life with all its glories lies in the fact of our union with Christ: "Christ in you, the hope of glory" (Col. 1:27). This then is the authority that Paul exercises to withstand those who would rob the church of salvation and hope.

This command from God and Christ which constituted Paul an apostle came to him as he had journeyed toward Damascus many years before. The words of Christ that brought Paul to faith and instructed him as to his ministry (Acts 26:16-18; cf. 9:4-6, 15) provided his call to apostleship. Paul himself is careful to explain that his authority was not due to men nor even to other apostles, but was from Christ Himself (1 Cor. 9:1). Of course, Christ and the Father should not be disassociated in this divine call (see Gal. 1:15-16).

The addressee.

> To Timothy, genuine child in faith: grace, mercy, peace, from God the Father and Christ Jesus our Lord (v. 2).

The position of Timothy is stated as that of a genuine child in faith. The King James translation "my own son," although undoubtedly true to the facts, is not an accurate rendering. The employment of the term "child" (*teknon*) is an indication of Paul's personal affection for Timothy. It is an intimate term of endearment when used in this way. *Teknon* also connotes nature and birth, and the following phrase *en pistei* (in faith) states the sphere in which this birth had occurred. Of course, Timothy was not Paul's physical child, for he had a Greek father (Acts 16:3). But in the realm of Christian faith, Timothy owed his spiritual birth to the agency of Paul. From materials in the book of Acts (already discussed in chapter 1), it seems certain that this birth in the realm of faith had occurred as the result of Paul's first ministry at Lystra. Furthermore, this spiritual birth of Timothy is described as genuine (*gnēsios*). The word used is the opposite of bastard (*nothos*). With the passing of the years, the genuine nature of Timothy's conversion was proved. His spiritual life was not illegitimate or abortive. He was a genuinely born-again child of God. This is the primary emphasis in the statement.

The prayer for Timothy desires for him three sweeping blessings from God the Father and Christ Jesus the Lord. The addition of the word *mercy* (*eleos*) is peculiar to the two epistles to Timothy, a fact leading some to question Paul's authorship. However, it is most unlikely that a forger would differ in so obvious a spot, when he could easily have copied Paul's usual formula. Yet no such limitation can be placed upon Paul.

The grace (*charis*) for which he prays is not just the grace that originally saves, for Timothy has just been addressed as a true child of God. Rather it is grace in its wider aspects, divine favor in its fullest form. The Christian needs the grace of God to sustain him constantly. That grace is what makes prayer possible and practical.

Mercy (*eleos*) is what Timothy and all believers need daily when conscious of failure. It is not necessary to imagine some glaring weakness on Timothy's part, to which Paul was subtly referring by this term. Fairbairn's comments are helpful here:

> He [Paul] knew how much he needed mercy for himself, not merely at the outset of his spiritual career, when he was rescued as a brand from the burning, but also when engaged in his work as an ambassador of Christ. He knew that, even when he was outwardly doing all, he was still spiritually coming short; that evil was more or less present with him, when seeking to do what was good; therefore he must ever feel himself a debtor to mercy. And could he wish his dear child and deputy to feel otherwise? . . . While they are ambassadors of mercy to others, let them never forget that they need to be themselves partakers of mercy—never more so than when they are engaged in the higher duties, and pressing the more sacred interests of the gospel.[3]

The peace (*eirēnē*) of God is the outcome of grace and

mercy experienced. It is that which keeps our hearts in confidence (Phil. 4:6-7). It is the daily, continual experience of the soul in harmony with God.

These three blessings for Timothy must proceed from above. The coupling by Paul of God the Father and Christ Jesus as co-bestowers of these divine blessings is clear indication of Paul's belief in the full deity of Christ.

Paul seemed to know what Timothy needed. Timothy's task in Ephesus was the most difficult he had ever faced. He needed all the gifts of God's grace. A tradition, recorded by Eusebius, says that Timothy was later beaten to death by a mob at Ephesus because of his arraignment of the idolatrous immorality of the worship of Diana. Paul's prayer for him was no mere stereotyped formula, but a fervent personal desire expressed to God on behalf of his faithful worker.

I. CHARGE CONCERNING SOUND DOCTRINE (1 Tim. 1:3-20).

A. *The danger to sound doctrine in Ephesus* (vv. 3-11).

When Paul established new churches, he did not leave his former churches destitute. He was continually concerned about their welfare, and expressed his concern by ceaseless prayer and constructive letters. That principle was stated by an ancient writer as follows: "To keep what has been gained is not a smaller virtue than to make new acquisitions."[4] The problem in Ephesus at that time was the serious threat to sound doctrine which was caused by the presence of some would-be Law-teachers who had infiltrated the church. These teachers were perverting true doctrine and thus were endangering the spiritual well-being of the believers. This opening chapter of Paul's letter sketches the problem, describes the teachers, and provides an introduction to the entire epistle.

1. Teachers who taught another doctrine.

Even as I exhorted you to remain in Ephesus while I was going into Macedonia, in order that you might

charge some not to teach different doctrine nor to hold
to myths and endless genealogies which present questionings rather than God's administration which is in
faith; and the goal of the charge is love out of a pure
heart and a good conscience and an unhypocritical
faith, from which things some having missed the mark
turned aside unto vain speaking, wishing to be Law-
teachers, not understanding either the things which
they speak or concerning what they strongly affirm (vv.
3-7).

a. Identification of these teachers.

Paul does not name the individuals, although he
quite likely knew who they were. Instead he refers to
them slightingly as "some" (*tisin*). It is suggested by
many commentators that this indicates the number to
have been few. However, this is not necessarily to be
inferred. More probably the expression is intentionally
vague so as to grant these teachers no standing whatever.

These persons also are described as desiring to be Law-
teachers (*nomodidaskaloi*). Apparently these men
attempted to be expositors of the Mosaic Law as it applied
to Christianity. However, they were ignorant of the subject they were discussing (*mē noountes*) and did not fully
understand the nature of the things which their confident
manner of teaching tried to indicate (*diabebaiountai*).
Their chief characteristic was their Judaizing tendency,
which would put the Christians under the full jurisdiction of the Mosaic Law. Those teachers showed their
ignorance by trying to mix law and grace. Yet those men
strongly affirmed their doctrine. Men often yell loudest
about that of which they know least.

Furthermore, those teachers have missed the mark
(*astochēsantes*) of the truth, and have turned aside (*ex-
etrapēsan*) to substitutes. *Astocheō* not only indicates
that the goal was missed, but that the aim was careless or
neglected. Those men missed the mark at which they
should have aimed. Thus they must have been nominal

members of the congregation at Ephesus, recognized as having professed faith at some time, but their current activity caused the apostle to state their case with unsparing severity. They were headed in the wrong direction. Their interests were not in maintaining a pure heart, good conscience, and sincere faith.

    b. The characteristics of their teaching.

       (1) Different doctrine (*heterodidaskalein*).

       This description of the false teaching was apparently coined by Paul, for it occurs only twice in the New Testament, both in 1 Timothy, and has not been found employed by any earlier writers. The prefix *hetero-* indicates that which is diverse, of a different type. (There is another Greek term *allos* which means another of a similar type. See Gal. 1:6-7: ". . . unto another [*heteros*, of a different type] gospel, which is not another [*allos*, of similar type]." In 1 Tim. 1:3 the choice is very meaningful.) It is not certain whether the infinitive should be translated "to teach different doctrine" or "to teach differently." Both would be true of these teachers, since to teach a doctrine different from that which Paul and the other apostles had proclaimed would be to teach in a far different manner from their divinely sanctioned preaching. The placing of a wrong interpretation upon the Mosaic Law is to teach differently from the orthodox teachers who rightly interpreted and taught sound doctrine.

       (2) Myths (*muthois*).

       The teaching of these errorists contained myths or fables, and the hearers must be warned not to give heed (*prosechein*). There is disagreement among expositors as to the reference of this term, some explaining these myths as Gnostic and others as Jewish. The fact that Paul terms such myths "Jewish" (*Ioudaikois*) (Titus 1:14) would seem to settle the matter in favor of the latter, especially since these errorists were would-be Law-teachers. Probably this is a reference to the numerous

legends which the Jews had added to the Old Testament.
Such legends are collected in the Talmud.

(3) Endless genealogies (*genealogiais aperantois*).

These genealogies have been regarded either
as Gnostic or Jewish. Some suggest that Paul refers to the
Gnostic teaching of aeon emanations under this name.
However, it is questionable whether such emanations
were ever called by this term, and furthermore, a full-
blown Gnosticism appeared a century after Paul's time. It
is more in keeping with the context to understand these
as Jewish genealogies. The Old Testament genealogical
lists were often amplified by the Jews. Names were in-
vented and whole tales were woven about them. The Jewish *Book of Jubilees* provides examples of that.

It is easy to see how the allegorizing of some parts of the
Old Testament would be appealing to the gentile world,
where Jewish and Palestinian references meant little. Yet
one can imagine how spiritually deadening that practice
would be in the church. Paul terms such handling of
genealogies as endless, for there can be no terminus to
such allegorizing. The only restriction would be the
amount of ingenuity possessed by the expositor.

Such genealogies and myths serve only to raise further
questions and cause new investigations (*ekzētēseis*). But
interpretations based upon the inventiveness of men can
never reach the settled state of God's truth. Consequently
they do not offer Christians anything useful for God's
administration. The KJV* has translated an inferior reading "godly edifying" (*oikodomian theou*), but the better
texts say "God's administration" (*oikonomian theou*). In
the realm of Christian faith (*en pistei*) God is administer-
ing the affairs of His children. He accomplishes this
through His Word, as it is proclaimed and taught by Spir-

---

*King James Version.

it-led men. But false teachers are not furthering the administration of God.

(4) Vain speaking (*mataiologian*).

Their teaching is further described as a vain speaking. The prefix *mataio-* signifies not just empty speech (*kenos*) but speech which is aimless, leading to no object or end.[5] It does not lead anywhere. There may be interesting matter in their speech but it does not accomplish anything in leading men along spiritual lines. This is the inevitable consequence of false teaching. It accomplishes nothing toward the edifying of the believer, and may lead him astray into deadening paths of human speculation. Paul never regarded the gospel as a matter of human speculation but as a divine revelation.

    c. Timothy's responsibility.

Timothy had been encouraged by Paul to stay on at Ephesus while he was journeying in Macedonia. The latter part of verse 3 is elliptical, the usual *houtōs* clause after *kathōs* being omitted. The reader must mentally supply some such clause as "so do I now." The apostle wished Timothy to continue on at Ephesus, just as he had previously, in order to deal with the dangerous situation which was developing.

(1) Timothy was to deliver a prohibitive charge.

He was told by Paul to charge the errorists not to teach their different doctrine. The verb "charge" (*paraggeilēis*) is a strong word of command, and the Greek tense employed here (an aorist) indicates a decisive action on Timothy's part. These men were to be given orders to desist immediately from their foolish interpretations.

(2) Timothy was to encourage a positive response.

Verse 5 contains the purpose of this instruction to Timothy. Paul states that the goal (*telos*) of this charge he is giving is to produce love. How different from the result of false teaching which produces strife and questionings!

Some expositors have considered the charge or "commandment" (KJV rendering) of this verse to be a reference to the Mosaic Law. However, the fact that this noun (*paraggelias*) is contained in the verb "to charge" (*paraggeilēis*) of verse 3, and is used again in verse 18 of this chapter to refer to Paul's charge to Timothy makes it more probable that the same significance is attached to each use of the word in this chapter. The noun *paraggelia* is never used in the New Testament to refer to the Old Testament law. E. K. Simpson states: "*paraggelia* . . . is not the proper term for the legal statute book."[6]

The goal of preaching, teaching, and warning men is to present the gospel of God's grace in Christ so as to call forth a response of faith and love. When the gospel is preached men see themselves as lost. Upon faith, sins are removed and new life and peace are brought in. The new nature of the believer causes him to love God, his fellow Christians, and lost men.

> Beloved, let us love one another, for love is of God; and everyone that loveth is born of God, and knoweth God. He that loveth not knoweth not God; for God is love (1 John 4:7-8).

Reference is often made to Romans 13:10 by those who regard the charge as meaning the Old Testament law. "Love worketh no ill to his neighbor: therefore love is the fulfilling of the law." It is true that such a one by love is uncondemned by the law, but the law did not produce this love. This passage does not teach that the Christian loves as a result of keeping the law, but quite the reverse. The believer's love is the product of his life in Christ, of grace and not law. But by this love he has carried out God's will. Thus there does not seem to be any compelling reason for making the "charge" of 1 Timothy 1:5 the Mosaic Law.

The love that Paul desires in the life of every Christian can come only out of a pure heart. The heart in Scripture symbolizes the essential part of man, and thus a pure heart indicates a cleansed life. This is the result of forgiveness secured at Calvary. Such a person can have a good conscience—one which is functioning properly and does not condemn. The Christian has Christ and His Word and now has a perfect standard by which his conscience can operate. When the conscience operates according to the proper moral standard and does not condemn because the life is clean, then it is termed a good conscience. With a conscience that is not condemning, the believer can have an unhypocritical (*anupokritou*) faith. This is faith that needs no mask to hide its insincerity. It is not mere lip faith, but a sincere trust of the heart. Sound doctrine, that is, a full gospel message declaring the whole counsel of God, will produce this kind of life in men and makes possible the greatest goal—love (see 1 Cor. 13:13).

2. Teachers who failed to use God's Law properly.

> But we know that the law is good, if one uses it lawfully, knowing this, that law is not laid down for a righteous man, but for lawless and disobedient ones, for ungodly and sinners, for unholy and profane ones, for father-smiters and mother-smiters, for murderers, for fornicators, for Sodomites, for kidnapers, for liars, for perjurers, and if any other thing opposes the healthy teaching, in accord with the gospel of the blessed God, with which I myself was entrusted (1:8-11).

Paul expands his description of the danger at Ephesus by showing that those false teachers not only taught other doctrine while claiming to be Law-teachers, but they also were using the Law improperly.

a. The law itself is good.

The term "law" (*nomos*) in verse 9 is without the article, a fact leading many to think that he refers to law in general, not just the Mosaic Law. It is certainly true that laws are necessary in human life for the restraint of evil, and if properly enacted and administered are a blessing to humanity. However, those who think this refers to the Mosaic Law have several factors in their favor. The preceding context (see v. 7) has been discussing certain would-be law-teachers who were certainly exponents of the Mosaic Law. Verse 8 does use the definite article with "law." Furthermore, the list of sins that appears in verses 9 and 10 seems clearly to follow the order of the Ten Commandments. Inasmuch as the Mosaic Law is the one discussed in the context, it is not obligatory to have the article in every instance for identification.

The adjective Paul employs to characterize the law is "good" (*kalos*). The usual significance of this term is outward attractiveness in addition to inward worth. The law is not to be condemned just because some men perverted it, especially if it is a law that God has given. Men everywhere recognize the sterling worth of the Mosaic Law (and the need of all law, for that matter). Paul had an enlightened conscience and recognized the excellence of the law. His conscience condemned the same things the law did. Furthermore, the purpose of the law, to lead men to Christ (Gal. 3:24), was unquestionably a good thing.

b. The law has an improper use.

The fact that law is good if used lawfully implies that it could be used unlawfully. Verse 9 states this wrong use: the application of law to a righteous man. Even using those terms in a general, nontechnical way, we can see the truth of his argument from human experience. Laws are not enacted because men are good, but because they are thoughtless, selfish, and criminal. A perfectly upright citizen needs no law, except to protect him from the depredations of his fellows, and to warn him against yielding to his own evil tendencies.

The context, however, which deals with men invading the church with their misinterpretation of the law, indicates that the theological meaning of "righteous man" (*dikaiōi*) must be understood. Since Paul is arguing that these law-teachers must be charged not to teach in the church as they have been, then his explanation that law is not for a righteous man must mean the member of the church. For a Christian to be called "righteous" is to say he is justified (exactly the same word in the Greek).

> For as by one man's disobedience many were made sinners, so by the obedience of one shall many be made righteous (Rom. 5:19).

> Who shall lay anything to the charge of God's elect? It is God that justifieth (Rom. 8:33).

Hence the impropriety of applying the law to Christians is obvious. The believer has died to the law's demands in the person of his substitute, Christ ("the end of the law . . . to everyone who believeth," Rom. 10:4). To bring the law into the church at Ephesus as a guide for Christians was to miss the purpose of the law. It was not designed to form motives of integrity. Christians have something far better: the Holy Spirit who continually guides from within.

    c. The law has a proper use.

        The chief excellence of the law was its unsparingness of evil and its glorious standard of right. The law speaks as loudly as ever to the sinner. From the order of terms in Paul's list of sins, it seems assured that he had the Decalogue in mind as he named a flagrant violator of each commandment. A study of the following table will show this. The sins listed are Paul's order.

1 Timothy 1:9-10	*Exodus 20:1-17*
Lawless and disobedient.	1. Thou shalt have no other gods before me.
Ungodly and sinners.	2. Thou shalt not make unto thee any graven image.
Unholy and profane.	3. Thou shalt not take the

name of the Lord thy God in vain.

4. Remember the sabbath day to keep it holy.

The first table of the Decalogue is covered in general terms by these three pairs of words. The examples of violators of the second table are more clearly seen in the next listing.

Father-smiters and mother-smiters.

5. Honor thy father and thy mother.

Murderers.

6. Thou shalt not kill.

Fornicators, Sodomites.

7. Thou shalt not commit adultery.

Kidnappers.

8. Thou shalt not steal.

Liars, perjurers.

9. Thou shalt not bear false witness.

Any other thing.

10. Thou shalt not covet. (Covetousness is hard to detect, and hence Paul does not name a flagrant example.)

The order of Paul's terms, especially the latter group, makes it very probable that he had the Ten Commandments in mind as he named various flagrant sins.

The fact that the Mosaic Law was intended not for righteous ones but for sinners is in accord with (*kata*, v. 11) the gospel message. For the gospel is the good news (*euaggelion*) that Christ died and bore the curse of the law, and believers in Christ are accounted as having died with Him. Kelly states the matter thus:

> If Christ died and bore its curse, and we too died with Him and now are no longer under law but under grace, the truth is kept intact, the authority of law is main-

tained, and yet we who believe have full deliverance. If we were really under law for walk, we ought to be cursed, or you destroy its authority.[7]

Hence the proper use of the law is to apply it to sinners to show them their sin and then to present the gospel with its message of salvation in Christ.

Paul terms the gospel with which he was entrusted "the gospel of the glory of the blessed God." Translations which weaken the phrase tēs doxēs to a simple adjective "glorious" are inexact and misleading. This is not a Hebraism but an assertion of God's glory, which is so evidently revealed in the Gospel. Fairbairn concisely expresses this:

> The gospel of God's glory is the gospel which peculiarly displays His glory,—unfolds this to the view of men by showing the moral character and perfections of God exhibited as they are nowhere else in the person and work of Christ.[8]

B. *The outstanding illustration of the results of sound doctrine* (vv. 12-17).

When Paul wished to give Timothy a most effective illustration of sound gospel teaching as contrasted with the disastrous effects of legalism, he related his own personal experience. His thanksgiving for the privilege of ministering the gospel reminded him of the utter difference of his former life, and he gave all credit to the mercy and grace of God who had provided the gospel.

> Thanks have I to the one who empowered me, to Christ Jesus our Lord, because he considered me faithful, having placed into service, formerly being a blasphemer and a persecutor and an insolent man: but I received mercy because being ignorant I acted in unbelief, and the grace of our Lord abounded exceedingly with faith and love which is in Christ Jesus (vv. 12-14).

1. Paul's former life of law-keeping was a life of unbelief.

His description of himself must not be attributed to

false humility or exaggeration, but was undoubtedly the way he felt about his past life. Those who live closest to God are usually the most keenly aware of their own faults.

Paul describes his past life by three terms, each term harsher than the one before. He had been a blasphemer (*blasphēmon*). Robertson traces this term either to the roots *blax*, stupid, and *phēmē*, speech, or to *blaptō*, to injure.[9] It denotes evil and injurious speech directed usually against God. Paul had spoken untruths against God and the Word. In Paul's case the blasphemy was particularly against Christ, since Paul thought he was honoring the God of his fathers (Acts 26:9). Furthermore, he had been a persecutor (*diōktēn*), pursuing God's people as far as Damascus. It seems likely that the unconverted Saul of Tarsus was the leader of the persecution described in Acts 8:1-3. Finally, Paul had been an insolent or outrageous man (*hubristēn*). He had committed all sorts of insulting and outrageous acts, even compelling Christians to blaspheme (Acts 26:11). Later Paul was to experience some of this insolent treatment at Philippi, for he uses a cognate participle to describe his shameful treatment (*hubristhentes*, 1 Thess. 2:2). Such treatment was also given to Christ: ". . . and shall be mocked, and spitefully entreated [*hubristhēsetai*], and spitted on" (Luke 18:32).

The factor that makes this testimony of Paul such a telling one in the light of the legalistic danger at Ephesus is that all of those previous traits of Paul occurred while he was a zealous exponent of the law. In fact, it may be asserted that the law produced those characteristics in him, as he became more and more a fanatical defender against its supposed enemies.

To complete the indictment against law-keeping as the producer of a righteous life, Paul admits that his former actions were done ignorantly because all the time he was in the realm of unbelief (*en apistiāi*).

His plea of ignorance was not an excuse for his guilt, however, though it does give the reason (*hoti*) why he received mercy. In the Old Testament a distinction is made between those who sinned through ignorance (including moral weakness) and those who sinned presumptuously ("with a high hand," Num. 15:30, ASV).* Atonement was available for the former group; none was possible for the latter. One clear passage is Numbers 15:27-31:

> And if any soul sin through ignorance, then he shall bring a she goat of the first year for a sin-offering. And the priest shall make an atonement for the soul that sinneth ignorantly, when he sinneth by ignorance before the Lord, to make an atonement for him; and it shall be forgiven him. . . . But the soul that doeth ought presumptuously, whether he be born in the land or a stranger, the same reproacheth the Lord; and that soul shall be cut off from among his people. Because he hath despised the word of the Lord, and hath broken his commandment, that soul shall utterly be cut off; his iniquity shall be upon him.

Hence Paul came under the first group. In spite of his crimes against God and the church, they were not the result of a determined set of his will against God (which the Old Testament calls "sinning presumptuously" and the New Testament calls the "sin against the Holy Ghost"). On the contrary, he thought he was doing God service. But his strenuous attempt to please God by law-keeping apart from the gospel resulted in blasphemy, persecution, and insolence.

    2. Paul's present life in the ministry was the result of mercy and grace.

In contrast to the sinful past, Paul now rejoices in his privileges of the present. He has a ministry to which Christ appointed him. This appointment was not the

---

*American Standard Version.

product of Paul's own abilities, but the enabling power to perform it was also supplied by Christ.

In receiving this ministry, Paul recognized that he had been the recipient of mercy (*ēleēthēn*, I was mercied). He had been spared a punishment that was deserved, and had felt the relieving hand of God. Coupled with mercy was grace (*charis*), the favor of the Lord, which was not granted on the basis of merit but freely given to the sinner. Along with the abounding grace were the gifts of faith and love.

3. Paul's conversion was planned as a pattern to future believers.

> Faithful is the word and worthy of all acceptance, that Christ Jesus came into the world to save sinners, of whom a foremost one am I. But on account of this I received mercy, in order that in me, a foremost one, Jesus Christ might show all his longsuffering, for a model of the ones about to believe on him unto life eternal. And to the King of the ages, incorruptible, invisible, only God, honor and glory forever and ever. Amen (vv. 15-17).

The formula, "faithful is the word," occurs five times in the New Testament, all of them in the Pastoral Epistles (1 Tim. 1:15; 3:1; 4:9; 2 Tim. 2:11; Titus 3:8). A similar expression, "these words are faithful and true," occurs twice (Rev. 21:5; 22:6). Apparently during the latter half of the first century, this formula was quite generally used to emphasize important truths. Here the reference almost certainly is to the statement of Jesus, uttered on several occasions (Matt. 9:13; Luke 19:10). Such truths as these probably were often repeated in the Christian assemblies, and were thus well known.

Paul refers to himself as a foremost of sinners (*prōtos*). The word *prōtos* may mean "first" either in time or in rank. This use in verse 15 (as well as v. 16) is obviously in the sense of rank. But is Paul guilty of extreme exaggeration in calling himself a first-rank sinner? (It should be noted that *prōtos* is anarthrous. He does not say "the" foremost of sinners.) There are no grounds for limiting the significance of "foremost" nor softening the connotation of "sinners" (*hamartōlous*). Hence we must take Paul's statement at face value. This was the way Paul felt about his life in view of the holiness of God. White expresses it well:

> In the experiences of personal religion each individual man is alone with God. He sees nought but the Holy One and his own sinful self. . . . And the more familiar a man becomes with the meeting of God face to face the less likely is he to be deceived as to the gulf which parts him, limited, finite, defective, from the Infinite and Perfect. It is not easy to think of anyone but St. Paul as penning these words; although his expressions of self-depreciation elsewhere (1 Cor. 15:9; Eph. 3:18) are quite differently worded. In each case the form in which they are couched arises naturally out of the context. The sincerity of St. Paul's humility is proved by the fact that he had no mock modesty; when the occasion compelled it, he could appraise himself (e.g., Acts 23:1; 24:16; 2 Cor. 11:5; 12:11; Gal. 2:6).[10]

No one can say he is too sinful to be saved since Christ has saved Paul. Furthermore, no Christian should regard any sinner as a hopeless case.

Paul indicates that his experience of God's saving grace was not only a blessing to himself but had a purpose of grace to others also. His case provided a pattern for future believers. The word *hupotupōsis* means an outline, sketch, example, pattern. It was used of a model which was placed before someone to be copied. Paul's case was an outline or pattern of Christ's long-suffering (*makrothumian*). This attitude of God is His restraining of His ardor (*thumos*) or rage against sin for a long period (*makros*). Just as Christ endured the blasphemies and persecutions of Paul for so long a time and did not smite him with judgment, so is He with all the world. Judgment is in abeyance during this age. If a sinner like Saul of Tarsus could be spared and receive salvation, so may other sinners.

Furthermore, to look at the positive side, Paul's case provided a pattern for those about to believe in Christ (*tōn mellontōn pisteuein ep' autōi*). No other conversion has been recounted so profitably to the winning of sinners to Christ. The account of Paul's conversion has been used to win Jews and gentiles. Paul gave his personal testimony many times. It appears, either extended or brief, no less than six times in the New Testament (Acts 9, 22, 26; Gal. 1, 2; Phil. 3; 1 Tim. 1). We still preach from it today.

No wonder Paul exults as he does in verse 17! A consideration of the great truths of sound doctrine often drew forth from Paul a doxology to God whom He now loved and served correctly. This doxology is one of the characteristic marks of Pauline authorship and is typical of his fervent spirit when thinking of salvation.

The great majority of commentators refer this doxology to God the Father. Only in rare instances does anyone understand the reference to be to Christ. However, the anarthrous use of *theōi* suggests that Paul is not attempting to isolate or distinguish the Persons of the Godhead, but is ascribing his praise to God in the generic sense, that is, the Triune God. If one must distinguish, then this writer must assert that some of the terms fit the Father more easily than Christ (e.g., "invisible," "only God"), but he feels that the explanation of the Triune God is the solution to the difficulty.

C. *The responsibility of the minister toward sound doctrine* (vv. 18-20).

Timothy is told to continue to promote sound doctrine and rebuke false teachers. By so doing he will keep his own faith in good condition and will avoid spiritual shipwreck.

1. The responsibility expressed by formal charge.

This charge I deposit with you, child Timothy, in

accord with the prophecies which led the way to you,
that you might wage in them the good warfare, holding
faith and a good conscience . . . (vv. 18, 19a).

The mention of "charge" (paraggelian) takes us back to
verses 3 and 5 where the same noun and cognate verb are
used. The charge as there explained was the command to
promote sound doctrine by the prohibiting of false
teachers and their doctrines. Again Paul emphasizes the
solemnity and importance of this matter by couching it in
this manner.

The expression "I deposit" (KJV, commit) is a banking
term (paratithemai) when used in the middle voice. The
deposit is the command to proclaim sound doctrine and
protect it from any adulteration by false teachers.

Such a charge is in perfect harmony with the prophecies which led the way to Timothy's present position.
The translation, "according to the prophecies which went
before on thee" (KJV) is not too clear. "According to the
prophecies which led the way to thee" (ASV) is better.
The participle employed is the present active of proagō,
to lead forward, lead the way. To understand these
prophecies or divine utterances in connection with
Timothy, one must consider another passage: "Neglect
not the gift that is in thee, which was given thee by
prophecy, with the laying on of the hands of the presbytery" (1 Tim. 4:14). Prophecies apparently led the way to
Timothy's ministry just as in the case of Saul and Barnabas (Acts 13:2). We are not told the content of these
prophecies, but on the basis of these passages, we conclude that they revealed what special gifts had been imparted to Timothy for his ministry at the time when the
elders laid their hands on him to set him apart for special
service. Hence Timothy was at Ephesus directing affairs
because of his divinely indicated spiritual gifts. Many
commentators wish to include in those prophecies the
preaching that brought Timothy to salvation, and some
include the Old Testament Scriptures that prepared his

heart for the gospel. Since the participle is a present tense, stressing continuing action of "leading the way," these further inclusions are certainly possible.

A practical consideration is seen here. Young ministers have often found relief from occasional discouragement by recalling their own call to the ministry and the time when their spiritual gifts were recognized by the church, and the elders laid hands on them, separating them to the work of the ministry.

As Timothy carried out the injunction of Paul, he would be campaigning as a soldier should in the good war, the campaign against the opponents of Christ and the gospel. But he must be careful in maintaining his own faith and conscience. This is a reference to the inward state of the minister. He must keep his own faith in good condition. He must be uncompromising on the matter of sound doctrine. The religious teacher who knows the truth but teaches falsehood, or allows it to be taught under his jurisdiction, will not have a good conscience, at least not at the outset. His conscience will condemn such perversion. However, persistence in such a course may dull the conscience so that it fails to be a helpful guide. Thus the minister should be very much concerned that his ministry is in accord with the standard of God's Word, in order that his conscience will be good, that is, it will function properly and have nothing to condemn.

2. The responsibility illustrated by two examples.

Which some having thrust away concerning the faith have made shipwreck: of whom are Hymenaeus and Alexander, whom I delivered to Satan in order that they might be disciplined not to blaspheme (vv. 19b, 20).

There were some religious teachers in the church at Ephesus who had rejected the gospel and adopted false doctrines, thus incurring a bad conscience. By their teaching they were making shipwreck of the faith, that is, the body of truth which comprises the Christian faith.

Since "faith" has the article (*tēn pistin*) it is best to understand it objectively, rather than "their faith." Although the great historical and theological facts of the gospel are settled and unchangeable, it is possible for heretics to wreck the message of the truth, and this has been done in various ways by teachers of error in every century. As previously intimated, some explain this statement as meaning "suffered shipwreck concerning their faith." Such a translation is possible, since the Greek may use the article as a pronoun at times. By this understanding, certain false teachers who abandoned the true doctrine of Christ and went after falsehood caused their own personal faith to meet with catastrophe. Such an interpretation of the verse indicates nothing concerning the possibility of a true believer being finally lost, since Paul's metaphor of shipwreck does not imply death. Paul himself experienced physical shipwreck on four occasions and survived each time (2 Cor. 11:25; Acts 27).

Two persons are cited as outstanding examples of men who did not stand true to sound doctrine. Hymenaeus is apparently referred to again in 2 Timothy 2:17, along with the mention of his error. He taught that the resurrection was already past. He probably spiritualized the doctrine and related it to conversion, and then denied any bodily resurrection. The other culprit was named Alexander, an extremely common name among the Greeks. Because it was such an ordinary name (not unusual like Hymenaeus), there are not sufficient grounds to identify him with other men of the same name. The man, Alexander the coppersmith (2 Tim. 4:14), has the added description, probably to distinguish him from the Alexander of 1 Timothy 1. Nor are there any compelling reasons for supposing him to be the same Alexander involved in the riot of the silversmiths (Acts 19).

Because of their falsity toward sound doctrine, Paul had delivered them to Satan for corrective discipline. The full significance of this action is disputed, and the lack of complete scriptural explanation must cause it to remain uncertain. However, some inferences can properly be drawn. Similar language is employed by Paul in dealing with the Corinthian church concerning the incestuous man. "To deliver such a one unto Satan for the destruction of the flesh, that the spirit may be saved in the day of the Lord Jesus. . . . Therefore put away from among yourselves that wicked person" (1 Cor. 5:5, 13). There the church was instructed to remove the offender from their company; that is, to excommunicate him.

Excommunication from the church places the offender back in the world which is Satan's domain. Hence to deliver unto Satan can be understood as removal back to the world, and this accords with other scriptural statements. "We know that we are of God, and the whole world lieth in the evil one" (1 John 5:19, ASV).

Such a removal from the church was corrective in its intent. If the false teachers were allowed to continue in their evil practices, they would not only lead others astray, but would delude themselves into a false sense of spiritual security. But removal into Satan's realm would cause the offenders to face the issues. If they were truly saved, the buffeting by Satan would cause them to see their error and forsake their sin.

II. CHARGE CONCERNING PUBLIC WORSHIP (2:1-15).

Now that Paul has sketched in an introductory way the problem facing the Ephesian church under Timothy's care, he proceeds to advise Timothy concerning the conducting of public worship. It is generally inferred by commentators that chapter 2 deals with problems of public worship. Some of the verses would be unintelligible or at least highly improbable if private devotions or household prayer were meant. For instance, verses 9 and 12 are more readily understood as referring to public meetings.

A. *Prayer in public worship* (vv. 1-7).

> I exhort therefore first of all that there be made en-
> treaties, prayers, petitions, thanksgivings in behalf of
> all men, in behalf of kings and all who are in suprema-
> cy . . . (vv. 1, 2a).

The connection to the preceding discussion is made
with the employment of *oun*, "therefore," indicating a
logical resumption of the foregoing material. In view of
the charge given to Timothy throughout chapter 1, and
restated in verse 18, Paul next enumerates a group of
directives to guide the young minister in carrying out the
charge. The expression *prōton pantōn* (first of all) goes
with *parakalō* (I exhort) and indicates the first of the
series of subjects which appear in the rest of the letter. (It
does not mean that entreaties are to be made first, followed by prayers, petitions, and thanksgivings.)

   1. The kinds of prayer.

   Four terms are employed to describe the function of
prayer. These terms are not mutually exclusive. Several
are synonyms. Rather than attempting the precarious task
of drawing hard and fast distinctions among them, it is
better to regard them as aspects or elements of genuine
prayer. It is highly probable that each of these aspects will
appear in every public prayer.

   a. Entreaties (*deēseis*).

   The root of this noun is the verb *deomai*, to
need. It considers prayer as an expression of our *needs,*
and implies the feeling of our great need of the gifts and
blessing of God.

   b. Prayers (*proseuchas*).

   This is the general term for prayer. It is always
restricted to prayers directed toward Deity, however. The
preceding word *deēseis* had no such restriction. Hence
proseuchē is a sacred word, and refers to prayer as a coming to God. The ideas of *worship* and *reverence* are its
distinctive features.

    c. Petitions (*enteuxeis*).

    This word occurs only twice in the New Testament, here and in 4:5. The translation (KJV) "intercessions" is inexact because it suggests pleadings in behalf of others, an idea not inherent in the word. The cognate verb form *entugchanein*, "to fall in with a person, to draw near so as to converse familiarly,"[11] indicates that the noun denotes an approach to God in confident, familiar prayer. The idea of petition in this term is also clearly established in the papyri.[12] Here the description of prayer is that of free access to God with childlike *confidence*. (But it is not necessarily on behalf of others. That idea comes from the context and is applicable to all aspects of prayer.)

    d. Thanksgivings (*eucharistias*).

    Thanksgivings should accompany prayer of every form (Phil. 4:6). No matter what his immediate condition, every Christian enjoys many undeserved blessings from God. Furthermore, unthankfulness is a great sin and is linked with unholiness by Paul (2 Tim. 3:2). Archbishop Trench has given us the thought that thanksgiving will persist even in Heaven, when all other forms of prayer have ceased because of the fruition of the things prayed for.

> As such it may, and will, subsist in Heaven (Rev. 4:9; 7:12); will indeed be larger, deeper, fuller there than here: for only there will the redeemed know how much they owe to their Lord; and this it will do, while all other forms of prayer, in the very nature of things, will have ceased in the entire possession and present fruition of the things prayed for.[13]

    2. The objects of prayer.

      a. All men.

    The "all men" (*pantōn*) is an unlimited expression. It cannot be restricted to all believers, for surely not all the kings mentioned next were Christians. This command for such intercessory prayer is in contrast to the

Jewish attitude toward gentiles. However, this command is a reasonable one, for who would pray for sinners if the church did not? Only Christians have a vital contact with God. If this command is carried out, no man is left unprayed for. We cannot pray too widely.

b. Kings and all who are in supremacy.

Paul singled out one group which should receive mention in our public prayers. These are the rulers, those who possess the greatest temporal power for good or evil. The term *basileus* (king) is the general designation for the supreme ruler and was applied to the Roman emperors by Josephus and the inscriptions.[14] It was general enough to apply to lesser kings as well. The group referred to as "all the ones being in supremacy" are the lesser officials appointed by the supreme ruler to govern various areas.

God Himself has given to human rulers this authority (Rom. 13), and Christians can assist them by prayer. It is significant that Paul singled out for special mention a group of persons who might be the most easily hated by Christians. These were the days of the infamous Nero. Christians were not wholeheartedly protected by the administrators in most areas. Consequently, believers had learned to fear the power resident in their governments. But lest that fear become hatred, Paul urged the antidote—prayer. Prayer for those who mistreat is still the finest safeguard against the sin of hatred. The Christian writers of the second and third centuries inform us that prayer for rulers always formed a part of the Christian gatherings.

3. The reason for prayer.

In order that we may lead a tranquil and quiet life in all godliness and dignity. This is good and acceptable before our Saviour God, who wishes all men to be saved and to come into full knowledge of truth (vv. 2b-4).

a. With respect to the church.

Such prayer will produce a tranquil and quiet

life for the church. This reason need not be understood as completely selfish, for if the church is at peace with outsiders, then the outsiders are experiencing peace also. God's blessings usually overflow the recipients, and affect others too. The terms *ēremon* and *hēsuchion* are synonyms, and not all agree on the distinctions between them. Vincent gives one of the clearest explanations:

> *Eremos* denotes quiet arising from the absence of outward disturbances: *hēsuchios* tranquility arising from within. Thus *anēr hēsuchios* is the composed, discreet, self-contained man, who keeps himself from rash doing: *ēremos anēr* is he who is withdrawn from outward disturbances.[15]

Since Christians must be subject to rulers who may persecute them, prayer is necessary to overrule them. Thus believers may be spared from troubles without and unrest within.

This manner of life must be exercised in the realm of godliness and dignity. *Eusebeia* (godliness) describes one's attitude and conduct as measured by God's standard. Godliness is a manner of life that properly reverences God. *Semnotēs* (dignity) refers to that quality of life which entitles one to respect among men. The translation "honesty" (KJV) should be understood in the sense of "honorableness." This term is a favorite one in the Pastoral Epistles. The dignity which so enhances the believer in his daily walk should not be overlooked in pastoral ministry.

      b. With respect to God.

         Such prayer agrees with God's desire for all mankind. The reason why we may pray for all men is because of God's action in providing salvation. Consequently, Paul refers to God by the title *tou sotēros hēmōn theou*, "our Savior God," an expression similar to 1:1. God as Savior has opened the door of prayer to men.

Furthermore, God wishes all men to be saved. The verb *thelō* is employed, which denotes a desire springing out of the emotions or inclinations, rather than out of deliberation (*boulomai*).[16] Hence this is a reference to God's moral will which applies to all men. However, this moral will of God may fail, and often does. Men sin, although God does not want them to. Consequently, if men are lost, it is because they opposed God's will which gave His Son to save them. This does not teach universalism, for God does not violate man's opportunity to choose. The passive voice of the infinitive *sōthēnai* (to be saved) may be suggestive. God wishes all men to be saved, that is, to experience salvation through the appointed channel of personal faith in Christ. If the text had used the active voice, "wishes to save all men," one would wonder why God does not then do so.

Through salvation by faith men can come into full realization of truth, and this is also God's will for men. *Epignōsis* is a richer term than *gnōsis*, and denotes knowledge which is the result of concentrating the attention upon (*epi*) a matter. English has no comparable term, so the translation "full knowledge" is used and then explained. Salvation places men in Christ who said, "I am the truth" (John 14:6). The Christian is thus in a position to enter into full experiential knowledge of Christ, and this is the key to full knowledge in every department of human thought. The anarthrous use of these terms stresses the quality of knowledge and truth rather than specific items.

4. The basis for prayer.

> For one is God; one also is Mediator of God and men, a man Christ Jesus, who gave himself a ransom in behalf of all, the testimony for its own seasons: unto which I myself was appointed, a proclaimer and an apostle—I speak truth, I do not lie—a teacher of gentiles in faith and truth (vv. 5-7).

Paul's next thought explains the basis upon which prayer can be made to God for the salvation and blessing of all men. These grounds for universal prayer center upon the Gospel which provides salvation available for all. Paul's thought can be analyzed as four arguments for universal prayer.

a. The unity of God.

"One is God." This was the central truth of the Old Testament. If there were many gods, men could be left to their own. But since there is only one God, and He desires all to be saved, then prayer to Him for all men is in order. If there is only one God, then He is the God of all men. All are responsible to Him. His expressed concern for the salvation of all should encourage men to pray.

b. The unity of the Mediator.

"One also is Mediator." The oneness of the Mediator is as fundamental to Christianity as the oneness of God to the Old Testament Jew. Since there is only one Mediator, then Christians have the responsibility of making Him known to all men. Some by their practice imply that Christ is "one" among many, and have included angels, saints, and the Virgin Mary as other mediators. That is exegetically impossible as seen in the preceding clause. To say Christ is one among many mediators is to say that God is one among many gods, a thought which hardly needs refutation.

This Mediator is a man: namely, Christ Jesus. The absence of the article with *anthrōpos* emphasizes the generic sense rather than the particular specimen. Our Mediator, although equally God, became man. Spence suggests that the humanity of Christ is specially mentioned because in His humanitysHe performed the work of Mediator, and also because His work affected the human race.[17] The incarnation of Christ answered the plea of Job 9:32-33.

c. The availability of the ransom.

Christ gave Himself as a "ransom for all" (*anti-lutron huper pantōn*). This is strongly reminiscent of Christ's own statement, "a ransom for many" (*lutron anti pollōn*, Matt. 20:28). The prefixing of *anti* emphasizes the idea of substitution. *Anti* signified substitution and its usual translation is "instead of."[18] That is confirmed by the findings in the papyri.[19] Thus by its very nature, this ransom is substitutional in character. Furthermore, it is available for all (*huper pantōn*). The announcement of this good news was to be made at the proper time. Before Christ ascended, He commissioned His followers to evangelize and make disciples. The proper season had arrived. During this age of God's grace, the testimony must be given out.

    d. The commission for gentiles.

        As a final argument to show the adequate basis for universal prayer, Paul points to his own commission which was to be a herald, apostle, and teacher of gentiles. This commission to Paul came from Christ, and specifically directed him to gentiles. Hence no racial or class distinctions are valid in the scope of the gospel (see Acts 9:15). Paul raised this issue, not to vindicate himself, but to show the divine interest in gentiles and rulers as illustrated by his own experience.

  B. *Men and women in public worship* (vv. 8-15).

    1. Conduct of the men.

> I will, therefore, the men to be praying in every place, lifting up holy hands, without wrath and argument (v. 8).

Having just discussed the place of prayer in public worship, Paul logically moves to those who will do the praying, and indicates the logical connection by the use of *oun*. The verb *boulomai* (I will) is stronger than *thelō*, and indicates a wish, intention, or purpose formed after deliberation.[20] (*thelō* denotes a wish seated in the emotions.) Thus we have Paul's apostolic directive to Timothy and the Ephesian congregation.

    a. Men should do the praying in public worship.

        The present infinitive *proseuchesthai* (to be praying) is in the emphatic place in the sentence, and stresses the fact that praying is to be an important and continual feature of Christian worship. The subject of this infinitive *tous andras* denotes men as distinguished from women (not just mankind in general, that is, *anthrōpos*). This directive from Paul is significant for at least two reasons. First, it shows that public praying in the first century was not restricted to elders or any clergy class, although there were elders in the church at that time. It was not limited to men with special gifts. Although in later hierarchical development, the practice of free prayer was abrogated, Paul himself placed no such limitations upon praying. Plummer traces the development of this restriction in prayer:[21]

All men (1 Tim. 2:8).

Extemporaneous prayer limited to "the prophets" (according to the *Didachē*).

The president of the congregation, that is, presiding elder (Justin Martyr).

Free prayer abolished altogether.

Second, Paul's statement indicates the male members of the congregation should be the leaders in public prayer. The word *anēr* definitely means men as distinguished from women. This restriction of public praying to the men is the general rule. However, Paul apparently did not mean that women cannot pray publicly, for he gave instruction on that very subject to the Corinthian church. "But every woman that prayeth or prophesieth with her head uncovered dishonoreth her head" (1 Cor. 11:5). The inference must be drawn that a woman could pray publicly if her head were covered. The restriction indicates that she must pray in such a way as not to usurp the place of the men. Therefore, this writer concludes that Paul means that men are to be the leaders in public prayers (1 Tim. 2:8). If women wish to engage in public prayer, they must not aspire to leadership, but must recognize the headship of the men.

The discussions in this chapter refer to the general worship service, as indicated by the references to teaching as well as praying. Consequently, a service convened for the special purpose of prayer is somewhat different. As long as men are in control of the service, the divine order is maintained, and women need feel no hesitancy in offering prayer.

    b. This directive holds good for public worship everywhere.

    Paul is not here urging men to pray wherever they might be, but says that wherever public prayer is offered, the men should be the leaders in it. It must be remembered that the first-century church had no special buildings for meeting, and consequently met in various homes of Christians. But regardless of the meeting place, this directive is to be followed.

    c. The prayers of the men are to be accompanied by a holy life.

    The use of the figure "lifting up holy hands" is dramatic and instructive. This is the only place in the New Testament where this figure is employed of prayer. Many see here a reference to one of the common bodily postures assumed by early Christians while praying. This posture is described frequently in the Old Testament (1 Kings 8:22; Psalm 28:2; 63:4; 134:2). However, Paul can scarcely be setting forth a particular bodily posture as being preferable, for his adjective *hosious* (holy) denotes a spiritual quality and indicates that he is using "hands" as symbolic of daily life. The adjective *hosios* means holy in the sense of unpolluted. Trench distinguishes it from *hagios* (holy, separate) by the following illustration:

> Joseph by reverencing the sanctity of marriage which violation would pollute, was *hosios*; by remaining aloof from the temptress and being devoted to God, he was *hagios*.[22]

Thus when men pray, they are to do so with spiritually unpolluted hands. This is another way of saying "an unpolluted life." The hands are an appropriate symbol of life and conduct since they are the bodily instrument for most of our activities. Only men whose lives manifest practical righteousness should pray in public. This is objective and can be observed by the church. Persons living openly in sin have no business offering public prayer, and should not be called upon to do so. "If I regard iniquity in my heart the Lord will not hear me" (Psalm 66:18).

      d. The prayers of the men are to be accompanied
         by a proper attitude.

      It is not unlikely that the excesses of evil rulers which were directed against the Christians caused wrath to arise in the hearts of the victims. But such wrath must gain no foothold when Christians come together to pray for their rulers. God's wrath is completely holy, but the wrath of man is too often based on personal feelings. "For the wrath of man worketh not the righteousness of God" (James 1:20). Man's wrath usually desires evil on others, but not God's. Luke 9:52-56 shows what man's wrath produces. How much better is the example of the believers in their prayer during persecution, "Lord, behold their threatenings" (Acts 4:29). All churches and believers can profit by this instruction.

      Prayer must be made also without argument or inward reasoning. The meaning of *dialogismou* in this passage is disputed. The King James rendering "doubting" is followed by many commentators. However, this meaning is not admitted by Liddell and Scott. It is undeniable that the usual significance of the term is reasoning, usually of argumentative or disputing nature. Frequently in the New Testament, there is an evil connotation. (In no New Testament passage is the meaning clearly "doubting.") The word itself may mean argument or disputing with others about their manner or subject matter for prayer, or it could mean argument or reasoning with oneself concerning the merit of such prayer. In this latter usage the element of doubt or lack of full confidence could be inferred. Inasmuch as the word is employed anarthrously, it is best to understand it as a reference to that spirit of argumenta-

tion or disputing, whether with others or within oneself, a spirit which has no place in true prayer.
2. Conduct of the women.
    a. Women are to dress in modest apparel.

> Likewise, women in well-arranged apparel, with modesty and sobriety, to adorn themselves, not in braids and gold or pearls or costly clothing, but that which is becoming to women professing godliness— through good works (vv. 9, 10).

Hōsautōs (likewise) links this paragraph to the preceding discussion, showing that the public worship service is still being considered. The exhortations to the women regarding dress are in view of their attire when attending worship. It is suggested by some, including Calvin, that they are to pray this way.[23] (cf. 1 Cor. 11:5, where women who pray are told to have their heads covered.) However, it does not seem necessary to limit the direction to this one activity.

The apparel is to be *kosmiōi*. This adjective is a cognate of the verb *kosmeō* which is also used in this sentence and is translated "to adorn" or "to arrange." Hence the apparel is to be "well-arranged." We would say it should be "in good taste." The well-grooming of the woman should never violate a proper sense of modesty. The word *aidōs* denotes reverence, respect, modesty. This coupled with *sōphrosunē*, sobriety, or a well-balanced state of mind, will protect the woman from vanity and worldly display. One's attire is the expression of tastes, interests, and even character. Consequently, the manner in which a woman dresses indicates a great deal about what sort of woman she is. Paul points out some of the more flagrant examples of poor taste in dress, which should not be emulated by the godly woman. Alfred Plummer quotes Chrysostom on this subject:

> And what then is modest apparel? Such as covers them completely and decently, and not with superfluous ornaments; for the one is decent and the other is not.

What? Do you approach God to pray with broidered hair and ornaments of gold? Are you come to a ball? to a marriage-feast? to a carnival? There such costly things might have been seasonable: here not one of them is wanted. You are come to pray, to ask pardon for your sins, to plead for your offences, beseeching the Lord, and hoping to render him propitious to you. Away with such hypocrisy![24]

The positive adornment which the godly woman is to assume is clearly given by the apostle. She is to adorn herself with good works. Her adorning, that which gives her attractiveness, is not to be costly array but exhibitions of Christian character. Scripture has more than one example of godly women whose good works have lived after them and have challenged succeeding generations. Phoebe was "a succorer of many" (Rom. 16:1-2). Lydia manifested Christian hospitality (Acts 16:14, 15). Dorcas dedicated her sewing talents to the relieving of the needy (Acts 9:36, 39). These displays of Christian character bless us all in the reading of them, although we know nothing about how the women were dressed. Every Christian woman should prize more highly a testimony to her Christian labors than a reputation as the best-dressed woman in the congregation.

It should be clear that Paul is not forbidding the wearing of any gold or pearls or expensive garments, any more than Peter in a similar passage was forbidding the wearing of clothes (1 Peter 3:3, 4). But those things are not to be the means whereby the Christian woman makes herself attractive to other Christians. Good taste should always prevail, and display for vanity's sake is out of place. Lenski says:

Paul is not insisting on drab dress. Even this may be worn with vanity; the very drabness may be made a display. Each according to her station in life: the queen not being the same as her lady-in-waiting, the latter not the same as her noble mistress. Each with due propriety as modesty and propriety will indicate to her both when attending divine services and when appearing in public elsewhere.[25]

b. Women are to learn in silence.

In quietness let a woman be learning in all subjection: but to be teaching I do not permit a woman, nor to have full authority over a man, but to be in quietness. For Adam first was formed, then Eve. And Adam was not deceived, but the woman, having been completely deceived, has become in transgression (vv. 11-14).

An exhortation is first given that women are to learn, not to teach. This action of the women has reference to their conduct in the public worship services. Twice Paul characterizes their demeanor by the noun *hēsuchia*, quietness. She is to conduct herself in a manner which does not writhe under authority. She is not to regard herself as unnecessarily imposed upon because of her sex. She is exhorted to assume the attitude of a disciple (*manthanetō*) and be continually learning.

The negative part of this exhortation is given next. The woman is not to do the teaching in the public worship service. The context is not discussing the possibility of women's teaching their children. This has reference solely to the function of the authoritative teacher of doctrine in the church. Wuest makes an interesting observation on the force of the present infinitive *didaskein* as follows:

Dana and Mantey in their *Manual Grammar of the Greek New Testament* (p. 199) have this to say on the subject: "The aorist infinitive denotes that which is eventual or particular, while the present infinitive indicates a condition or process. Thus *pisteusai* (aorist) is to exercise faith on a given occasion, while *pisteuein* (present) is to be a believer; *douleusai* (aorist) is to render a service, while *douleuein* (present) is to be a slave; *hamartein* (aorist) is to commit a sin, while *hamartanein* (present) is to be a sinner." Thus, *didaxai* (aorist) is to teach, while *didaskein* (present, 2:12) is to be a teacher. Paul therefore, says, I do not permit a woman to be a teacher.[26]

The role of teacher in New Testament days was an authoritative office. The teacher was the declarer of doctrine. Another name for "teacher" was "rabbi" (John 1:38). Christ Himself as a man was recognized as one who held this office (John 3:2). Consequently, teachers were among the early officials in the church, exercising their function of declaring the Word of God (Acts 13:1; Eph. 4:1). Such a responsibility is denied to women. Nowhere in the New Testament is a woman presented as a teacher in the church. The case of Priscilla is no exception, for she was with her husband in the home and both of them instructed Apollos (Acts 18:26).

That does not mean that a woman cannot ever do any kind of teaching. Paul himself declares that women can teach other women and the young (2 Tim. 3:14; Titus 2:3). But it does mean she cannot assume the role of authoritative teacher of Scripture, in which role she would exercise dominion over men. This text does not prevent women from teaching Sunday school classes. Such teachers are under the doctrinal authority of "the teacher," that is, the pastor of the congregation. It does not forbid the ministry of women on mission fields, provided they do not take to themselves the doctrinal authority which belongs to the male head of the mission. The positive teaching is that women are to conduct themselves at public gatherings of believers in a manner which recognizes the God-appointed submissiveness to men.

The explanation for such an exhortation is then given. Paul uses two historic reasons to explain why women are not to assume the authority of a teacher. Some feminists explain Paul's prohibition as directed solely against a local situation in which women had usurped authority from men and had used their position to teach falsehood.[27] It is then implied that as long as those problems were avoided, women were not prevented from teaching. Yet it is most significant that Paul lays down no conditions here that would allow such exceptions.[28] Nor does he accuse the women at Ephesus of teaching falsehood. The apostle's reasons were based upon God's order of creation and the subsequent Fall, at which God made a further indication of His will regarding the order of the sexes.

The first reason lies in creation. "Adam first was formed, then Eve." Hence the very chronological order of creation proves that Eve was not intended to direct Adam. Paul uses the same argument: "Neither was the man created for the woman, but the woman for the man" (1 Cor. 11:9). Man is the generic head of the race. God "called their name Adam" (Gen. 5:2). It is probable that *prōtos* bears the idea of rank in the passage, and this makes the argument even clearer. "For Adam, as chief one, was formed, then Eve." If God had intended for a woman to have authority over man, then there was a time in history when it *could not* have been so!

Paul's second reason is the Fall. It was Eve who was utterly deceived by the serpent, but Adam was not deceived at all. This is forcefully indicated by the apostle who employs the compound *exapatētheisa* in the perfective sense to describe Eve's lapse, whereas the simpler form is used of Adam and then made negative (*ouk ēpatēthē*). Paul does not aver that the woman was mentally, morally, or spiritually inferior to man. But it was she who was deceived in the matter of doctrine. By taking leadership over the man, she ate first and then gave to her husband to eat. Thus the Fall was caused, not only by disobeying God's command not to eat, but also by violating the divinely appointed relation between the sexes. Woman assumed headship, and man with full knowledge of the act, subordinated himself to her leadership and ate of the fruit (Rom. 5:19). Both violated their positions. This subordination of woman to man is not Paul's invention. It is rooted in the very nature of the sexes and was put there by God Himself. Disaster comes when that relationship is violated.

Some interpreters do not accept this explanation of

women's subordination in the church. In addition to the feminists who reject all biblical authority, there are some within the church, including ones claiming to be evangelical, who argue that women have been wrongly held down, and that this passage should be understood differently.

Advocates of a wider role for women usually base their understanding upon the following principles: (1) Galatians 3:28, ". . . there is neither male nor female: for ye all are one in Christ Jesus," is alleged to be the definitive New Testament statement, and obliterates all functional distinctions between the sexes in the church.[29] (2) Genesis 1 and 2 are regarded as contradictory, or else Genesis 2 is explained as a poetic description of Genesis 1. The only reliable account of creation is Genesis 1, where the differentiation of the sexes is not elaborated.[30] (3) The Pauline passages regarding women's role in the church and in society are explained as culturally influenced and are not to be "absolutized."[31] Some frankly assert that Paul was guilty of "distortion,"[32] had "failed to grasp the full impact of his own teaching,"[33] or was clearly wrong in his interpretation of divine truth regarding women.[34]

The obvious meaning of 1 Timothy 2:11-14, however, is by no means destroyed by such arguments. In rebuttal, one may begin by first appealing to the nature of Scripture, and the hermeneutical principle which logically follows. If "all Scripture" is the product of God's revelatory breath to man (2 Tim. 3:16), then Scripture must be without error in all its parts as long as God is true. So-called "limited inerrancy" is really no inerrancy at all, for the character of God would allow Him no mixture of truth and error if all Scripture is God-breathed. Consequently, one must follow the normal rules of grammatical and historical interpretation, understanding the import of the passage in its obvious sense. Admittedly incidental cultural elements must be recognized as such (for example, "sandals" in Mark 6:9), but to treat the entire principle involved as cultural and temporary is a violation of sound hermeneutics. Most careful interpreters acknowledge that 1 Timothy 2:11-14 clearly teaches a subordinate role for women in the church.[35] Hence the problem is really one of biblical authority.

Second, Paul's teaching in this passage can be understood as consistent with his other statements. In particular, Galatians 3:28 offers no obstacles when it is understood that the oneness there described is spiritual and ontological, not functional. It was Paul's teaching that every believer is an equal sharer of new life in Christ and is thus an equal participant in the Body of Christ—the church. Functionally, however, Paul also taught that differences were to be recognized. For instance, not everyone was qualified to be an overseer or a deacon (see 1 Timothy 3).

Third, to regard Genesis 1 and 2 as contradictory is arbitrary and violates the clearly-indicated teaching of the New Testament toward the Old Testament in general and these passages in particular (John 10:35; 1 Cor. 11:8-12). Surely it is a reasonable understanding to view Genesis 1 as the general statement of creation, and Genesis 2 as the more detailed description of human origination. Therefore, even though Paul's counsel here may run counter to certain trends in today's society, it is clearly the instruction of the apostle for the conduct of the church.

Having clearly stated woman's subordinate position in the public functions of the church, does Paul wish to imply that she is too low to be saved? Does her prominent place in the Fall render her incapable of salvation in the fullest sense? Lest anyone should think that Paul had such an attitude toward women, the next verse clearly answers any suspicions. There is salvation for women, even though they are in subjection to men. This is in contrast to many other religions which place women below the level worth saving.

> But she shall be saved through the childbearing, if
> they remain in faith and love and sanctification with
> sobriety (v. 15).

All commentators agree that verse 15 affirms salvation
for women, even though they may not hold positions of
authority in the congregation. However, the interpretation of the phrase *dia tēs teknogonias* (through the childbearing) is difficult and has produced variety of opinion.
The different renderings of this passage in the common
English versions indicates something of the problem. The
KJV says "saved in childbearing." The ASV says
"through her childbearing," and the marginal reading is
"through the childbearing." The RSV* says "through
bearing children," and the marginal reading is "by the
birth of the child." This writer has encountered the following:

Four views on childbearing (1 Tim. 2:13).

Physical salvation in childbirth view. This view explains the reference as physical salvation for women
through the sufferings of childbirth. This view is held by
Ironside, Simpson, and others. In the words of its proponents we find the following:

> On the other hand, there seems to be a great deal of
> comfort here for prospective parents. I cannot help but
> believe that this has reference to the hour of her trial,
> when she shall be preserved in childbearing. . . .[36]

> Many a godly woman had dreaded the pangs of tra-
> vail; so it is not unfitting that, to relieve the pressure of
> the doom, Paul should assure Christian matrons of the
> coveted boon of *eutokia*, safe delivery, provided that
> they abide in faith and love, amid the throes of
> parturition.[37]

The glaring weakness of this interpretation is that it is
not always true. Many godly women have died in childbirth. To hold this view we are compelled to say that

*Revised Standard Version.

such women were deficient in faith or love or sobriety. How cruel! And how baseless! Scripture no more promises physical safety for every faithful woman in childbirth than it promises good health to every Christian man.

Spiritual salvation through childbirth view. This view explains the verse as teaching salvation of the soul through bearing children. This interpretation could not be found clearly stated by any author available to the writer, but he has seen the viewpoint referred to. Sometimes it is taught that if a woman dies in the process of childbirth, her soul will be saved. One Catholic writer infers that childbirth secures salvation in the following words: "Motherhood is sanctifying, though not the only means by which women may be sanctified and saved."[38]

However, the end of the verse refutes the idea that this speaks of women who die in childbirth, for they must remain in faith and love. Such would be impossible if they died. Furthermore, the granting of spiritual salvation on the basis of childbirth is contrary to scriptural teaching that salvation is given to sinners solely on the merits of Christ's substitutional atonement.

Spiritual salvation in the home view. A great host of commentators hold that this verse teaches that women will experience salvation equally with men through fulfilling their function in the home, just as men function publicly in leadership in the church. Many include ideas of child rearing as well as childbearing in their understanding of the term. White states:

> So St. Paul, taking the common sense view that childbearing, rather than public teaching or the direction of affairs, is woman's primary function, duty, privilege, and dignity, reminds Timothy and his readers that there was another aspect of the story in Genesis besides that of woman's taking the initiative in transgression: the pains of childbirth were her sentence, yet in undergoing these she finds her salvation.[39]

This view holds that *dia* (through) indicates accompanying circumstance. Others within this category give it full instrumental force. Apostolos Makrakis writes:

> Woman's main work is childbearing and child rearing; moreover, if she rears her children in the faith and love of God, if she observes the sanctity and prudence of marriage by avoiding God-hated adultery, she will be saved; but upon neglecting these her duties, she will be lost.[40]

The chief defect of this explanation is its inadequacy. It is true that women may be saved while being housewives and mothers. But this fails to give a satisfying explanation of *dia*. If woman was instrumental in causing the Fall, then we would expect Paul to explain whether that removed her from equal enjoyment of salvation, and if not, how such salvation was effected. Yet we must avoid the extremes of seeing here salvation by means of her childbirth, or else softening *dia* so that it tells us nothing whatsoever about how salvation is possible for women.

Spiritual salvation through the Incarnation of Christ view. This view holds that the reference is to salvation through the Incarnation of Christ, as promised to Eve (Gen. 3:15). The proponents of this view emphasize the article *tēs* and the usual force of *dia*. Among those holding this view are Ellicott, Clarke, and Gurney. Some who hold the third view see in the passage "another and deeper reference" which includes the idea of the fourth view.[41] The arguments in support of this interpretation as the correct understanding of the passage are presented in some detail:

Arguments Supporting Writer's View

The context has Eve under discussion, and she must be understood as the subject of the verb *sōthēsetai* (she shall be saved). Furthermore, verse 15 is connected closely to the thought of verse 14 by the use of the postpositive conjunction *de*. This close relationship has been indicated with a comma between the verses by Alford, a semicolon by Nestle's Greek text, and a colon by the ASV. Hence the verse begins with a reference to Eve, who had precipitated the Fall. Consequently, it is pertinent to consult the Mosaic narrative to aid in the problem. Genesis 3:15 indicates that the serpent's victory was not to be complete and unalterable, for God said: "I will put enmity between thee and the woman, and between thy seed and her seed; it shall bruise thy head, and thou shalt bruise his heel." Thus it would be the "seed" of the woman who would bruise the serpent's head and bring about salvation. It did not refer to childbearing in general, but to the Christ to come. This promise was fulfilled when Jesus Christ, the promised "seed," purchased redemption at Calvary.

A spiritual catastrophe is the subject of verse 14, and spiritual deliverance is to be expected as a part of the discussion. Thus, even though Eve precipitated the Fall, she can be saved, for God promised deliverance through the "seed" to come. To explain the salvation of verse 15 as physical safety is out of keeping with the spiritual disaster under discussion.

The definite article tēs which appears with "childbearing" indicates a definite and particular event, rather than childbearing in general. This is certainly the more obvious inference to be drawn from the presence of the article. The Greek language had a very simple way by which to indicate childbearing in general. All that was necessary was to omit the article. This would throw emphasis upon the quality or idea in the noun, rather than individualizing it. The presence of the article makes the Incarnation viewpoint the more probable.

The preposition dia marks the channel connecting salvation to the first woman. *Dia* is derived from *duo* (two) and indicates a connection or channel between two points. Here *dia* marks the channel between Eve in her fallen condition and salvation. This channel is "the childbearing." It was "through" the seed of the woman that salvation was possible for her, and for all women. While it is true that the "bearing" of the Child was not the absolute means of salvation, it was the channel through which salvation reached her, an idea which is perfectly expressed by the ordinary meaning of *dia*. The incarnation of Christ is a more worthy and likely channel to bring salvation than the fulfilling of home duties.

The verb *sōzō* is more probably to be understood in this passage of spiritual salvation. Although it is true that *sōzō* can be used in the sense of physical safety, and is so used in the New Testament, Paul does not so use it in his epistles. In not one of his thirty-one uses of the word (including Hebrews and this passage) can it be shown indisputably that physical saving is meant, unless this be the exception. This would eliminate the first view.

To finish his sentence, Paul widens his thought from Eve, his illustration, to all women, who are the subjects of his practical exhortation. Just as Eve was saved through faith in the "seed" to come, so all women may experience full salvation through this same channel (that is, faith in the "seed"), even though they are not leaders in the church.

Inasmuch as salvation in Scripture is not a theological abstraction but an intensely practical matter as well, Paul adds the clause: "if they remain in faith and love and holiness with sobriety." These women under discussion are already believers and part of the church. They have been saved by faith in Christ. Saved women will manifest their condition in daily conduct. Thus these qualities of life are the evidence to all observers that such women are truly saved, just as certainly as are the men. One writer paraphrases the verse thus:

> But she, Eve, shall be saved ultimately, on the same plane and through the same channel as man, that is, through the childbearing, the incarnation of Christ, and this includes all women abiding in that hope, the evi-

dence of which is faith, charity, and holiness with sobriety.[42]

III. CHARGE CONCERNING CHURCH OFFICERS (3:1-16)

Only two church officials are mentioned in the New Testament: overseers (also called elders) and deacons. There is a difference between the gifts given by Christ to the church, such as apostles, prophets, evangelists, and so forth (Eph. 4:11), and the offices to be held in the church (Phil. 1:1). The offices are to be filled by the local congregations, and thus the qualifications for persons to fill these offices are properly given by Paul in this pastoral letter. A man may possess both gift and office. Paul was an apostle and an elder. So was Peter. But it is the offices that are under discussion here.

A. *Office of the overseer* (vv. 1-7).

The *episkopos* (overseer) is the same official as the *presbuteros* (elder). It is generally admitted that the two are to be identified during the first century. Only in succeeding years as the church expanded was the overseer (often translated "bishop") set over many elders and made an administrative officer over an area. In the New Testament several passages indicate the identity of the two names.

> And from Miletus he sent to Ephesus, and called the *elders* of the church, and when they were come to him, he said unto them. . . . Take heed therefore unto yourselves, and to all the flock, over the which the Holy Ghost hath made you *overseers*. . . . (Acts 20:17-28).

> For this cause left I thee in Crete, that thou shouldest set in order the things that are wanting, and ordain *elders* in every city. . . . For a *bishop* must be blameless. . . . (Titus 1:5-7).

In both of these passages it is clear that the two terms are used synonymously. Any attempt to make the overseer of a higher rank than the elder is arbitrary and completely unwarranted by New Testament and first-century usage.

That the overseer and the deacon are the only two officers of the New Testament church is indicated by several factors. They are the only two offices of which qualifications are given (1 Tim. 3; Titus 1). They are the only officers mentioned in Paul's official greeting to the church at Philippi: "To all the saints in Christ Jesus which are at Philippi, with the bishops and deacons" (Phil. 1:1).

The term *presbuteros* (elder) is the earlier designation, and was probably derived from the synagogue, in which the chief officials bore this title. The word itself emphasizes the maturity and dignity of the office. The New Testament lays no stress on the age of the officer, but the term came from Jews who did. The designation *episkopos* (overseer) emphasizes the duty or function of the office.

When the term "overseer" or "bishop" (*episkopos*) appears in the New Testament, we must disengage ourselves from modern ideas of "bishops" who exercise authority over many pastors in many churches. In view of the qualifications set forth in this chapter, the bishop was one who engaged in public teaching and functions of oversight in the congregation. Therefore, his closest modern equivalent is the pastor, who oversees a congregation of believers and teaches them the Scriptures. Such a person possesses the New Testament office of the overseer or elder, and also should be manifesting the spiritual gift of the pastor and teacher.

1. Nature of the office.

> Faithful is the word: if someone reaches after an overseership, he desires a good work (v. 1).

There is some disagreement among scholars whether the formula, "Faithful is the word," belongs with 2:15 or 3:1. There is no grammatical reason and no strong hermeneutical reason why the attachment of the formula to the following statement (3:1) should not be accepted. This is the same usage that Paul employed in his first use of the expression in 1:15. Of the other three uses of this phrase in the Pastoral Epistles, one is clearly used with what follows (2 Tim. 2:11), one with what precedes (Titus 3:8), and one is ambiguous (1 Tim. 4:9).

      a. It is an office which may be rightfully desired by the believer.

Two strong verbs depict the yearning for this office which is commended by Paul. *Oregō* means to reach out after, and the middle voice employed here indicates that the subject is reaching after this object for himself. Such a yearning is described by a second verb *epithumeō*, to desire, to fix the ardor or passion upon a thing. Here it is used in the good sense of strong desire.

This godly desire for the responsible task of overseership, if controlled by the Spirit of God, may deepen into a sacred conviction. Such a desire is the motive for preparation in college, Bible school, and seminary. Of course, desire for this task merely for the prestige or honor involved is not praiseworthy, but if longed for in the will of God is to be commended.

      b. An office which involves oversight.

The overseership is denoted by the word *episkopē*, from a root which means to look upon, inspect, oversee (*episkopeō*). The English translation "office of a bishop" may mislead some to an improper emphasis. It is not the office which is emphasized, but the function of overseeing. This oversight will be exercised by the officer within the local congregation. As stated before, the New Testament knows nothing of a bishop over other ministers. On the contrary, Scripture does reveal that the Ephesian church had several bishops in the one congregation (Acts 20:28). Elders (an equivalent name) were chosen within the local churches of Asia Minor (Acts 14:23). Therefore the overseeing with which this bishop will be concerned will be directed toward members of the local congregation, not toward lesser clergy within a diocese. Furthermore, it must not be thought that Paul is here calling for the initial organization of the Ephesian church. Acts 20 reveals that this church aljeady had bishops. Rather, Paul is instructing the church that only qualified men are to fill this office whenever vacancies or new needs occurred.

The New Testament does not give a list of the full duties of the overseer. However, many examples of such a function are mentioned in various passages. Some examples are:

Visiting those in need (James 1:27).
Feeding the flock of God (1 Peter 5:2).
Being examples to the flock (1 Peter 5:3).
Protecting the flock from enemies (Acts 20:29-31).

   c. An office that involves work.

It demands the output of energy (*ergon*). The overseership is not a mere honor to be enjoyed. Every theological student and every other aspirant to the task should note well Paul's statement. It is a good work, but it is work. One of the duties of the overseer is teaching. He must be "able to teach" (v. 2). To do this one task well requires serious work in preparation. And this is not his only duty.

   d. An office which is worthwhile.

Paul says it is a good work. The adjective he employs is *kalos,* which means not only good intrinsically, but outwardly also. It is attractive to beholders. The overseership is not only beneficial to the one possessing it, but if properly exercised is appreciated by those who behold it. Sincere Christians recognize the high calling of their minister, and thank God for it.

  2. Qualifications for the office.

It will be noted in these verses that the great stress is on moral and spiritual qualities. Also it should be realized that all these requirements, except "apt to teach" and "not a novice," apply to all Christians. There is just one standard for laity and ministers. Yet as Lenski very clearly states:

> Yet we may note that in the case of the members of the congregation faults may be borne with which cannot be tolerated in ministers, for they are to be examples of the flock (Phil. 3:17; 2 Thess. 3:9; 1 Peter 5:3). A man who aspires to the ministry must be of proved character.[43]

The various qualifications may be grouped in numerous ways. It is difficult to find any rigid order in Paul's list. The following classification by the writer may be thought arbitrary, but it follows Paul's order with one exception (*philoxenon* and *didaktikon* are reversed) and may serve as an aid to the memory.

   a. General qualification.

   It is necessary therefore for the overseer to be blameless. . . .

He must be a blameless male. The adjective *anepilēmpton* is derived from *lambanō*, to take hold of, *epi*, upon, and the alpha privative which negates the quality. Hence the word means "not to be taken hold upon" or "irreproachable." This means a great deal more than just not a criminal. His conduct should be of such a nature that no handle is given to anyone by which to injure his reputation. The following list explains the various aspects of conduct involved. Of course, this does not mean he must be perfectly sinless. But it does refer to consistent, mature Christian living which gives no occasion for public reproach.

It is also clear from this statement and from succeeding ones that the overseer must be a male. Every adjective used in this list is masculine. The name "overseer" is masculine. The use of the expression "husband of one wife" proves that men are being referred to. The duty of superintending the church (v. 5), which is the very nature of the office, excludes women (according to 1 Tim. 2:11-14, see comments). Thus we find no women elders or bishops in the New Testament.

b. Moral qualification.

. . . husband of one wife . . .

In the Greek text this expression is qualitative (since it is without the definite article), and thus it could be rendered "a one-woman man." The adjective "one" receives the emphasis in the phrase, the inference then being that the bishop must have nothing to do with any other woman. All marital sins disqualify a man from an overseership.

The interpretation of this short phrase has been disputed from the earliest times. The writer has encountered the following:

Five Views on the "Husband of One Wife" (1 Tim. 3:2).

Marriage to the church view. One Roman Catholic view is that the "one wife" is the church, to which the bishop must consider himself married. This view is referred to in *Lange's Commentary* on this passage.[44] Of course, this is an obvious and rather clumsy attempt to protect the Romish doctrine of celibacy for priests. However, there is no warrant for spiritualizing this part of the passage when every other term in the list is understood literally. In all fairness, it must be said that this is not the view of all Roman Catholics. The more usual explanation by Catholics is that priestly celibacy was an ecclesiastical law enacted later as a helpful disciplinary measure, and that 1 Timothy 3:2 refers to a prohibition of polygamy.

Prohibition of polygamy view. This view, which understands the passage as prohibiting polygamy, has a special appeal today, since polygamy does not exist in most western countries, and thus we are not compelled to settle vexing problems of frequent divorce as a disqualification for the ministry. Certainly, Paul regarded polygamy as unlawful for any overseer. He forbade it for all believers, not just the leaders of the church (1 Cor. 7:2). But is this all that Paul meant? Polygamy at this time was forbidden in the empire, although some of the Jews are known to have practiced it, and even many Romans found ways to circumvent the law. There is no evidence from these days that any polygamists ever entered the church. Hence it is hardly to be expected that a special prohibition was needed to exclude them from overseerships, since there were probably none in the membership. More help is found in the phrase of 1 Timothy 5:9 regarding widows as "a wife of one husband." This is the same Greek expression except for the switch of terms. Whatever one means, the other must mean. If 3:2 means polygamy, then 5:9 must mean polyandry. Yet is there any reason to suppose that the prevailing sexual sin of women was their having many husbands simultaneously? Were polyandrous women so plentiful that this was the one moral qualification to be considered? It is doubtful if polyandry was practiced at all in the empire during those years. Therefore, this viewpoint is rejected as not being the full explanation of the apostle's words.

Prohibition of remarried widowers view. A very common view, especially in Europe, refers this to remarried widowers. It holds that a bishop may marry once, but if the wife dies, he may never marry again. There are numerous variations of this view, but all agree on prohibiting second marriages. The "Apostolic Constitutions" allowed a man already married to be ordained, but if he were single when ordained, he must remain so all his life.[45] The chief weakness of this view is the lack of harmony with the tenor of Scripture teaching on the subject of marriage. Nowhere in Scripture (including Paul's epistles) is remarriage after the death of the wife depicted as forbidden or even morally questionable. Paul advises widows to remarry (1 Tim. 5:14). If 3:2 prohibits widowers from second marriages if they wish to be overseers, then 5:9 prohibits widows from remarrying if they wish to be enrolled. Would Paul then advise young widows to marry again if such was questionable, or would remove

them from the possibility of special aid in their later years
(5:14)? It seems most unlikely. Paul's clear teaching was
that death of the partner dissolved the marriage bond, and
the remaining partner was free to marry in the Lord (Rom.
7:1-3). To cast suspicion upon the holiness of a second
marriage is to impugn what Scripture nowhere denies,
and reflects the spirit of asceticism which arose early in
the church and has plagued her for twenty centuries. The
argument of Plummer that a second marriage is a sign of
weakness on the part of the minister is unfortunate.[46] The
same thing could be said of the first marriage.

A further weakness of this view is the fact that this is
the only moral requirement mentioned for overseers. Was
this the greatest sexual sin? Was this the only one to be
looked for in the candidate for the eldership? Because of
Scripture teaching on remarriage after the death of one
partner, and the inherent improbability that this was the
only moral item that mattered, this view is most unlikely.

Exclusion of unmarried overseers view. This interpretation holds that only married men are eligible for the
office. I was unable to find anyone holding this view, but
some commentators mention it. The weaknesses of this
view are inescapable. Such an understanding does not
properly represent the force of the adjective "one" (*mias*)
which is placed first. The overseer must be the husband
of "one" wife, not "many." Paul does not say he must be
"husband of a wife." This latter expression could be easily stated in Greek by the mere omission of *mias*. Furthermore, to take this as a demand that the overseer be
married logically obligates the interpreter to understand
that verse 4 demands that the overseer have children. Yet
most expositors hesitate to go that far. Finally, we have
the example of Paul himself who was an elder (cf. 1 Tim.
4:14 with 2 Tim. 1:6, where Paul is one of the presbytery),
and yet was unmarried. (The possibility that Paul was a
widower must remain just that. It cannot be conclusively

demonstrated.) He saw nothing wrong with his unmarried state (1 Cor. 7:7-8, 17).

Prohibition of divorce view. This view refers the phrase to a prohibition of divorce or any other marital infidelity in persons chosen for the overseership. I feel this view is the most reasonable. It is known that during the first century divorce was very common among Romans and Jews, and could be easily obtained. In the early days of the church, the bulk of the membership in gentile areas had come from paganism with its moral vices. When congregations were organized, the overseers were chosen from among the mature men, who usually were married men with families. (As Lenski points out, there were no seminary graduates awaiting calls.)[47] Although it is true that the blood of Christ cleanses the vilest sinner, and all true converts can become members of local churches, not every member is qualified for holding the highest office. That is why this list of qualifications was necessary. Consequently, when men were to be considered for this high office, there must be no record of divorce or other marital infidelity in the candidate, even before his conversion. A very practical reason for this restriction is seen. Extremely embarrassing complications might occur in the church if the minister's divorced wife, mistresses, illegitimate children, or children of other marriages should come to light. Since such a condition would at least lay him open to reproach, it would violate the general qualification of blamelessness. There must be nothing in the life of the overseer that would prevent his ministering spiritually and helpfully to any and every person. Another reason why the moral (marriage) qualification can reach back to the unsaved state is because this is God's standard for all society, not just for the church (Matt. 19:8).

Does this restriction remove from true candidacy a man who was previously divorced on the one scriptural ground of adultery in the wife, and has remarried? Undoubtedly this is a problem. However, it appears to me that such is the only proper and practical understanding. If a man has remarried after divorce, many of the same complications just noted could occur and lay the ministry open to censure. Remarriage after divorce can hardly be understood as constituting the candidate as a "one-woman man." The view explained here includes all other forms of infidelity to one's wife. Adultery without divorce excludes one from the overseership. The qualitative nature of the terms employed by Paul emphasizes the general nature of the restriction.

The phrase by Paul is stated positively. The overseer must be a one-woman man. He must be devoted to her and give her all the love and consideration that a wife deserves. It means more than merely not divorced, although this is the objective fact which can be checked on by the church. When divorced and remarried persons are saved, they should rejoice in their salvation, and should serve the Lord faithfully in every way they can. But they should not aspire to be overseers.

    c. Mental qualifications.

      . . . sober, sound-minded, orderly . . . able to teach. . . .

      (1) Sober (*nēphalion*).

      Etymologically, this term means abstaining from wine entirely, and is so used by Josephus. It had also a metaphorical usage in the sense of spiritually sober, temperate, calm, and sober in judgment. It is not certain which meaning is intended here, but it is probable that the wider meaning of sobriety in judgment (not merely in the use of wine) is to be employed. The abstinence from wine is referred to later in the list. The overseer must be sober in judgment so as not to be diverted by false teaching.

      (2) Sound-minded (*sōphrona*).

      This adjective means a quality of mind which is serious, earnest, sound. It does not mean the minister should be long-faced, but he should be earnest. He should have the balanced judgment to relegate fun to its proper place. The overseer, especially if he is young, must avoid the reputation of a clown. Young people may think such a preacher is funny, but they won't come to him for spiritual help.

(3) Orderly (kosmion).

This adjective is a cognate of kosmeō, to arrange, and kosmos, world (an orderly arrangement, not a chaos). It refers to a life which is well-ordered, the expression of a well-ordered mind. Orderliness refers not only to the structure of his sermons, but the nature of his habits, whether physical, moral, or mental. The ministry is no place for the man whose life is a continual confusion of unaccomplished plans and unorganized activity.

(4) Able to teach (didaktikon).

The adjective does not mean "teachable," but "apt at teaching." The RSV renders it "an apt teacher." It refers to the imparting of knowledge to others. The personal companions of Christ were dying, and thus arose the need for teaching the material which they had received. Teaching was necessary to impart the doctrines of the faith, to feed the flock, to rightly divide the Word of truth. Although the ability to teach demands a certain inherent mental capacity, it also assumes a knowledge of what is to be taught. That knowledge is obtained and expanded by education. Here is authority for Christian education. Any man who shows himself incapable of successfully teaching others is not qualified for the eldership.

d. Personality qualifications.

... hospitable ... not beside wine, not a striker, but gentle, not fighting, not a money-lover. . . .

(1) Hospitable (philoxenon).

The root of this word means "loving strangers." The overseer must be such a person. In that day there were not many suitable accommodations for Christian travelers. The inns along the road were the scenes of brawls and vice. Consequently, there would be abundant opportunity for the leader of the Christian congregation to display this needed virtue. Persecution, poverty, and the plight of widows and orphans gave additional opportunity for hospitality to be exercised. The overseer must set an example for his flock.

(2) Not beside wine (mē paroinon).

This is the literal translation of the Greek term. From the original meaning of one who sits long beside his wine there came the meaning of one who becomes quarrelsome after drinking. The first meaning could include the second. The overseer must not be a drinker.

(3) Not a striker (mē plēktēn).

This is derived from the verb plēssō, to strike, and denotes a pugnacious, quick-tempered individual who strikes back with his fists when annoyed.

(The phrase "not greedy of filthy lucre" is omitted in the best texts.)

(4) Gentle (epieikē).

The ideas of patience, forbearance, and yielding are to be understood in this word. This sort of personal disposition will avoid much contention and will make the overseer's work more effective. People do not enjoy being domineered.

(5) Not fighting (amachon).

This adjective denotes the person who is not contentious. Such a person is not offensively aggressive. He will not insist on his rights. He keeps his temper under control.

(6) Not a money-lover (aphilarguron).

The etymology of the term is arguros, silver, money; and phileō, to love, with the alpha privative. The overseer is not to have his attention fixed upon the monetary rewards. How frequently has the church suffered in reputation as well as in spiritual growth through the covetousness of some of her leaders. Furthermore, the poverty of many Christian ministers still does not remove this temptation from them. In a materialistic world, the elder must wage an unceasing battle to keep material things in their proper perspective. The love of money often leads to other sins. Calvin quotes the old Latin proverb: "He who wishes to become rich also wishes to become rich soon."[48]

e. Domestic qualification.

> . . . superintending his own house well, having children in subjection with all dignity (but if anyone knows not to superintend his own house, how shall he take care of God's church?). . . .

The way in which a man controls his home reveals his capacity for leadership and government. This ability is most obvious when there are children in the home. This does not demand that an overseer must have children (although this would be the usual situation), but if he does, they must be controlled. The administrative ability required to cause a home to function smoothly will also be necessary if one is to superintend a church. Deficiency in these matters at home disqualifies a man from serving in a ruling capacity in the church.

When children are in the home, they are to be controlled with dignity. (It is the father who displays the dignity.) The kind of father who cuffs his children around will usually treat church members in similar fashion. Even in the close association which exists among members of a family, there must be a dignified and respectful relationship maintained.

f. Christian experience.

> Not a novice, lest having been puffed up with pride he might fall into the Devil's judgment.

The word "novice" (neophutos) means "newly planted," and is to be understood in the spiritual sense here. The overseer must not be a new convert. Maturity in the faith is essential. The Ephesian church at this time had been in existence at least twelve years, and spiritually mature men could be found. In the case of Crete, such a qualification was not given (Titus 1) because it was apparently a new work and the ideal could not be insisted upon. Today, there is scarcely any excuse for placing a novice in situations of such responsibility, inasmuch as Christianity has spread to an extent that qualified men are more readily available.

The great danger to the novice is that his sudden elevation is likely to cause him to inflate with pride (*tuphoō*). The root of this word is *tuphos*, smoke, and perhaps the ideas of foggy, smoky thoughts as the result of pride are to be understood. If such conceit occurs, the judgment that was meted out to Satan for his pride may happen also to the novice. *Tou diabolou* (of the devil) is an objective genitive. It means the judgment that the devil experienced, not a judgment that the devil brings upon novices, for the devil does not judge. Conceit might smother his young faith, and he would be like the seed that fell among the thorns and was eventually choked.

g. Reputation.

> And it is necessary also to have a good testimony from those outside, lest he fall into reproach and the Devil's snare.

Since the world is the group from which he must win new converts, the overseer must be careful to keep his reputation unbesmirched. This, of course, refers to the testimony to his life since conversion. Here can be seen another indication that the overseer or elder is taken from the local congregation, and is not an administrator with headquarters in a distant city.

The reproach (*oneidismon*) may refer to the accusation men might make against him, and the snare of the devil (*pagida tou diabolou*) refers to the pitfalls Satan lays to

trap the unwary. *Tou diabolou* is here a subjective genitive.

The statement of White is particularly astute, and is
given here in full:

> St. Paul's attitude toward *them that are without* is
> one of the many proofs of his sanity of judgment. On
> the one hand, they are emphatically outside the
> church; they have no *locus standi* in it, no right to
> interfere. On the other hand, they have the law of God
> written in their hearts; and up to a certain point, their
> moral instincts are sound and their moral judgments
> worthy of respect. In the passage before us, indeed, St.
> Paul may be understood to imply that the opinion of
> "those without" might usefully balance or correct that
> of the church. There is something blameworthy in a
> man's character if the consensus of outside opinion be
> unfavorable to him, no matter how much he may be
> admired and respected by his own party. The *vox
> populi* then, is in some sort a *vox Dei*: and one cannot
> safely assume, when we are in antagonism to it, that,
> because we are Christians, we are absolutely in the
> right and the world wholly wrong. Thus to defy public
> opinion in a superior spirit may not only bring discred-
> it, *oneidismos*, on oneself and on the church, but also
> catch us in the devil's snare, *viz.*, a supposition that
> because the world condemns a certain course of action,
> the action is therefore right and the world's verdict may
> be safely set aside.[49]

B. *The office of the deacon* (vv. 8-13).

Likewise [it is necessary for] deacons [to be] dignified, not double-tongued, not holding to much wine,
not shamefully greedy of gain, holding the mystery of
the faith in a pure conscience. And let these be tested
first, then let them serve, being unaccused. . . . Let
deacons be husbands of one wife, superintending children and their own houses well (vv. 8-10, 12).

1. Nature of the office.

Information is very scant in the New Testament concerning the office of deacon. The exact nature and duties

of the office are nowhere set forth in any systematic way. However, the New Testament is very clear that there was such an office. From the title given to the office (*diakonos*) and from the cognate verb employed in verse 10 (*diakoneitōsan*), it is concluded that the nature of the office is a ministering or serving. A *diakonos* in the ordinary sense was one who executed the commands of another, a servant, attendant, minister. It seems almost certain to me that the title of the office, and probably the office itself, was derived from the choosing of the seven in Acts 6. Since the epistles reveal the existence of deacons from the earliest days of the church (Rom. 12:7; Phil. 1:1; etc.), it is not illogical to trace the beginnings to the Jerusalem church. Although the name *diakonos* is not used in Acts 6, the cognates *diakonia* (twice) and *diakoneō* (once) are used. The function of the seven was to assist the apostles, and in 1 Timothy 3, their qualifications are listed along with the overseers, thus showing their close association with the chief officers.

  2. Qualifications for the office.
    a. Personal character.

      (1) Dignified (*semnous*).
      This term means worthy of respect, stately, dignified. It is a positive term, perhaps explained by the three negative phrases that follow. It denotes a seriousness of mind and character. Their service will be done in the name of the whole congregation, and thus is not to be lightly undertaken. (The word does not mean austere or unbending, however.)

      (2) Not double-tongued (*mē dilogous*).
      Persons who spread conflicting tales among the congregation are not to be selected as deacons. Since the ministrations of such an officer would conceivably take him on constant rounds of visitation, a double-tongued person would spread havoc in short order. This officer must know how to bridle his tongue.

(3) Not holding to much wine (*mē oinōi pollōi prosechontas*).

It is an incontrovertible fact that wine was the common beverage in that part of the world in that era. It still forms the basic beverage in some parts of the world where modern means of water purification are not employed. But the deacon must be one who was careful not to abuse this usage. He must be noted for sobriety. He must not be holding his interests and attention toward wine.

It is extremely difficult for the twentieth-century American to understand and appreciate the society of Paul's day. The fact that deacons were not told to become total abstainers, but rather to be temperate, does not mean that Christians today can use liquor in moderate amounts. The wine employed for the common beverage was very largely water. The social stigma and the tremendous social evils that accompany drinking today did not attach themselves to the use of wine as the common beverage in the homes of Paul's day. Nevertheless, as the church grew and the Christian consciousness and conscience developed, the dangers of drinking came to be more clearly seen. The principle laid down elsewhere by Paul that Christians should not do anything to cause a brother to stumble came to be applied to the use of wine. Raymond states it this way:

> If an individual by drinking wine either causes others to err through his example or abets a social evil which causes others to succumb to its temptations, then in the interests of Christian love he ought to forego the temporary pleasures of drinking in the interests of heavenly treasures.[50]

Certainly in present-day America, the use of wine by a Christian would abet a recognized social evil, and would set a most dangerous example for the young and the weak. To us, Paul would undoubtedly say, "No wine at all."

(4) Not shamefully greedy of gain (*mē ais-chrokerdeis*).

We infer that the office of deacon gave the holder opportunity to yield to this impulse. If his work involved the distribution of alms to the needy, there was a chance for embezzlement. Anyone who has access to church finances has opportunity to act dishonestly. Erdman has stated: "Judas was not the last treasurer who betrayed his Lord for a few pieces of silver."[51]

b. Spiritual life.

Although the deacon is not required to have the gift of teaching, he does need to be settled in his faith. He is required to be holding the "mystery of the faith." In Paul's use of the term *mustērion* there is always the idea of something previously hidden but now revealed. The genitive *tēs pisteōs* (of the faith) is a descriptive or defining genitive which explains what that mystery is. The mystery is the body of truth that comprises Christian faith.

The great truths of the faith are not to be held as theological abstractions, but are to be properly employed in daily life. To hold the mystery of the faith in a pure conscience is so to live in the light of Christian truth that the enlightened conscience will have no cause to condemn. A pure conscience indicates a pure life.

Although the primary task of the deacon is not to teach, his ministrations will require him to bring spiritual comfort to others. Thus his own spiritual life must be pure.

c. Christian experience.

Candidates must first be tested before being selected as deacons. The verb is a present imperative (*dokimazesthōsan*) which does not call for a formal test (an aorist would be needed) but a constant observing or testing, so that when deacons are needed, qualified ones may be nominated as candidates. Persons who have been under observation by the church for an adequate length of time can then be termed "unaccused" if no disqualifying trait has appeared. There is no warrant here for appointing a recent convert as deacon to "get him active in the work."

d. Morality.

The same moral standard is required of deacons as for overseers. They are to be husbands of one wife, that is, no record of divorce or other marital misconduct.

e. Domestic relations.

A similar requirement regarding home life is demanded of overseers and deacons. No place is more indicative of a person's real Christian character than his home. At home sham and all pretense are dropped, and a man can be seen for what he is. This requirement in the case of the deacon is probably not so much to demonstrate ability in rulership as it is an evidence of Christian character.

3. Qualifications for the female deacon.

> Likewise [it is necessary for] women [to be] dignified,
> not slanderous, sober, faithful in all things (v. 11).

There is difference of opinion as to the reference of these words. Do they refer to the wives of deacons (as the KJV suggests), or to an established office of the deaconess? The writer will present arguments supporting the view that a separate office of deaconess is meant, and by these arguments will refute other ideas.

There were deaconesses in the first-century church. Phoebe is called a *diakonon* (Rom. 16:1). Since there were such persons, this chapter presenting the qualifications for church officers is the logical place to discuss the selection.

The grammatical structure of the passage indicates a transition to another class. The use of *hōsautōs* (likewise) makes this very clear. A brief table may be helpful.

"It is necessary for the overseer to be blameless" (v. 2).

"[It is necessary for] likewise, the deacons [to be] dignified" (v. 8).

"[It is necessary for] likewise, women [to be] dignified" (v. 11).

The employment of *hōsautōs* (likewise) clearly indicates three classes under consideration.

The term "wives" is the simple word "women" (*gunaikas*), and is so translated in the ASV. Since the title *diakonos* is used as both masculine and feminine (see Rom. 16:1), it could not be employed here without causing confusion with the previous group. Consequently, the general term *gunē* was used and the reader is left to infer "women deacons."

This cannot refer to all the women in the church. This context deals with officials in the church. The general instruction for all the women was given in the previous chapter.

This cannot be limited to the wives of deacons. There is no pronoun used with *gunaikas* to relate them to the deacons, nor is there even an article which might be used in that sense. Thus there is no grammatical connection between the women of verse 11 and the deacons of verses 8-10. Rather, *hōsautōs* marks another group. If this requirement refers to the wives of deacons, it is strange that no such statement is made with regard to the wives of overseers. It seems more likely that the wives of deacons are covered by the requirement that the deacon should superintend well his own household (3:12).

Of course, it is often a very convenient arrangement when a husband and wife can each qualify as deacon and deaconess. But there is not sufficient warrant in this passage to demand that this must be the case every time. If it be recognized that there is such an office as deaconess and that such is referred to in this passage, then it cannot be demanded also that *gunaikas* be understood here as wives. The interpreter must make his choice.

    a. Dignified (*semnas*).

        The same dignity is demanded of the women as the men.

 b. Not slanderous (*mē diabolous*).

 This adjective is used substantively as a name for the devil (*ho diabolos*), who is the chief slanderer of God and the people of God. The deaconess must not partake of this characteristic of Satan. She must not be a "she-devil." If her official duties would cause her to circulate among the congregation, she must avoid improper speech.

 c. Sober (*nēphalious*).

 This term was also used of the overseer (v. 2). Whether the metaphorical use of sobriety in judgment, or the literal meaning of abstinence from wine is meant is not certain. However, the rather obvious parallelism with the terms in verse 8 would suggest the literal meaning here.

Deacons (v. 8)	*Deaconesses* (v. 11)
"Dignified"	"Dignified"
"Not double-tongued"	"Not slanderous"
"Not holding to much wine"	"Sober"

 d. Faithful in all things (*pistas en pasin*).

 This general reference includes trustworthiness in her ecclesiastical duties, as well as domestic affairs. She must be faithful to her husband, to her family, to Christ, and to the church.

 4. The encouragement for deacons.

> For the ones who have served well are obtaining for themselves a good standing and much boldness in faith which is in Christ Jesus (v. 13).

Two promises are held out to deacons (including their feminine counterparts). Some refer this verse to all the officials just discussed, but the reference seems to be to deacons, because of the conjunction *gar* and the use of the verb *diakoneō*.

a. They obtain a good standing.

The proper interpretation of this verse depends upon our understanding of *bathmos*. It has the following uses: (1) a step; (2) rung; (3) base; (4) degree in rank, standing. The meaning of standing or degree of respect seems to be the thought here. Ellicott lists several interpretations of this verse.[52] One view refers it to an advance in ecclesiastical office. Deacons who serve well may be promoted to higher office. Although that may often be the case, it does not harmonize with the latter part of the verse, which refers to spiritual blessing, not ecclesiastical promotion. Furthermore, it seems to be a most unusual argument for Paul to use as an inducement to deacons. A more plausible view is that this refers to a good standing in the eyes of God and men. The deacon who has served well for some length of time (aorist participle) is progressively obtaining or acquiring for himself a good standing. He is achieving a respected reputation in the church. He is also laying up treasures in heaven, so that in the day of Christ he will have a good standing when rewards are distributed.

b. They obtain much boldness in Christian faith.

The word "boldness" (*parrēsian*) contains the idea of confidence and assurance. It is often used in the sense of boldness in speech, and the example of Stephen, one of the Seven who preached in the synagogues, comes to mind. Here the idea seems to be that deacons who perform well have as a consequence real confidence in the sphere of their Christian faith. They can approach God boldly in prayer, knowing that no sin or carelessness in spiritual matters is barring the way. Such spiritual boldness or confidence will also assist them in further spiritual labors.

C. *The importance of this charge to the church* (vv. 14-16).

1. The charge was important because Paul could not be there personally to direct this church.

> These things I write to you, hoping to come to you more quickly. . . . (v. 14).

Since Paul was absent, it was important that these written instructions be heeded. "These things" probably refer primarily to the selection of officials to function in the church. Paul had hopes of visiting Timothy even more quickly than circumstances would probably allow (or perhaps "more quickly than you can initiate these regulations for officers").

2. The charge was important because the conduct of affairs in the house of God was Timothy's responsibility.

> . . . but if I should delay, in order that you may know how it is necessary to conduct yourselves in God's house, which is the church of the living God, pillar and support of the truth (v. 15).

Because of the possibility of Paul's delay, Timothy must carry on as his official representative and see that the affairs in the church at Ephesus were organized and carried on properly. The infinitive *anastrephesthai* is a present middle, and denotes the conducting of oneself in general activity. The middle voice indicates that the subject is involved in the action of the verbal. Since there is no expressed accusative subject for this infinitive, it is questioned whether Timothy alone is to be inferred or the entire congregation. In view of the context, which discusses the organization of the church, plus the fact that the infinitive is not limited by any subject and thus must be understood in its widest sense, we refer the notice to a general statement regarding general church conduct. However, the singular subject of *eidēis* (know) indicates that Timothy must know these regulations in order to effect them.

The church, which is designated "God's house," (*oikōi theou*) is the spiritual house of believers (in its visible or local aspect) built upon Christ, the great foundation, in which house God dwells. It is not a reference to any church building, since such had not come into being. The church is the pillar and support of the truth. It upholds in the world the truth that God has revealed to men. The translation "support" for *hedraiōma* is preferable to "ground" or "foundation."

      3. The charge was important because of the greatness of the mystery of godliness, which is the possession of the church.

> And confessedly great is the mystery of godliness:
>> Who was manifested in flesh,
>>> Was justified in Spirit,
>> Was seen by angels,
>>> Was proclaimed among nations,
>> Was believed in the world,
>>> Was taken up in glory (v. 16).

Verse 16 delineates the content of "the truth" that has just been mentioned as being upheld by the church. Here it is called the "mystery of godliness." *Mustērion* is used in the same sense as in verse 9, and denotes a secret which has been revealed. Here it describes God's revealed secret which produces in men the life of godliness.

"Confessedly" (*homologoumenōs*) must be understood as limited to the church. Only believers are able to acknowledge the statements that follow. Perhaps the next lines were an early creedal confession. Certainly their rhythmical structure suggests some sort of formal usage of these words, whether as a confession or an early hymn.

The next six lines are introduced by *hos* (*theos* is rejected by almost all scholars). The content shows that Christ, the divine Son of God, is the subject of each clause. Various analyses are made of these lines, some dividing into couplets, others into trilogies. Some attempt to trace a chronological arrangement. This writer divides the poem into three couplets because of the contrasting pairs at the end of each two lines, but does not press any consecutive or chronological order in the series.

Christ was manifested in flesh. The preincarnate Son assumed humanity in order to effect salvation (John 1:14). He was pronounced righteous in the realm of His spirit. There is disagreement over the identification of "spirit." Is it the Holy Spirit, Christ's own human spirit, or His divine nature? Those interpreting the phrase as the Holy Spirit treat the preposition *en* as instrumental, and point to other scriptural uses of "flesh" and "the Holy Spirit" in combination (as in John 1:14, 32).[53] Those referring the phrase to Christ's human spirit emphasize a strict parallelism with the previous phrase "in the flesh" (a reference to his outward physical being).[54] The view that interprets "Spirit" as Christ's divine nature sees the phrase as a contrast to His human nature referred to as "in flesh."[55] All things considered, this writer concludes that the Holy Spirit is being referred to. The Spirit was the one who vindicated Christ's claims when men were too blind to recognize them. Such occurred at the baptism (Matt. 3:15-17), resurrection (Rom. 1:4), ascension (John 16:7, 10), and on other less prominent occasions. Of course, this vindication demonstrated that Jesus possessed a divine nature. Hence a combination of the Holy Spirit and the divine nature may well be involved in the fullest meaning of the phrase.

The next antithesis is between angels and nations. The mighty angelic hosts were witnesses to Christ during His earthly ministry at various times (birth, temptations, agony in the garden, resurrection). Yet the wonder of the gospel is that its proclamation and application were not to mighty angels but to men. And these men were not just Jews, members of a specially favored race, but are found in all nations.

The third couplet makes the contrast between the world and glory. Only Christ is able to join these two. The proclamation of the gospel has caused faith in Christ to occur in this sinful world. Yet Christ Himself did not partake of sin. Rather He was taken up in connection with glory. His resurrection, ascension, and second coming are all depicted as aspects of the glory in which Christ now moves (Luke 24:26; Acts 1:9; Matt. 25:31). Where He is and what He is becomes our glorious prospect and living hope.

IV. CHARGE CONCERNING FALSE TEACHERS (4:1-16).

Chapter 1 was a general introduction to the letter, and discussed the legalistic doctrines of some would-be law-teachers. Chapter 4 gives much more detail concerning some later heretical teachers, and explains their origin and content of teaching.

A. *The appearance of false teachers* (vv. 1-5).

> But the Spirit explicitly says that in latter seasons some will depart from the faith, holding to deceiving spirits and teachings of demons, in hypocrisy of lie-speakers, ones cauterized in their own conscience, forbidding to marry, to abstain from foods, which things God created for partaking with thanksgiving for those who believe and have recognized the truth. Because every created thing of God is good, and nothing to be thrown away, being received with thanksgiving: for it is sanctified through God's word and petition (vv. 1-5).

1. The time of these teachers.
   a. It is revealed by the Spirit's revelation.

All prophecy is produced through the inspiration of the Holy Spirit, whether in the Old or New Testaments (2 Peter 1:21). Hence the prophecy concerning false teachers and apostasy came from the Spirit. Paul says that this information from the Spirit was given explicitly or distinctly (*rētōs*). It was not couched in symbolic, hard-to-understand language, but was expressly and clearly stated. When did the Spirit reveal the coming apostasy? One can find such predictions in the Old Testament (Dan. 7:25; 8:23). The same information is given by

Jesus and recorded in the gospels (Matt. 24:4-12). The apostles wrote of it (2 Thess. 2:3-12; 1 John 2:18; 2 Peter 3:3; Jude 18). The present tense of the verb is used (*legei*), which links the speaking by the Spirit to the time of Paul's writing. One may conclude that the Spirit at that moment communicated the information to Paul, or it may be inferred that the apostle means the continual stream of the Spirit's prophesying, beginning in the Old Testament and continuing to the time of the apostles.

    b. It will occur in latter seasons.

    This is not the same expression as "last days." The term "last days" or "last hour" refers to that whole period of time beginning with Messiah's first coming. Whenever the term is employed in the Old Testament, Messianic days are always involved. Yet it cannot refer solely to the second coming, for the New Testament indicates that we are now in the last days (Acts 2:16-17; Heb. 1:2; 1 John 2:18). Hence the expression is a broad term which includes the whole period of time between the first and second advents, and prior to the "age to come." (Time in Scripture is reckoned in relation to the coming age.) The word employed in 1 Timothy 4:1 is *kairois*, seasons, or shorter segments of time. The plural is used to show that these seasons will be recurring from time to time. The adjective *husterois* (latter) indicates that these seasons were future at the time of writing. Many of these seasons of apostasy are now past, but others will come. This does not refer to the final apostasy of 2 Thessalonians 2, but to the intermittent experience of the church throughout this age. Acts 20:29-30 foretells this same thing to the same church.

    2. The description of these teachers.

    Three parties are involved in the apostasy: the victims, the demonic source, and the human agents.

    a. They cause their victims to abandon the faith.

    Those who follow the false teachers are denoted by the indefinite "some" (*tines*). Not all will be affected at any one time, but there will be some. Those who are victimized will depart from the faith. The verb "depart" (*apostēsontai*) is the source of our word "apostatize," and denotes a "standing away from" the original position. This departure is from "the faith" (*tēs pisteōs*), the body of truth. Thus these victims are nominal Christians whose submitting to this error reveals their true nature. They now depart from the body of truth which constitutes Christianity, to which they once gave assent.

  b. The source of their teaching is evil spirits and demons.

  The first designation "deceiving spirits" (*pneumasin planois*) denotes those who are wandering away from the truth and are leading others to do so. Some think these deceiving spirits are the false teachers, but most others regard them as synonymous with the demons mentioned in the next phrase. The latter seems most likely inasmuch as the human agents are mentioned in the next verse. The existence of evil spirits who influence men is told in Scripture (e.g., Beelzebub, John 8:44; 1 John 4:1-6). The expression "teaching of demons" (*didaskaliais daimoniōn*) should be understood as a subjective genitive: demons' teachings (not teachings about demons). Those teachings are not about demonology. On the contrary, they are concerned about earthly matters. The same warning concerning demonic doctrine is given in James 3:15: "This wisdom descendeth not from above, but is earthly, sensual, devilish" (*daimoniōdēs*). Scripture plainly teaches that satanic power can get hold of a man's mind and will. The cases of Judas (John 13:2, 27) and Peter (Matt. 16:23) are well known. Satan will control the great Antichrist (2 Thess. 2:9). Thus Satan is constantly at work in the world, seeking to corrupt and pervert the proclamation of the truth.

  c. The human agents who mediate this apostasy are hypocritical lie-speakers.

This fact is obscured by the KJV which causes *pseudologōn* to be understood as a participle (i.e., "speaking lies") modifying *daimoniōn* (demons). However, there are difficulties in this view, not the least of which is the fact that Scripture does not seem to attribute conscience to demons. Yet these *pseudologoi* have a conscience. Both ASV and RSV have treated the term properly as a substantive, "liars" or "men that speak lies." These are the human agents who, motivated by the evil spirits, victimize the unwary with their hypocritical teaching. These correspond to the demon-inspired false prophets of 1 John 4:1. Such errorists must work in the realm of hypocrisy in order to palm off their lies. The etymology of *hupokrisis* indicates the assuming of a mask as an actor. Certainly these false teachers must make themselves appear different from what they really are. It may be the case that many false teachers are unaware of the hypocrisy of their action. Some have gone so far that lying becomes second nature to them, because the standard of truth in God's Word has been abandoned. They feel no qualms because their conscience has been seared.

The description of the conscience of these mediators of demonic teaching as cauterized has called forth several explanations. The participle *kekaustēriasmenon* belongs to the medical world. Hippocrates used the term *kaustēr* to mean "cauterizing apparatus."[56] Because of Paul's close association with Luke, it is not difficult to see where he derived the term. This writer has encountered the following:

Four Views of the Cauterized Conscience (1 Tim. 4:2).

Callous from constant violation view. This interpretation holds that their conscience is past feeling and callous from constant violation. "Who being past feeling have given themselves over unto lasciviousness" (Eph. 4:19). Although this may be true, the use of the strong word *kaustēriazō* demands a more violent and radical experience than mere repeated violation. To sear or cauterize is to burn a portion of the body, with the result that it loses sensitivity. But it is not a gradual process.

Ownership marks of Satan view. Their conscience bore the ownership marks of Satan, just as Paul bore in his body "the marks of Jesus" as Christ's bondservant (Gal. 6:17). (See also 2 Tim. 2:19, for a description of the Lord's seal.) Just exactly what this means is not explained by the proponents, although the *Expositor's Greek Testament* lists it as a plausible explanation.[57]

Self-condemnation view. This view holds that the marks of crime were burned into them so that they were self-condemned. Ellicott states it thus:

> They felt the brand they bore, and yet with a show of outward sanctity (comp. *hupokrisei*) they strove to beguile and to seduce others, and make them as bad as themselves.[58]

This view understands the participle as middle instead of passive. However, even though it may be true, it does not fully explain what the branding is.

Radical act of perversion view. The conscience has been made insensitive to right and wrong because of some radical act of perverting the truth. The conscience is man's sensitiveness to right and wrong based on his standard. If the standard is perverted, then its action becomes altered. It is cauterized and fails to respond. The verb *kaustēriazō* depicts this perversion of truth as a violent and radical action. The writer suggests that act to have been the time when the religious teacher deliberately turned away from the instruction of God's Word and permitted Satan's demonic hosts to take control of his mind and thought.

  3. The Teaching of these teachers.
    a. Forbidding to marry.
      A false asceticism is the key emphasis of their teaching. How often has this sort of ascetic teaching, under the guise of a more spiritual religion, arisen to

plague mankind! The Essenes and Therapeutae in the days before the church, the Gnostics during the early centuries, Roman Catholicism with its celibacy for priests down to the present hour—all are examples of this practice. Yet it is in contradiction to the purposes of God. It impeaches God's institution of marriage. Such doctrine is typical of the evil one who has always been the great opposer of God's will.

   b. To abstain from foods.

   This grammatical construction is an example of zeugma, and is legitimate. There is no need to imagine some missing verb, such as "commanding." The meaning is obvious and clear. (Another example of zeugma in this epistle is in 2:12.)

   Numerous historical examples exist of groups who have denied the rightful partaking of certain foods. (*Brōma* means solid food in general, not merely animal meat.) Judaizers, Gnostics, Catholics (Fridays, Lent), Seventh-day Adventists, and all types of ascetics have promoted this error. Paul faced it squarely in his epistle to the Colossians (2:21-23). The error arises from a false conception of our physical bodies, supposing that they are evil just because they are physical, and therefore to deny their normal appetites is thought to be praiseworthy. Yet Christ clearly taught that "not that which goeth into the mouth defileth a man; but that which cometh out of the mouth, this defileth a man" (Matt. 15:11).

   Consequently, vegetarianism is not a means of sanctification. On the contrary, if it is observed on religious grounds, it is a disrespect of God. To make a distinction between various kinds of wholesome food (or marriage), on the grounds that the rejection of some and the use of others is meritorious, is illogical and unscriptural. Paul says it is demonic.

   This does not mean that the unmarried state might not be more convenient under certain conditions, or that fasting for a season might not have its place (1 Cor. 7:5). But even on such occasions, it is not the fasting or the celibacy which is meritorious in itself, but rather the concentration of energy and attention on prayer or some other spiritual duty. But even then, the abstinence from those privileges must be only temporary.

4. The refutation of these teachers.

Refutation is accomplished by disproving their doctrines. The plural relative pronoun *ha* indicates both of the preceding teachings involving marriage and food, and the refutation should be understood to apply to both.

> *a.* These challenged privileges were created by God for partaking by men.

Both marriage (Gen. 1:28) and foods (Gen. 1:29; 9:3) were given by God to men. It is the obligation of men to partake of these privileges with gratitude. To cast reflection upon their sanctity is to dispute the wisdom, purpose, and morality of God, and to thwart His intention.

> *b.* These challenged privileges were intended for saved people.

The use of only one article shows that one group of people is meant by the expression, "those who believe and have recognized the truth." They are the believers who by faith in Christ have come to know Him who is the Truth. Thus they are in possession of a deeper spiritual knowledge than the unconverted. Of course, in pre-Christian times these believers would be the sincere and righteous Jews. Here Paul is thinking primarily of Christians.

Food and marriage are for the propagation and sustenance of human life. In a very special sense these privileges apply to saved people, for sinners are under sentence of death and will not need marriage or food. It is only the grace of God that keeps the sinner in life and thus gives him additional opportunity to repent and believe the gospel. Satan and his demons are completely wrong in saying that these privileges are not for believers. They were originally given to Adam and Eve in a saved (holy) state. In contrast, the unbeliever has even his pure things tainted with impurity, because of his heart condition, his motives, and his manner of reception (Titus 1:15).

      c. These challenged privileges are intrinsically good.

      Paul states that every created thing (*ktisma*, result of the act of creating) is good (*kalon*). Moses stated this after his description of the days of creation (Gen. 1:12; etc.). Christ reiterated the truth that food cannot defile (Mark 7:15). Even the Old Testament distinctions between ceremonially clean and unclean animals, which were useful until Christ, are now finished (Acts 10:15). The person who argues that marriage or eating is a moral or spiritual flaw is calling something evil that God has pronounced good.

      d. These challenged privileges are sanctified through the Word of God and through prayer.

      The verb *hagiazetai* is a present passive, and means "continually being set apart for a holy purpose." This is the great safeguard against license or abuse of God-given privileges. The two great means to this end are God's Word which teaches men the holy and rightful purpose of marriage and food, and the petitionary prayer (*enteuxeōs*) of the partaker that he may use these privileges in the proper way. Many have seen here an apostolic encouragement for prayer before meals. Hence this is not indiscriminate license for the believer to use these privileges as he sees fit, but as God's Word reveals.

  B. *The duty of the minister toward false teachers* (vv. 6-10).

    1. Constructive teaching.

      Suggesting these things to the brethren, you will be a good minister of Christ Jesus, being nourished in the words of the faith and of the good teaching which you have closely followed. And the profane and old-womanish myths be declining (vv. 6-7a).

The responsibility of the spiritual leader in constructively teaching his people involves positive and negative aspects. He must know what to teach and what to ignore. Paul answers both problems.

The minister should place before the brethren the correct doctrine. "These things" of verse 6 refers to the matters of verses 1-5, the false doctrine with its decisive answer in true Biblical doctrine. Nearly all commentators agree that the term "suggesting" (*hupotithemenos*) is a mild one. The minister can do much to win support to true doctrine by a moderate manner of presenting the truth. This does not mean compromising. But it does mean a calm and logical explanation of biblical teaching. This is especially becoming in a younger minister, where dogmatism and a domineering spirit are most unpleasing. It is also a mark of good ministry to place under the attention of (*hupotithēmi*) the congregation what the Spirit expressly speaks. By shifting the responsibility to what the Word and the Spirit say avoids personality clashes between the minister and his people. The issue can no longer be between the minister and his people, but it will then be between God and the people. This is the function of the minister.

The term "minister" (*diakonos*) employed here is not used in any official or technical sense of "deacon," but in the general sense of minister or servant. To serve Christ effectively, in the capacity that Timothy was, demanded much personal feeding upon the Word of God. He must be thoroughly conversant with the sum total of Christian belief ("the faith").

Paul advised Timothy to decline to involve himself in disputes about profane and old-womanish myths. While he must meet demonic teaching head-on and refute it with Scripture, he must not fritter away his time with silly religious trivia. False doctrine must be met with true doctrine; silly myths merit disdain. The imperative *paraitou* means to beg off, refuse, decline (see Luke 14:18). He

must not even bother to argue against them. These myths
had no spiritual value and are of the type that senile
women tell to children for entertainment. The profitless
myths devised around Old Testament themes are known
to history. It is not devoid of significance how many religious myths contrived by women are still with us.
Madame Blavatsky, Annie Besant, Ellen G. White, and
Mrs. Eddy are well-known examples.

   2. Godly living.

> But exercise yourself toward godliness. For the bodily
> exercise for a little is profitable; but the godliness for all
> things is profitable, having promise of life which is
> now and that which is to come. Faithful is the word
> and worthy of all acceptance (vv. 7b-9).

Paul employs the language of the gymnasium to encourage Timothy to keep on the path of godly living.
Gumnaze is a present imperative and means, "keep on
exercising." The verb is derived from the adjective *gum-
nos* (naked) and denotes the practice of the athlete in
removing his clothing in order to exercise. The Christian
is to exercise himself spiritually toward godliness. He
should strive to live in a godly manner himself, and encourage others to do likewise. This is a great antidote for
heresy.

He illustrates godly living by a comparison with the
athletic world. "The bodily exercise for a little is profitable." Disagreement has arisen over Paul's meaning in the
expression "bodily exercise" (*hē sōmatikē gumnasia*). It
is hardly to be supposed that he means the preceding
ascetic practices of forbidding marriage and certain foods.
Paul would say such practices are suicidal, not profitable
even for a little. Some say he means certain practices
which are a useful discipline toward godliness. Such
matters as refusing to let physical appetites rule the will
are understood here. However, Paul's contrast is not between two kinds of asceticism, but between asceticism
and godliness. The most likely explanation is that he

means ordinary physical exercise. The expression was literally used in the sense of gymnastic exercise, and the illustration would naturally come to his mind because he had used the verb *gumnazō* as a metaphor in the previous clause.

The difference between gymnastic exercise and godly exercise is expressed by the phrase "for a little" (*pros oligon*). Gymnastic exercise is profitable for a little extent and for a short duration. Paul does not state which idea he meant, and perhaps he meant both, since he next explains godliness as being profitable for all things (extent), both in this life and in the life to come (duration). Gymnastic exercise affects chiefly the physical part of man, and lasts only a little while when compared to the far-reaching effects of godliness. Spiritual exercise profits the body, soul, and spirit, and brings value in the present life as well as the age to come. By godliness Paul means that conduct of life which is according to the standard of the Word of God (1 Tim. 3:16). The power for such a life is supplied by Christ living within.

Paul confirms this matter by using the formula, "Faithful is the word." The two previous occurrences of the formula (1:15; 3:1) have referred to statements which follow it. Here it is not absolutely certain, but most scholars prefer to relate it to the previous clause. The use of *gar* (for) in the next verse seems to indicate this, since it serves to introduce supporting or affirming data, rather than the content of the *logos* itself. Furthermore, verse 8 seems more likely to have been a well-known and quoted saying than does verse 10.

3. Faithful laboring.

> For unto this we are laboring and striving, because we have set our hope on the living God who is Saviour of all men, especially of believers (v. 10).

The life of godliness, which is so profitable for time and eternity, is the apostle's goal. Toward this end (*eis touto*) he labors to the point of weariness and exhaustion (*kopiō-*

men) and strives as fervently as any athlete in the games
(agōnizometha). Such energy is not pointless or ineffective, however, for Paul has the confidence that his faith
rests on the right foundation. The God whom he trusts is
the Savior of the world, and in a special sense, of believers (cf. 1:1, where God is called "Saviour").

The statement that God is the Savior of all men has
evoked a variety of interpretations. Purdy lists the following four as being the most clearly defined.[59]

Four Views of the "Saviour of All Men" (1 Tim. 4:10)

Universalist interpretation. This view holds that all
men will eventually be saved spiritually and brought
back into fellowship with God. None will experience
eternal punishment. The special sense in which God is
Savior of believers is their earlier experiencing of the
blessings of salvation and their escape of even temporary
corrective punishment by God. However, the biblical
doctrine of eternal punishment refutes this view.

Providential interpretation. This view takes the term
"Saviour" in its lower sense of preserver, deliverer. God
saves all men in that He gives them life, sends sun and
rain and fruitful seasons. Believers are the subjects of a
special providence of God. The adverb "specially"
(malista) demands that the believers enjoy in the highest
degree what all men enjoy to a limited degree. It is doubtful that Paul would lower the term "Saviour" in regard to
believers to the mere temporal. Yet this must be the case
if the general sense of the first clause means a temporal
Savior. Furthermore, the spiritual aspects of salvation are
certainly in this context, so that this view seems unlikely.

Potential-actual interpretation. This view holds that
God is the Savior of all men, for He desires to save all, and
provided in Christ salvation for all. However, this poten-
tially universal salvation becomes actual only to those
who believe. This understanding is in accord with the

facts of biblical doctrine and has many advocates. However, the adverb *malista* (specially) does offer a problem, since its ordinary meaning demands that all men must enjoy to some degree what believers enjoy in the highest degree. This is hardly possible in the potential-actual interpretation.

Temporal-eternal interpretation. This view looks upon God's salvation as one. As applied to unbelievers it includes preservation and deliverance from various evils and the bestowal of many blessings during this life. To believers, however, this salvation does not end with earthly life but goes on for all eternity. Purdy explains thus:

> God is the Saviour of all men in that on a temporal basis he gives them life and strength, awakens within them high ideals, provides for their pleasure and sustenance, and graciously allows them to live for a time in the light of His countenance.
>
> God is specially the Saviour of believers in that he has a special call for them, answers their prayers, and provides for their well-being, not only in this life, but also in the life which is to come.[60]

This view seems to be the best one, because it gives the proper force to *malista*. It is in agreement with the temporal-eternal elements of the context (e.g., 4:8), and employs *sōtēr* (Savior) in a valid way. Thus Paul finds in the saving function of God the great impetus for faithful laboring in a world which sometimes brings adversity.

C. *The encouragement of the minister toward a constructive ministry* (vv. 11-16).

After describing in some detail to Timothy the false teachers and their ascetic emphasis, along with a directive to combat their influence in the church, Paul now adds a paragraph of personal encouragement. Good advice is given whereby Timothy can make his ministry even more effective.

1. In public life.

Continue charging these things and teaching. Let no one despise thy youth, but continue becoming a model for the believers in word, in conduct, in love, in faith, in purity. While I am coming, continue giving heed to the reading, to the exhortation, to the teaching (vv. 11-13).

  a. He should command and teach sound doctrine.

Specifically, it is the material concerning false teachers and their errors that Paul refers to by "these things." Timothy, in his capacity as spiritual leader, is to order certain behavior on the part of the congregation. The first imperative (*paraggelle*, continue charging) indicates a command to be given, and the present tense reveals the continual obligation to give such orders. The second imperative (*didaske*, continue teaching) orders the instruction of the congregation on the moral and spiritual principles involved. The godly minister must always base his commands on what "the Spirit expressly says." Therefore, a fundamental element in his ministry is the continued teaching of the Word of God in order to safeguard his people from false teachers and their doctrine.

  b. He should maintain the respect of his people.

Timothy is not to allow any to set him aside or discount his ministry on account of his youthfulness. Some of the elders at Ephesus may have been much older than Timothy. Some of those heretical teachers whom he must refute may have been older than he. Of course, one must not overstress the "youth" idea. Timothy must have been at least thirty years old at this time. He was chosen to be Paul's companion on the second journey (variously dated in the proximity of A.D. 50), and was certainly no less than sixteen at the time. If 1 Timothy was written in A.D. 63, then he must have been no less than thirty years of age. There is abundant evidence that the term *neotēs* was applied to men till the age of forty. Youth is a relative concept anyway. White remarks: "Forty is reckoned old for a captain in the army, young for a bishop, very young for a Prime Minister."[61] For such a responsible and important position, Timothy was youthful. Yet any who despised him for his youth were inexcusable. The word "despise" (*kataphroneitō*) means to "think down upon," and indicates an inferior estimation.

However, there was something Timothy could do to win their respect, in a way that the mere issuing of orders would never do. He could live before the believers in a manner above reproach. This statement does not suggest that Timothy had been careless about his conduct. The present imperative denotes a continuance in a course of activity. "Continue becoming a model." This is of necessity a process. One does not set himself up before men and say, "Watch me; I am a model." Rather, he must live consistently day by day so that Christian observers may increasingly realize the display of Christian character that is unfolding before them. Paul lists five outstanding realms in which Christian people should be able to follow their minister as an example: speech, conduct, love, faith, purity. Unwavering devotion to these Christian virtues will do much to remove the force from any criticism because of youth.

    c. He should carry out a balanced scriptural ministry.

The three terms, reading, exhortation, and teaching, are all used with the article, and it is most likely that these are all public functions.

There may be a logical sequence in the terms. The reading (*tēi anagnōsei*) most certainly refers to the public reading of the Scripture during the services. The art of doing this effectively is greatly neglected in our own day. It should be cultivated. All who treasure the Scripture as God's revelation to man should give the reading of it a prominent place in public worship. In Timothy's day the Old Testament comprised by far the largest part of sacred literature. However, various portions of New Testament writings were beginning to appear and can be understood as included in the matter for public reading.

The exhortation (*tēi paraklēsei*) was probably the customary encouragement of the people to carry out the injunction of the Scripture just read. This custom had been followed in the synagogues (Acts 13:15), and was carried over into the church.

The teaching (*tēi didaskaliāi*) refers to the formal instruction of the people based on the Word of God, whether on the passage just read, or on some other. The teaching is directed primarily to the intellect, whereas the exhortation is largely aimed at the moral sense of the hearers. Perhaps we need not completely disassociate these two terms but regard them as aspects of religious instruction, based on the Scripture.

2. In personal life.

> Continue neglecting not the gift which is in you, which was given to you through prophecy, with laying on of the hands of the presbytery. These things continue caring for, be in these things, in order that your progress may be manifest to all. Continue taking heed to yourself and to the teaching; keep remaining in them; for doing this, both yourself you will save and the ones hearing you (vv. 14-16).

a. He is to take care of the gift he possessed.

The nature of the gift (*charismatos*) is indicated by the employment of the term elsewhere in the New Testament. *Charisma* is used twice in the Pastoral Epistles, and fourteen times in Paul's other epistles. The only other New Testament occurrence is 1 Peter 4:10. It always means a gift of grace, bestowed by the Lord for some special ministry. These "charismatic gifts" are explained by Paul as being distributed to various believers so that the church will benefit. "Having then gifts [*charismata*] differing according to the grace that is given to us, whether prophecy, let us prophesy according to the proportion of faith . . ." (Rom. 12:6). "Now there are diversities of gifts [*charismatōn*] but the same Spirit. . . . But all these worketh that one and the selfsame Spirit, dividing to every man severally as he will" (1 Cor. 12:4-11).

Thus Timothy had received a gift from the Holy Spirit which he was now urged to exercise. It is not revealed what his gift was. According to the list in 1 Corinthians 12:28, we need not suppose that his gift was necessarily miraculous. Many have suggested that the ability to teach, discern error, and administer the church as a pastor may have been Timothy's spiritual endowment.

Paul urges Timothy, "Neglect not the gift." The use of the present imperative (*mē amelei*) to express the prohibition, rather than the aorist subjunctive, has led many to infer that Timothy was dilatory in his work. Paul is then understood to say, "Stop neglecting the gift." Most grammarians concur that this is the more frequent connotation of the present imperative with *mē*. However, this general usage was not an irrevocable distinction. Robertson shows how *mē poiei*, while usually meaning "stop doing," can also mean "continue not doing."[62] Moulton says:

> But does *mē amelei* in I Timothy 4:14 require us to believe that Timothy *was* "neglecting" his "charism"— *mēdeni epitithei* and *mēde koinōnei* in 5:22, that he was warned to stop what he was hitherto guilty of? May we not rather say that *mē amelei* is equivalent to *pantote meleta* or the like, a marked *durative*, with a similar account of *mēde koinōnei*?[63]

In view of the tremendous responsibility that Paul reposed in Timothy it is incongruous to imagine that he was a vacillating, dawdling, lazy person, listless in the performance of his duties. It is more reasonable to see in this expression a litotes in which a positive command is expressed negatively.

The reception of Timothy's gift is next described. It was

bestowed upon him "through prophecy with laying on of the hands of the presbytery." "Through" (*dia*) denotes the channel by which the gift was given to Timothy. This means, or channel, was prophecy. In the New Testament, prophecy was that inspired utterance which was itself a gift (1 Cor. 12:10). The gift was bestowed and made known to Timothy by an inspired prophet who revealed what the gift was. This revelation to Timothy through prophecy was accompanied by the imposition of hands by the body of elders. *Meta* (with) does not denote agency but accompaniment. The imposition of hands was thus a symbolic action accompanying the reception of the gift. The laying on of hands was a symbolic practice used in the Old Testament for ordaining special officers (Num. 27:18, 23), for symbolizing the transfer of guilt from the sinner to the sacrificial animal (Lev. 16:2), and for the bestowal of blessing (Gen. 48:14, 20). In each case it symbolized the transfer of something. In the New Testament, the symbolism also refers to the communication of some blessing, but the laying on of the hands is always symbolic, not efficacious. In 1 Timothy 4:14 the action symbolizes the communication to Timothy of the spiritual gift, but the act itself did not produce the gift. Paul's preposition *meta* shows it was only an accompanying circumstance.

The use of the aorist for the verb *edothē* (was given) points to some historic moment when this event occurred. Most likely it was the time when Timothy was formally set aside for his special ministry. The place and time are not indicated. We infer that Paul was one of the elders who had a part in this rite (2 Tim. 1:16). Fairbairn states:

> The prophecy, therefore, is to be viewed as the distinct enunciation of God's will in respect to Timothy's qualifications—his spiritual as well as natural qualifications for the evangelistic office; and the formal designa-

tion of him by the presbytery was the church's response
to the declared mind of God, and appropriate action to
carry it into effect.[64]

The value of using his gift is next stated by Paul. By
exercising his ministry in the power of his gift, Timothy
would display the progress which he had made since the
time when the hands had been laid upon him and the gift
had been given. No one could then find any fault in
seeing such great responsibility in the hands of a young
man. Both imperatives are durative, stressing the continuing obligation. He must continually be caring for
(*meleta*) the matters of teaching and ministry. He must
continually be (*isthi*) in the realm of these matters.
Robertson paraphrases *en toutois isthi* as being "up to his
ears" in them.[65] A constant attention to the work of the
ministry removes many a criticism before it begins.

   b. He is to take heed to himself.

      H. A. Hoyt gives a significant outline of this
verse. The minister must care for his own character ("thyself"), creed ("doctrine"), and conduct ("continue in
these things").[66] Any minister must first prepare himself
if he is to bless others. He must prepare not only his
sermons but himself. Both imperatives are present tense,
showing that Timothy is to continue doing those things. It
is probable that the definite article with "teaching" (*tēi
didaskaliāi*) is used in the pronominal sense as "thy
teaching," in view of *seautōi* (thyself). Paul is here discussing doctrine as Timothy must handle it, not the body
of truth per se.

By careful attention to his personal life and ministry,
Timothy will save himself and his hearers. Some have
hesitated to interpret *sōseis* in this passage in its usual
Pauline sense of spiritual salvation, because it is predi-
cated of Timothy rather than of God. Such expositors refer it to a saving from difficulties,[67] or from demonic
teaching.[68] However, the basis for such a view is not
sound, for Scripture clearly indicates that salvation of the

soul has a present aspect in which we are commanded to "work out your own salvation with fear and trembling, for it is God which worketh in you" (Phil. 2:12-13). John Calvin, one who was certainly not biased toward minimizing God's part in salvation says:

> Nor ought they to think it strange that Paul ascribes to Timothy the work of saving the Church; for, certainly, all that is gained to God is saved, and it is by the preaching of the gospel that we are gathered to Christ. And as the unfaithfulness or carelessness of the pastor is ruinous to the Church, so the cause of salvation is justly ascribed to his faithfulness and diligence. True, it is God alone that saves; and not even the smallest portion of his glory can lawfully be bestowed on men. But God parts with no portion of his glory when he employs the agency of men for bestowing salvation.[69]

Inasmuch as the context discusses doctrinal and practical matters relative to spiritual salvation (cf. v. 10), it is most likely that such is in view. By a careful attention to his own spiritual condition and ministry, Timothy and all ministers are "working out" their own salvation, and are bringing the message of salvation also to others.

V. Charge Concerning Various Members of the Congregation (5:1—6:2).

In addition to addressing public gatherings, the minister must deal with individual members. The matters now discussed are not doctrinal, but practical. The first two groups will be considered not in a verse-by-verse exposition but by a topical study, since this method seems more suitable to Paul's epistolary style in this section.

A. *The pastoral care of old and young members* (vv. 1-2).

> Do not sharply rebuke an old man, but exhort as a father, younger men as brothers, older women as mothers, younger women as sisters in all purity (vv. 1-2).

1. The persons involved.

The mention of the four groups makes it clear that the *presbuterōi* is not an official but an old man. (The official "elder" is mentioned in v. 17.) Since Timothy was a comparatively young man, these designations are particularly significant to him. His parishioners will be comprised of many people older than he, and many, like himself, of younger age.

2. The nature of the pastoral care.

a. It must not be a harsh or disrespectful rebuke.

The verb *epiplēxeis (epiplēssō)* means much more than rebuke in the sense of admonition. It literally means to strike with blows. Figuratively used here, it means to smite with words rather than fists. Admonition is necessary for all, but a disrespectful, roughshod assault upon an older man by a minister who is younger merely lays the accuser open to rebuke. All vindictiveness and bitterness must be avoided, if the minister would manifest the spirit of Christ in his duties.

The Bible places much stress on respect for age, especially in the Old Testament. In the earliest days of the church, as is often true today, believers were a closely knit group, because they were more or less rejected by pagan friends or synagogues. Such close associations tend to erase the common courtesies which Scripture indicates as necessary. Consequently, a reminder is appropriate that there is no place for disrespect, even when a rebuke is warranted.

b. It should be a comforting, encouraging, and admonishing entreaty.

All these ideas are contained in the imperative *parakalei*. This verb supplements *epiplēssō*. Old men do not have the liberty to do anything they please, merely because they are old. There may come occasions for correction. When so, the matter must be handled by the minister in a way that comforts and encourages along with the admonition. The same verb is understood with reference to the other groups: older women, younger men and women. Probably *epiplēxēis* (sharply rebuke) is to be implied with reference to them also, being used with the fi4st term only because the impropriety would be seen most clearly with the older man. The very practical reason for this advice is that proper dealing with such cases will make the offenders more inclined to heed the admonition.

3. The manner of pastoral care.

    a. It should be performed with such consideration for others as is proper in a family.

The minister should not only assent to the theological truth that all believers are spiritual children of God the Father, and thus are brothers and sisters in Christ, He should also treat them in his ecclesiastical dealings as considerately as members of his own family circle. When admonition or encouragement becomes necessary, he should be as respectful to the elderly ones as to his own parents, and as considerate of the others as of his own brothers and sisters.

    b. It should be performed with all purity where young women are involved.

Logic as well as grammar indicates that the phrase *en pasēi hagneiāi* (in all purity) belongs with "younger women" (*neōteras*). This is not a warning only against acts of immorality (such would of course be understcod), but against any breach of propriety. Even if immorality is not involved, thoughtlessness or indiscretion will ruin the ministry of any pastor, regardless of his eloquence. When his pastoral duties require him to deal with young women, he should behave as he would want other men to act toward his own sister, or as he would act toward his sister. This warning is most significant, for at this very point many young men on the threshold of long and fruitful service have lost their usefulness.

B. *The pastoral care of widows* (vv. 3-16).

Honor widows who are actually widows. But if any

widow has children or descendants, let them learn first
to act reverently toward their own house and to give
recompense to their parents, for this is acceptable before God. But she who is actually a widow and has been
left alone has hope set upon God and is continuing in
the entreaties and the prayers night and day. But she
who is living in pleasure is dead while living. And
these things continue charging, in order that they might
be blameless. But if anyone does not provide for his
own ones and especially ones of his household, he has
denied the faith and is worse than an unbeliever. Let
not a widow be enrolled having become less than sixty
years, wife of one husband, being testified to in good
works, if she has reared children, if she has entertained
strangers, if she has washed saints' feet, if she has
assisted afflicted ones, if she has followed closely every
good work.

But younger widows be declining, for whenever they
behave wantonly against Christ, they wish to marry,
having judgment because they set aside the first faith.
And at the same time also they learn [to be] idle, while
going about the houses, and not only idle but also tat-
tlers and busybodies, speaking the things which are not
necessary. I will, therefore, for younger ones to marry,
to bear children, to rule households, to give not any
starting point to the adversary for the sake of reviling.
For already some have turned aside after Satan.

If any woman believer has widows, let her assist
them, and let the church not be burdened, in order that
it may assist those who are actually widows (vv. 3-16).

The material regarding widows will be considered under a topical arrangement. Every statement in these verses
will be treated, however.

1. The kind of widows.

The problem of the proper care of widows arose early in the church. Acts 6:1 is the first recorded instance of
difficulty. There were no organized institutions to care
for the problem. It is most likely accurate to say that all
such institutions are the result of Christian influence,

either direct or indirect. Women could not find ready employment of an honorable kind. Therefore, the church faced the problem from the beginning.

Paul distinguishes several kinds of widows. The five groups he mentions are not completely independent of each other. However, each group calls for special treatment.

a. The widow who is actually bereft (vv. 3, 5, 16).

Paul calls such widows *hē ontōs chēra*, "the genuine widow," or "the one actually a widow." This group is characterized by more than loss of husband. The description of the widows follows.

(1) She is completely alone, without husband or family to provide support.

The noun *chēra*, widow, is just the feminine form of the adjective *chēros* used as a substantive, and means bereft, robbed, having suffered loss. Thus a *chēra ontōs* is a woman who is truly bereft, not only of husband, but of other family assistance as well. The participle *memonōmenē*, "left alone," (v. 5) reinforces this idea.

(2) She has hope set on God.

These actual widows whom Paul discusses are Christian women. Only to them does the church bear the special responsibility that is outlined in this chapter.

(3) She lives a godly life.

She continues in entreaties and prayers night and day. Not only is this widow a believer, but she must also be a spiritual woman whose life of piety is evident.

b. The widow who has a family (v. 4).

This widow is considered separately by Paul because her problem of livelihood is different. This family may consist of children or other descendants, but she is not completely alone, as is the widow previously mentioned.

c. The widow who is living in pleasure (v. 6).

The present participle *spatalōsa* denotes a continuance or course of life, and is derived from the noun *spatalē,* riotous, luxurious living. Such a widow, though physically alive (*zōsa*), is spiritually dead (*tethnēken*— perfect tense indicating present condition).

d. The enrolled widow (vv. 9, 10).

The verb *katalegō* means to set down in a register, to enroll. We are not told the purpose of this enrollment. It certainly was not merely equivalent to church membership, for it is most unlikely that a widow under sixty years of age would be denied church membership, other factors being favorable. The possible purpose of this enrollment will be discussed later, under the subject, "The treatment of widows." At this point we conclude that the enrolled widows composed a portion of the group first described as widows actually bereft. A description of the enrolled widow is given.

(1) She must be at least sixty years old.

In view of the explanation regarding younger widows (v. 11), this age limit must have been intended to safeguard against the possibility of remarrying.

(2) She must have had a blameless married life.

The same marital standard was true of the enrolled widow as of the overseer (3:2) and the deacon (3:12). There must have been no divorce, polyandry, or other marital adulteration.

(3) She must have a reputation for good works.

The list Paul enumerates are not duties that she must now perform, but are works to which she has received testimony already by others. Before a widow was enrolled, she must be testified to in the matter of good works. Five of these areas of godly living are mentioned. The use of *ei* (if) to introduce each clause may indicate indirect questions, such as were asked at the time when her enrollment was being considered. It must not be supposed that in each of these characteristics the widow must have excelled. The fifth one, "if she has followed closely every good work," is too broad to insist upon a rigid fulfillment in every case. Consequently, it is not necessary to infer that a childless widow could never be enrolled. It is more likely that these are the realms where testimony to a woman's life might occur, and there must be no adverse testimony to her life in these fields. Of course, if she had no children, then such a question would not apply to her.

(a) Reared children (eteknotrophēsen).

This is particularly the woman's responsibility, and here her godliness and moral standards are readily displayed. To rear children well is worthy of highest praise.

(b) Entertained strangers (exenodochēsen).

The lodging of guests is largely the responsibility of the woman in the home. It is she who usually expresses the geniality and simple kindnesses which are the true indications of hospitality.

(c) Washed saints' feet (hagiōn podas enipsen).

The usual interpretation of this phrase makes it a picturesque reference to hospitality. There are serious objections to this explanation, however. Hospitality has just been mentioned by the apostle in the preceding clause. Furthermore, it is difficult to see why he restricted it to the saints if hospitality were meant, since all strangers should be the objects of our gracious spirit. To take the phrase literally, and then explain it as the custom of washing guests' feet at the door, is a most unusual characteristic for a woman. This custom was carried out by servants or the host, not by the woman of the house. White states:

> . . . it is natural to suppose that the story told in John 13:5-14, and the Master's command to do as He had done, was known to St. Paul and Timothy.[70]

Since the action is restricted to the saints, and is considered an important indication of a widow's godliness, it is best understood as a reference to the ordinance of washing the saints' feet, as given by Jesus Himself (John

13). Her participation in this ordinance would indicate her devotion to Christ and her desire to obey His commands (John 13:14, 17). Perhaps this one ordinance was picked by the apostle because it most clearly demonstrates the individual's willingness to follow unreservedly the Lord's commands, even to the point of personal inconvenience, and thus reveals her spiritual nature (John 13:17).

      (d) Assisted afflicted ones (*thlibomenois epērkesen*).

The assistance may have taken many forms, but whatever the form, the spirit of Christian love was manifested.

      (e) Followed closely every good work (*panti ergōi agathōi epēkolouthēsen*).

This general statement sums up the description of the enrolled widow. We are reminded of the woman Dorcas (Acts 9:36, 39) who was noted for her good works as a seamstress, to whom the widows bore testimony.

    e. The younger widow (vv. 11-15).

These widows are less than sixty years old, and perhaps should be thought of as the remaining members of the first group who are not included with the enrolled widows. Because of the younger age, special discussion is devoted to them.

  2. The treatment of widows.

    a. Widows who are truly helpless (group one) are to be honored by the church (vv. 3, 16b).

The verb *timaō* is used, which means to assess a value, bestow honor upon. These godly widows whom Paul defines as being completely bereft of husband or family and thus dependent upon God are to be given respect and sympathy by the church. Whether financial aid is involved cannot be determined by *timaō*, but must be explained by the context. Here it seems best to understand *timaō* in its usual sense of respect, which of course would include financial assistance where necessary, regardless of the age of the widow. A church cannot truly "honor" a widow, and let her suffer financial need. Individual cases must determine the direction which the honoring must take.

     b. Widows who have families (group two) are to be supported by them, in order that the church might not be burdened (vv. 4, 8, 16a).

     (1) Performance of this work is an obligation for families.

     The obligation is laid upon children (*tekna*, v. 4), descendants (*ekgona*, v. 4, a general word which refers to offspring, and can be broadly understood as grandchildren), and upon woman believers who have widows in their households (*pistē*, v. 16). Because of the context the women believers should probably be understood as Christian women whose husbands are unbelievers and thus would not recognize the authority of Paul's charge, or else Christian widows who have sufficient means to relieve other widows in their families.

     (a) It was commanded by God in the Old Testament.

     Caring for parents or grandparents is acceptable conduct with God, for it was so stated in the fifth commandment. Jesus emphasized the importance of this obligation (Mark 7:9-12). Such filial care is a reverent action (*eusebein*) and cannot be lightly treated by any son or daughter.

     (b) It is proper gratitude for care received from parents.

     By caring for a widowed mother or grandmother, the son shows appreciation for the sacrifice and tender care he received at the hands of his parents. He should also remember that old age comes upon all, and eventually he may be dependent upon his children for care.

     Ironside records the Jewish tale of the young Jew who

had housed his aged father until his young wife finally demanded that he be sent to the poorhouse. After fruitless discussion, he took his father on the way. At last he had to drag his protesting father. When they reached a certain tree, the father refused to be dragged farther, and cried, "You can't drag me past this tree, because this is as far as I dragged my father!"[71]

　　　　(2) Failure in this work is a denial of Christianity.

　　　　To shirk this filial responsibility is to deny one of the articles of the Christian faith (*tēn pistin* is articular, v. 8). (Such passages as Eph. 6:2; Mark 7:9-12; Exod. 20:12, are involved in the denial.) Furthermore, such a denial places the shirker in a position even worse than the unbeliever (*apistou*). He is worse for at least two reasons. First, it is worse to claim to possess the true teaching and then flagrantly deny it, than to make no such claim. Second, even unbelievers assent in principle to the filial obligation referred to here. Matthew 5:46-47 suggests that even sinners feel a family devotion and responsibility.

What is the responsibility of the church toward widows whose families do not support them? Paul does not discuss that possibility. He rather emphasizes what should be the proper thing, that families should care for their own ones, and not shift the responsibility to the congregation. However, it should be obvious that the church could not stand idly by if a Christian widow were in material need.

　　　　c. Widows who live in pleasure (group three) are not the responsibility of the church to support (vv. 6-7).

　　　　Such widows are spiritually dead and need to be converted to Christ. Of course, the church bears the same responsibility to worldly widows as to all other unbelievers, but the church does not owe them the same respect and sympathy that the godly widows deserve.

Verse 7 is best taken in connection with verse 6. Pleasure-loving widows must be warned of the grave consequences of their conduct, and all widows should beware of stumbling into such a trap.

d. Widows who meet certain qualifications (group four) may be enrolled by the church (vv. 9, 10).

It is known from church history of the second, third, and fourth centuries that a Widow Office existed in the church, whose primary function was prayer and works of mercy.[72] However, it cannot be shown without much addition to the text that such was Paul's intent here, although it is easy to see how such an office could have developed later.

In this passage it should be observed that no duties are listed. The qualifications stated are all to be evident before this widow is enrolled. Furthermore, the context has to do not with what the widow should do for the church, but what the church should do for the widow. Also, the age of the enrolled widow indicates that her years of laboring were largely if not completely past. In that era, a woman of sixty years was in the aged and infirm class, and any service she might render must of necessity have been strictly limited. Fairbairn avows:

> There is no proper evidence whatever to show that such widows as those here mentioned by the apostle were invested with any sort of office, or were called to do anything but such pious and free-will service as their own hearts might prompt, and their limited opportunities might enable them to perform.[73]

The purpose of the enrollment has still not been explained, and it must be quickly added that the matter is obscure. To hazard a guess, it seems possible that this enrollment was for the purpose of dispensing regular support for the older widows who would in all likelihood not remarry. Since such support was done in apostolic times (Acts 6:1), these regulations by Paul to Timothy would serve as a guide in determining who was eligible for regu-

lar support. (Of course, this would not bar a younger
widow from receiving temporary assistance in time of
need, on the basis of v. 3.) Because of the godly characteristics of such women, they would continue to bear a good
testimony (vv. 1, 10), and exercise the ministry of prayer
(v. 5).

> e. Younger widows (group five) must not be en-
> rolled (vv. 11-15).

As previously explained, these widows must be
considered as the remaining members of group 1, ones
not yet sixty years old. Though they may be godly, and
equally bereft of husband and family, they must not be
enrolled along with the older widows. Three reasons are
given for this prohibition.

> (1) Because of their youth.

Enrollment should be declined to widows
under sixty because their younger age involves special
problems. Paul here speaks along very practical lines. Because of their youth, the normal desire for husband and
family would be more likely to assert itself. The verb
katastrēniaō means to feel the impulse of sexual desire, to
behave wantonly toward. Paul finds nothing wrong with
marriage (see v. 14) but he argues that the enrollment is
for those who most probably are past the age of marrying.
If, as has been suggested, the enrollment indicated full
support, then to include women in this group who are
only temporarily widowed, and still possessed of youthful vigor, would not provide a practical grouping. Younger widows are likely to have a divided allegiance or
attention.

Paul goes on to explain what direction this youthful
vigor of the young widow may take. Her wanton behavior,
arising from sexual impulse, may take her away from
Christ if she marries. It is most easily understood if this be
viewed as marriage to a pagan, since the marriage of a
Christian widow to a Christian man is not condemned but
encouraged (v. 14). If a young widow who professed

Christianity married in wanton rebellion against Christ, she is said to have set aside the "first faith" (tēn prōtēn pistin). This is usually explained as a pledge not to remarry, which the enrolled widow took (in accord with a classical usage of pistin). However, it is difficult to see why this would be called the "first" faith, since such an expression would lead one to suppose the original faith in Christ. Furthermore, this view is based on the hypothesis that the enrolled widow must never remarry, due to the phrase "wife of one husband." However, that is a most uncertain interpretation of the phrase. It appears far more likely that the judgment (krima) resting upon a widow, who marries without regard to Christ, is a judgment which she incurs because she has set aside the very principle of godliness and separation from sin which she professed to accept when she became a Christian.

  (2) Because enrollment might produce idleness and other faults.

  If enrollment involved full support without working, the younger, more active widows would have more time for meddling. Idleness can be a great curse. Inasmuch as the younger widows might not have their attention fully centered on Christ, their visits in various homes could produce more troublesome results.

  (3) Because their duty is to marry and maintain homes.

  Here Paul specifically encourages remarriage of widows, with no hint of disapproval. This same endorsement is given by Paul (1 Cor. 7:39), where the one stipulation added is that she must marry a Christian. (This restriction reinforces our interpretation that the remarriage of a wanton widow was to a pagan, v. 11.) This is woman's primary function, and no ascetic celibacy for its own sake can possibly be more holy. The woman for whom it is possible should look forward in the will of God to marriage, children, and the managing of a household. Of course, Paul gives this as advice. He cannot command a woman to get married, since she is not the only one involved in marriage. But remarriage for young widows is a solution to the problems he has previously sketched. Some widows had already allowed Satan to lead them into sin, and Paul desires to safeguard the testimony of the church and the widows.

There is always a demand upon the church for aid, and usually church funds are limited. Therefore, great care and wisdom must be employed in dispensing such funds so that benefit will go to those most truly in need. Especially is this warning needed in this present day when the prevailing sentiment is, "Somebody owes me a living."

C. *The pastoral care of elders* (vv. 17-25).

The elders *(hoi presbuteroi)* now discussed are the officials, not merely older men (see 5:1, for the discussion of the older men). The context makes this obvious.

1. The honoring of elders.

> The elders who are superintending well, let them be deemed worthy of double honor, especially those who are toiling in word and teaching. For the Scripture says: thou shalt not muzzle a threshing ox; and: worthy is the workman of his pay (vv. 17-18).

The qualifications for overseers or elders were given in chapter 3. Now Paul sets forth to Timothy the way these elders were to be treated by the congregation. It was Timothy's responsibility to see that these matters were carried out.

    a. Those to be honored are those who superintend well.

The basic or essential function of the elder (overseer) was the superintending of the congregation (see 3:4-5). His function is that of the spiritual ruler of the local church (whatever he may be called in modern terminology), and is commonly called "pastor" in most churches. The adverb *kalōs* (well) refers to that which is done excellently, in a commendable way. The work of the elder must not be taken for granted by the congregation. Evaluation must be made and when real excellence appears, it should be recognized and commended.

b. Those to be honored are those who are toiling in preaching and teaching.

The participle *kopiōntes* is a present form from *kopiaō*, to work hard, toil, grow weary. The verb stresses the idea of labor to the point of weariness. The particular area of superintendence mentioned is the realm of preaching and teaching. The anarthrous form *logōi* has reference to the general function of speech in connection with the elder's ministry. The term *didaskaliāi* is more limited and denotes the particular aspect of teaching or instructing, as distinguished from exhorting, admonishing, comforting, and other forms of preaching. This verse does not give sufficient warrant for the Reformed view of two classes of elders, those who ruled and those who taught. Every elder engaged in teaching (3:2). However, some would do so with more energy and excellence than others. The differentiation in this verse is between those who do the work perfunctorily and those who labor to the end of strength in performing their function. The labors of a godly elder must not be overlooked or minimized.

c. These elders are to receive double honor.

The expression *diplēs timēs* (double honor) has caused much discussion. Many explanations have been offered, some of which are nothing more than curiosities. One such example was the third-century practice of placing a double portion of meat before the presbyters at the love feasts.[74] A more reasonable explanation has understood the phrase as meaning double pay, perhaps twice the pay of the sixty-year-old widow, or of deacons. However, there is no scriptural statement regarding pay of deacons, and the matter of pay for widows is somewhat obscure. Also, it is hardly to be supposed that Paul meant *diplēs* (double) to be taken in a strictly mathematical sense.

Another explanation views the double honor as one honor for age (i.e., an old man) and another honor for the office (eldership). While this may be true, it seems unnecessary. It takes the term *presbuteroi* in an ambiguous sense of both old man and officer, and this is unlikely in verse 17.

Some view the phrase as a reference to honor plus honorarium. In view of the following verse, pay certainly seems to be involved in the *timē*. However, to define the twofold honor as rigidly as this infers that the elder who functioned without great excellence received respect but no pay—a rather curious arrangement, and not usually admitted by the holders of this view.

The writer holds that the double honor for the laboring elder implies a comparison with those who serve professionally, without undue exertion or distinction. One honor goes to him because of the position which he occupies. Extra honor goes to him if he serves with distinction. Here is a responsibility laid upon congregations to express appreciation for pastoral work done well.

What is included in *timē*? The word means honor, price, compensation. The usage of *timē* in the sense of pay or price is well established. (Matt. 27:6, 9; Acts 4:34; 7:16; 1 Cor. 6:20 are clear examples of this use.) Since the next verse employs a quotation used elsewhere by Paul (1 Cor. 9:9) to argue for the right of the minister to be supported by those whom he benefits, the idea of remuneration must be included in *timē* here. Thus the writer concludes that the double honor refers to a proportionate increase in respect and appreciation, which includes adequate remuneration, for those who excell in their superintending and teaching ministry.

d. This honoring has scriptural support.

Paul adduces two quotations to clinch his point. The first is Deuteronomy 25:4, which he also uses in 1 Corinthians 9:9. It refers to the humane custom enjoined upon the Jews of allowing the ox, which walked over the grain to separate kernel from chaff, to eat some if it desired. Fairbairn comments astutely here:

> The passage respecting it is taken from Deuteronomy 25:4, and is one of a series of directions enjoining kind and considerate behavior. It is the only one that has immediate respect to the lower animals; all the rest bear on the conduct that should be maintained toward one's fellow creatures, and especially toward those who might be in the unhappy position of bondmen; so that we can scarcely suppose this somewhat exceptional instruction could have been designed for the exclusive benefit of oxen. We may rather suppose it was intended, by carrying the injunction to cultivate a tender and beneficent disposition so low, to make it all the more sure that such a disposition should be exercised toward brethren of one's own flesh, most especially toward those who were laying themselves out in self-denying labors for the public good. It is therefore a perfectly legitimate application which is made of the passages here, and in I Corinthians 9:9, to the laborers in the Christian ministry.[75]

The second quotation is the statement of Jesus as recorded in these exact words in Luke 10:7 (and in a slightly altered form in Matt. 10:10). No other meaning can be gotten from Paul's construction than that he places both quotations on the same level (joined by *kai*, and) and terms them Scripture (*hē graphē*). Paul wrote this letter in A.D. 62-63, and Luke's Gospel was probably written before A.D. 60. Hence this verse is further evidence that the writings we call New Testament Scripture were recognized as such during the lifetime of their writers, and we may suggest in many cases from the time of writing.

Paul thus has shown from the Old and New Testaments that proper honoring and remuneration of elders is a scriptural principle. Of course, it may not be the plan of wisdom for a pastor to attempt to impose bluntly this teaching upon his congregation in order to better his own lot, without adequate foundational instruction. However, any pastor can see to it that the principle is taught by his own example in urging proper remuneration for guest ministers who visit his pulpit. This removes suspicion of selfishness, and will help to drive home the force of this passage to the congregation.

2. The discipline of elders.

> Against an elder do not receive an accusation, except on the basis of two or three witnesses. The ones sinning before all rebuke, in order that the rest also may have fear. I solemnly charge before God and Christ Jesus and the elect angels that you guard these things without prejudice, doing nothing according to partiality (vv. 19-21).

a. Discipline must be founded on fact, not rumor.

No charge against an elder (officer, not just old man), which would involve a public rebuke or other disciplinary measures, must be even entertained unless there are several witnesses on which to base this accusation. This follows the Mosaic command (Deut. 17:6), which was reiterated by Christ (Matt. 18:16). These witnesses are not thought of as appearing at the trial, but rather at the time when the disciplinary process is first contemplated. Unless the evidence is sufficient and practically certain, no action should be initiated against an elder.

This safeguard of the elder is a wise one. No person is more subject to Satan's attack in the form of gossip and slander than God's servant. If every accusation necessitated full investigation, the elder would have time for little else. Therefore, no elder should be brought to trial on the accusation of one person, for even charges of which an elder is acquitted can damage his work. How often has a godly pastor been remembered as "that preacher who was in some sort of trouble," even though he may have been exonerated!

b. Discipline must be administered in the sight of all the church.

Verse 20 shows that the preceding safeguard for elders was not intended to be a protection for evil men. The connection of *enōpion pantōn* (before all) is uncertain, some referring it to the preceding *hamartanontas* (sinning), and others to the following *elegche* (rebuke). However, the rest of the verse makes it clear that the public disciplining is involved so that others may profit, and therefore it is simpler to understand the command to be, "Rebuke before all." A public disciplining is especially appropriate if the sin was of a public nature. People will then have a respect for the church and will search their own lives, when they see that even leaders are not exempt from discipline for sin.

The substantive participle *tous hamartanontas* (the ones sinning) is a present, perhaps stressing the flagrant condition of the offender.

     c. Discipline must be administered without prejudice against or partiality toward the elder.

Paul uses a most solemn mode of expression to urge serious consideration and fairness in carrying out these injunctions. He reminds Timothy of the presence of God the Father and Christ and elect angels who are witnessing his administration of the church. Paul's interest in the holy angels (ones who did not leave their first estate, Jude 6) as observers of the church is indicated elsewhere (1 Cor. 4:9; 11:10).

The term prejudice is *prokrima*, a prejudgment, or decision arrived at before the facts are properly considered. Partiality is *prosklisis*, an inclination toward someone. When disciplining of elders is called for, it should be done with all fairness and with the absence of personal like or dislike.

  3. The selection of elders.

     Lay hands on no one hastily, neither share in other people's sins. Keep yourself pure. No longer be a water-drinker, but use a little wine on account of your stomach and your frequent weaknesses. The sins of some men are evident, leading the way unto judgment, but some also they follow after. Likewise also the good works are evident, ant those which are otherwise are not able to be hid (vv. 22-25).

    a. Haste must be avoided in selection, for those who ordain hastily are responsible for their conduct.

There is disagreement as to the reference of the words "lay hands on no man." Does this refer to the original ordination of elders, or to the restoration of a penitent elder to his former position? Many modern expositors, because of the immediate context, decide for the latter interpretation. However, the earliest exposition (Chrysostom) explains it as ordination. Furthermore, there is no evidence at all that the laying on of hands was employed to restore elders in the apostolic age. Inasmuch as the laying on of hands is known with certainty to have been used in the ordination of elders (and the other two uses in the Pastorals refer to ordination), the writer adopts that viewpoint and sees no lack of harmony with the context. By exercising care when an elder is selected, the possibility of future need for disciplining is greatly reduced. Paul seems to mean that failure to exercise this caution implicates those responsible for hasty ordination in the sinful effects of their unwise choice. Of course, even after careful examination, those who ordain may find that they have been deceived. Certainly, if they have used every precaution available to them, they are not held responsible by God for the sinful lapse of an erring elder. But if they, out of partiality or haste, born of failure to take seriously the nature of the eldership, have ordained hastily, then guilt to some extent must rest upon them. Timothy is to keep himself spiritually pure from blame on this score.

Here occurs a personal note to Timothy, advising him to use a little wine for the sake of his frail health. It appears that the thought came to Paul's mind when he said, "Keep yourself pure." He then expanded the thought to explain that asceticism at the expense of health does not keep one pure. In that day wine was employed as a medicinal agent for many ailments. This has been true in medical practice until very recent times. Water was unsafe to drink in many parts of the world, and yet Timothy apparently was refraining from any use of the common beverage, wine, lest he might be thought of as a *paroinos* (3:2). Paul urges that the medicinal purpose was a valid use, and should not be avoided when his health called for it. However, Timothy's weak stomach is no argument for drinking liquor today.

A practical observation may be made here. Paul's urging of wine as a medical remedy for illness certainly refutes the curious notion which some have today that the only biblical means for curing disease is through the prayer of faith. Paul recognized that medicines are useful for God's people.

      b. Haste must be avoided in selection, for their character will be revealed with the passing of time.

Paul explains that the wise choosing of elders is not an impossible task. Churches and their leaders need not fear implication in sins of elders, if they allow time to elapse before ordaining. The reason is that character manifests itself sooner or later. Some men's sins are clearly evident, as if preceding them into the final judgment, but in the case of others, the sins are not immediately discovered. This is also true of good works. Some are clearly evident; others come to light later. But eventually nothing will be hid. Therefore, time must be allowed to pass before a candidate is finally selected. This will avoid the necessity of disciplining later.

  D. *The pastoral care of slaves* (6:1, 2).

    As many as are under a yoke as slaves, let them regard their own masters worthy of all honor, in order that the name of God and the teaching might not be blasphemed. And the ones having believing masters, let them not despise [them] because they are brethren, but let them serve the more because they are believers and beloved, ones who are taking hold of the well-doing. These things continue teaching and exhorting (vv. 1-2).

A large proportion of the problems in the early church were the result of the institution of slavery. The Christian church knows no such distinctions, and therefore conflict between liberty in Christ and the current social system was bound to occur. Paul deals with this problem in several passages, not on the basis of theory, but with regard to the individual's responsibility for Christian conduct in whatever state he chanced to be. Paul did not preach revolution, but by proclaiming the gospel of Christ, which issues in a life of godliness, he accomplished much toward eventually ridding much of the world of this evil.

1. A slave should serve his unsaved master respectfully.

   a. The manner of this service.

   Verse 1 obviously refers to Christian slaves with pagan masters, since verse 2 distinguishes Christian masters. The term *despotēs* (master) is the technical correlative of *doulos* (slave). *Kurios* (lord) would have been a wider, less technical designation.

   These slaves, who probably formed a large proportion of the gentile church, as well as of the general population, were to account their masters deserving of every honor and respect. Their new-found liberty in Christ gave them no warrant for less faithful service.

   b. The reason for this service.

   Failure to show the pagan master proper respect was likely to cause blasphemy of God's name and of Christian doctrine. Not only would the offending slave be beaten, but the gospel and the Lord would be blamed by the unconverted for causing the misconduct.

2. A slave should give his Christian master even more service, and not look down upon him.

   a. The manner of this service.

At first glance this admonition might seem unnecessary, but practical experience has shown that trouble often arises at this very point. The admonition is expressed negatively and positively. A Christian slave (Paul could admonish no other kind) must not despise his Christian master. The imperative *kataphroneitōsan* is composed of *phroneō*, to think, and *kata*, down. The slave must not look down on such a master. For those who in the nature of the social system were subjugated to masters, the freedom from such class distinction in the spiritual life might well cause them to imagine that such freedom extended also to civil relationships. A Christian slave might soon come to despise his Christian master, who did not grant him freedom. Yet we know that Christian slaveowners were not compelled to free all their slaves (notice Philemon). Realization of equality in Christ must not become a cause of disrespect.

The positive admonition is expressed by *mallon douleuetōsan*, let them serve the more. *Mallon* is not to be regarded as corrective ("rather"), but as intensive ("the more"), since to say "let them rather serve" is a meaningless and unnecessary addition. The intensive use "more" is common (Rom. 5:15), being the basic connotation of the word. This does not mean that the slave of an unsaved master does not need to give as much service, but it does indicate that the slave of a Christian master has even more reason to render service. There should be greater motivation, arising from the spiritual relationship which unites the two.

   b. The reason for this service.

The fuller service which a Christian master can expect is due to motivation of the slave by the common faith and brotherly love. Since the masters are believers and beloved ones, a relationship exists for the slave which does not if the master is a pagan.

The last phrase *hoi tēs euergesias antilambanomenoi* is capable of several explanations. *Antilambanō* means to lay hold of, help, seize. *Euergesia* means well-doing, or a good deed done. The phrase must refer to the masters. It could then grammatically mean that the masters who are recipients of this good service are believers and beloved ones. Or it could equally well mean that these Christian masters are themselves engaging in (taking hold of) this beneficial activity toward their slaves. The explanation that *tēs euergesias* refers to salvation in Christ ("the benefit") is far-fetched.

Although slavery does not exist in America, the responsibility of conduct is the same for employees and employers in principle.

VI. CHARGE CONCERNING THE MINISTER HIMSELF (6:3-21a).

As Paul nears the end of this letter to Timothy, he makes a number of admonitions, some of which are almost a recapitulation of previous material. However, his purpose is different. The fact that he is speaking more personally accounts for the rather loose grouping of thoughts in this final chapter.

A. *The minister is charged to avoid improper motives* (vv. 3-10).

If anyone is teaching different doctrine and does not come to healthy words, the ones of our Lord Jesus Christ, and to the teaching which is in accord with godliness, he is puffed up, knowing nothing, but being sick concerning questionings and wars about words, out of which are coming envy, strife, blasphemies, evil suspicions, constant wranglings of men corrupted in the mind and deprived of the truth, supposing their godliness to be a means of gain. But the godliness with contentment is a great means of gain. For nothing brought we into the world, because neither are we able to bring anything out. But having sustenance and coverings, with these things we shall be sufficed (vv. 3-8).

Paul warns Timothy by pointing out the examples of false teachers whose actions may be accounted for by wrong motives.

1. The evidence of wrong motives.
   a. The person who teaches different doctrine.

Modern indifference to doctrine is not an apostolic trait. Paul exhibits no toleration whatever toward those who deviate from the well-defined standard of truth, the gospel message (see 1:3-20, for Paul's treatment of the same subject from a different standpoint). This different doctrine (heterodidaskaleō) is further explained as a failure to assent to (proserchetai, come over to, the root of the word "proselyte") the words of Christ, who is the great person of the gospel. These words are those which supply spiritual life and health (hugiainō) to the believer.

   b. The person who does not assent to the teaching which produces a life of godliness.

This goes beyond mere teaching to one's living. Paul's terming of didaskaliāi (teaching) as tēi kat' eusebeian (in accord with godliness) shows that he was thinking of Christian teaching in the light of its fruits. True doctrine based upon Christ issues in genuine piety and godliness of life. If a man's motive in preaching and teaching is wrong, sooner or later this evidence of wrong doctrine and wrong living will appear. Therefore, when these evidences do appear, the cause of the trouble must be sought in the motive of the false teacher. Paul next mentions two of the most frequent wrong motives.

2. The nature of wrong motives.
   a. Pride.

The verb tuphoō means to inflate, besmog, puff up with pride (see 3:6), and refers to the inflated ego of the individual who claims the right to teach different doctrine from that revealed by Christ. That this is pride is clear from the next phrase, "knowing nothing." Moreover, the pride revealed in false teaching is a sickness (*nosōn*, being sick) in contrast to the healthy words of true doctrine (*hugiainousin*, healthy). The symptoms of this disease of pride are listed by Paul. Questionings, wars over words, envy, strife, blasphemies, evil suspicions, constant wranglings—these are the indications of men proud of their schemes and intellect. Every sort of strife is mentioned; which are the products of fleshly minds, not the fruit of the Spirit. The men engaging in these things are in a state of corruption (perfect participle) with respect to the mind (accusative of specification). They are also in a state of deprivation (perfect participle) of the truth. This means that they formerly possessed the truth of the gospel, but allowed pride or other factors to rob them of their possession. (To say they formerly possessed the truth implies nothing as to whether they had personally appropriated the truth and had been truly converted. It merely says they had contact with the truth at one time, but no longer possess it.)

　　b. Desire for gain.

　　This is a second injurious motive that Paul warns against. It may be in operation along with pride in the same individuals. This desire for gain is not mentioned just incidentally as a part of pride, however, for the thought is developed further in the succeeding verses.

　　The presence of the article with *eusebeian* (godliness) makes it clear that "godliness" is the subject. Common sense also confirms this understanding of the passage. (It is extremely doubtful if anyone ever thought that gain was godliness, but the reverse is often inferred.) Thus Paul says the false teachers are "supposing their godliness [article used as possessive pronoun] to be a means of gain." How often the Christian church has been plagued by this sordid, materialistic view that their profession of

Christianity (that is, their godliness) was to be a source of personal gain to these individuals. Tetzel and the papacy, with their sale of indulgences, is a noted example. Simon Magus is another instance. And how many religious workers of recent times have capitalized on the financial! We should contrast the spirit of Paul, who refused on some occasions to take his daily bread from his converts.

3. The prevention of wrong motives.

(The clause *aphistaso apo tōn toioutōn*, "from such withdraw thyself," which is used in the KJV is not in the best manuscripts, and is rejected by modern textual critics.)

The Christian should find his contentment is true godliness, for this is a means of gain which material acquisitions can never be. The word *autarkeia* (from *autos*, self, and *arkeō*, suffice, be content) signifies a satisfaction or sufficiency in oneself, not connected with outward circumstances. Paul is not praising poverty, or declaring property a crime. He merely says that real contentment, which is independent of poverty or wealth, finds its satisfaction in the spiritual blessings which come to the soul of him whose life is godly.

This explanation is reinforced by a moment's reflection on birth and death. When we were born we brought no material possessions with us. The reason is (*hoti*) that we must leave this life the same way. Thus the gaining of material acquisitions must be of only temporary significance. Therefore, the few things we actually need while on earth need not unduly disturb the minds of godly people. Paul's statement reminds us of Job 1:21: "Naked came I out of my mother's womb, and naked shall I return thither."

If Christians have food to eat (*diatrophas*) and coverings for their bodies (*skepasmata*, a broad term for covering which may include the idea of shelter), then the anticipated outcome is contentment (future tense of *arkeō*).

This godliness is a way of gain, although not of material

gain as corrupted men have supposed. Actually, to Paul's way of thinking, it is the only way of achieving eternal gain. For if we die as we were born, without material possessions, then the only thing that has been gained during this life which will remain for the life to come is godliness, which has laid up treasures in heaven. This knowledge should cause us to be content with the possession of sufficient food and clothing, and to center our attention on the life of godliness.

4. The results of a wrong motive.

> But the ones desiring to be rich are falling into temptation and a snare and many senseless and harmful lusts, ones which sink the men into destruction and perdition. For a root of all the evils is the love of money, which some reaching after have been caused to wander from the faith and pierced themselves with many griefs (vv. 9-10).

Paul picks the one motive of desire for riches as his illustration, and shows the terrible results of it. These persons to whom he refers are not necessarily wealthy, but are desiring or intending to be wealthy. *Hoi boulomenoi* designates those whose desire is centered in the will and reason rather than in the emotion (*thelō*). These persons are willfully determined to accumulate wealth. As such, Paul says they have placed themselves in a most dangerous position. This illustration is intended to warn the minister against falling victim to this evil motive. If this seems unnecessary, it should be realized that often Christians get the idea that their lot in life ought to be somewhat better financially than others. Paul refutes this idea. Because this sinful motive of desire for wealth is so common, one of the qualifications for the overseer was that he should not be a money-lover (3:3).

Six results of desiring to be rich are listed.

a. It causes falling into temptation.

The present tense of *empiptō* is used, suggesting a continual falling, not just once but over and over again.

To fall into temptation means more than just to be tempted. Jesus was tempted, and men are pronounced blessed if they endure temptation. But falling or entering into temptation indicates a yielding under the test. To the one whose supreme purpose is to acquire wealth, there are always opportunities of a questionable nature whereby he can take advantage and acquire still more wealth.

b. It causes falling into a snare.

This carries the illustration a step farther and pictures the victim who fell as now caught in a trap (*pagis*). Satan prepares such traps for men, especially ministers (3:7).

c. It causes falling into many senseless and harmful lusts.

The desire to be rich produces other desires which are also evil. How many other sins are an outgrowth of avarice? Such sins as theft, dishonesty of various kinds, and even immorality can spring from a desire to be more influential and powerful than others.

Such lusts are senseless (*anoētous*) for they cannot be logically defended, nor do they bring real satisfaction. They are also harmful (*blaberas*), for they do great damage to one's character and spiritual life, and they dissipate one's energies and call away one's interest from spiritual activity.

d. It causes men to sink into destruction and perdition.

The verb *buthizō* (sink) is used in its only other New Testament occurrence in Luke 5:7, to describe the sinking of the boat overloaded with fish. Here it is used metaphorically to describe the downward and inevitable course which proceeds from an evil motive. *Olethron* and *apōleian* both refer to destruction, with perhaps the latter being the more intensive. Ellicott explains *olethron* as referring to destruction in a general sense, whether of body or soul, while *apōleian* refers to the destruction of the soul.[76] This precise distinction is not admitted by all, however. These terms refer not to the place where punishment will occur (that is, hell), but to the result which will finally occur. The soul which has yielded to the love of money will be eventually marred and ruined for all eternity. These terms denote the eternal punishment of the wicked. (They do not mean annihilation.) All who call themselves Christians should consider carefully the ultimate end of such a sinful course and remove from themselves this sinful desire.

　　　　e. It causes a wandering from the faith.

　　　　This idea is introduced by the observation *riza gar pantōn tōn kakōn estin hē philarguria*. The great difficulty of translating the anarthrous *riza* (root), and of properly understanding the force of *pantōn* (all), has hindered our appreciation of this statement. Shall we accept the KJV, "the love of money is the root of all evil," or the ASV, "the love of money is a root of all kinds of evil"? The word "root" (*riza*) is without the article and introduces the clause. Thus it is emphatic and qualitative. In English we most naturally would employ an article. If we employ the definite article "the root," we make the expression misleading, suggesting that it is the only root of evil, a statement which is opposed to experience. If we say "a root," we sacrifice the emphasis of the statement. All things considered, it is best to say "a root," and understand that Paul is thinking of money-love as root (qualitative) rather than fruit. It is viewed as source rather than product in this context.

　　　　Pantōn is used distributively (predicate position) with *tōn kakōn*, and thus bears the meaning "all kinds of evils." Since experience seems to show us that some evils are the results of other roots, it is best to understand Paul's meaning to be that from the root of money-love results only evil, not good, and these evils can be of every type. To take *pantōn* (all) in its widest sense, there is no type of evil which cannot arise from this root of money-love.

This evil root is termed *philarguria* (money-love). Vincent observes, "It is not the *possession* of riches, but the *love* of them that leads men into temptation." Riches can be the source of much that is good. But the desire for riches, which characterizes the lives of those Paul mentions, is evil and only that. We must not forget the solemn words of Jesus which set the service of God as the opposite of the service of mammon, the money god (Matt. 6:24).

Such desire causes men to be led astray or made to wander from (aorist passive of *apoplanaō*) the faith. This further explains the acts of falling into temptation, a snare, destruction, and perdition, mentioned by Paul previously. Those acts are explained as a wandering from the faith.

f. It causes many griefs.

What these griefs (*odunais*) are must be concluded by the reader. They are the pains the sinners bring upon themselves (*heautous*), as if plunging a sword into their own bodies (*periepeiran*). They are not the final tortures of the lost, but the present griefs which accompany the avaricious person. Pangs of conscience, disillusionment, spiritual unrest, and many other unhappy accompaniments, are the product of this course of life.

B. *The minister is charged to maintain a proper walk* (vv. 11-16).

1. The nature of a proper walk.

But thou, O man of God, continually flee these things; and continually pursue righteousness, godliness, faith, love, patience, meekness (v. 11).

a. It is a continual fleeing from evil.

The present imperative (*pheuge*, flee) denotes durative action. The minister must continually flee from unworthy motives, which Satan will constantly put in his path. There is no safe distance at which one can stop fleeing. Especially must the young minister, who is often underpaid, beware of the temptation of desiring money.

The designation "man of God" (*anthrōpe theou*) is one often employed of prophets (e.g., 1 Sam. 2:27), characterizing the individual as belonging to God and representing Him. However, there is no reason to suppose that the term bears any technical sense here, for 2 Timothy 3:17 shows that it can be applied to any Christian. Timothy is reminded that the minister (as is every Christian) is a man who belongs to God, rather than one whose heart is possessed by desire for wealth.

b. It is a continual pursuing of godliness.

Again the present imperative is used (*diōke*), denoting the positive aspect of which fleeing is the negative. For the Christian, these should be two aspects of the same thing. He should flee evil by pursuing good. By pursuing the good, he will thus be fleeing evil. The six virtues are in three pairs.

(1) Righteousness (*dikaiosunēn*).

This is not the imputed righteousness, which is the possession of the believer in its complete form on the merits of Christ's death, but rather practical righteousness. This too is produced by God through the Spirit, but the individual must present himself to the control of the Spirit. Righteousness never loses its forensic sense, and here the life of the believer is viewed as God will declare it.

(2) Godliness (*eusebeian*).

This term is closely allied with righteousness, and also refers to the daily life of piety and reverence to God, but does not carry the connotation of God's verdict.

(3) Faith (*pistin*).

Faith which is to be continually pursued is that sustaining faith for the various needs of life. It is the confidence which enables believers to trust God in everything.

(4) Love (*agapēn*).

Love is often paired with faith in the New Testament. It is a fruit of the Spirit (Gal. 5:22), and the essence of Christ's new commandment (John 13:34). The love mentioned here by Paul is unrestricted, and includes love directed toward God and men.

(5) Patience (*hupomonēn*).

Hupomonē (from *menō*, remain, and *hupo*, under) refers to an enduring or a remaining steadfastness under trials. It always is used with reference to things, and is not merely a quality of personality (such as *makrothumia*, longsuffering, can be). Whatever the difficulty may be, God's child and especially a minister must pursue the development of a patient enduring of the trial.

(6) Meekness (*praupatheian*).

This term denotes meekness of feelings, and supplements *hupomonē* in describing the minister's attitude toward opponents and adversity in general. Not only should he endure and not waver, but he also must maintain gentleness of temper. He should not exhibit that proud, self-assertive, swaggering demeanor, which unsaved men admire as manly. He should rather display the demeanor of his Lord (Matt. 11:29; see Matt. 5:5).

2. The performance of a proper walk.

> Be contending in the good contest of the faith; lay hold of the eternal life, into which you were called and did confess the good confession in the presence of many witnesses. I charge in the presence of God who gives life to all things and Christ Jesus who testified before Pontius Pilate the good confession, that you keep the commandment spotless, blameless . . . (vv. 12-14a).

a. It is a continual contending in the good contest of the faith.

Agōnizomai (contend) and *agōn* (contest) are terms derived from the athletic field. The athletic figure is a favorite one with Paul (see Phil. 3:13-14). The contest is the one which belongs to the faith (*tēs pisteōs*), that is, the contest which one enters when he becomes a Christian. This contest is good (*kalon*), whereas the love of money is evil (*kakon*). Here is a real challenge for men and women. (Simpson shows that *agōnizomai* is also used in a military sense, but the athletic figure is more typically Pauline.)[77]

    b. It is a taking hold of eternal life.

       The imperative *epilabou* is aorist, indicating an act of grasping, not a course of action. The eternal life does not refer to the prize at the end of the race, for Timothy is told to grasp it now, although he is urged to keep on contending in the contest. Nor can we infer that Timothy does not already possess eternal life, since he is called "man of God," had been called by God, and had confessed his faith. Rather, the exhortation was for him to lay hold of that eternal life that he had and use it. He is to live in the light of his great possession. He is to make it practical in daily life. For the one who has really laid hold on eternal life, earthly treasures do not seem so important.

    The good confession (*tēn kalēn homologian*) of Timothy is most easily understood as his confession of faith in Christ for salvation, a confession which was reinforced by his consistent Christian life. At that time he had responded in faith to the effective call of God for salvation (*eklēthēs*).

    c. It is a solemn keeping of the truth of God.

       Paul solemnly commands the keeping of a proper Christian walk by calling attention to two great witnesses in whose presence every minister constantly moves.

    God is first mentioned as a witness. He is characterized as the continuing life-giver (present participle of *zōiogoneō*, to make alive, or preserve alive). Thus God is not only watching, but is the one who has bestowed eternal life, and is sustaining Timothy as he fulfills his ministry.

Christ Jesus also witnesses our Christian life. Paul reminds Timothy that just as he had confessed the good confession, it was Christ who bore the original testimony before Pilate, and since Christ did so in spite of personal suffering, so He encourages us to walk courageously in harmony with our confession.

What was the good confession to which Christ testified before Pilate? An examination of the gospels shows that He confessed that He was King of the Jews, or Christ (Matt. 27:11; Mark 15:2; Luke 23:2-3; John 18:37), and that He had a kingdom whose source was not of this world (John 18:36). This confession of the identity and source of Christ, to which Jesus Himself gave the original testimony, is the same confession men make in order to be saved. "These are written that ye might believe that Jesus is the Christ, the Son of God; and that believing ye might have life through his name" (John 20:31). Paul terms Christ's confession "good" (kalēn) because it contains the great truths which make possible salvation for men. Thus it is the Savior-Christ who is vitally interested in the ministries of His servants.

The commandment (tēn entolēn) that Timothy must keep has been variously explained as the gospel, the injunctions in this letter, the Word of God, or Christ's new commandment. Inasmuch as nothing in the context serves to limit the reference, it is best to understand the commandment as the obligations which are upon believers as a result of the gospel (singular). Several passages help us here. "If ye keep my commandments, ye shall abide in my love" (John 15:10). "Ye are my friends if ye do whatsoever I command you" (John 15:14). "Teaching them to observe all things, whatsoever I have commanded you" (Matt. 28:20). Timothy's conduct is to be in such harmony with the standard in the Gospel that he will be spotless and blameless.

3. The incentive for a proper walk.

> . . . until the appearing of our Lord Jesus Christ, which at His own seasons He will show, He who is the blessed and only Potentate, the King of those reigning and Lord of those ruling, the only one having freedom from death, inhabiting light unapproachable, whom no one of men has seen nor is able to see: to whom honor and might eternal. Amen (vv. 14b-16).

The great incentive for Christian living is the second coming of Christ. Paul does not state unequivocally that Timothy will live until the Lord's appearing, but he must regard it as possible. The term *epiphaneias* refers to the visible and glorious display when Christ returns and is vindicated among men. At that time, the validity of the good confession will be demonstrated to all, and any suffering which Christians are called upon to undergo will be turned into joy as the enemies of God are put down. Of course, these blessings will begin for Timothy at the rapture of the church, but the great public vindication in view here will occur at the epiphany, or visible manifestation of Christ to the world.

This appearing of Christ has not been dated for us. The time lies in the counsels of God. Jesus Himself said: "Of that day and hour knoweth no man, no, not the angels of heaven, but my Father only" (Matt. 24:36). Even Christ Himself during the days of His humiliation did not know when it would occur (Mark 13:32). Just prior to the ascension, Jesus repeated this truth: "It is not for you to know the times or the seasons which the Father hath put in his own power" (Acts 1:7). Since the knowledge of the time of the epiphany lies with God the Father, it is best to regard the Father as the subject of the verb *deixei* (will show), and the one denoted by the doxology which follows.

As intimated above, there is some difference of opinion as to who is meant by the designation "blessed and only potentate," and the other descriptions which follow. A few writers, among them Chafer and Ironside, have suggested that Christ is meant. This is based on a similarity of expression here and in Revelation 19:16, in which latter reference to the "King of kings and Lord of lords" is Christ. (This is a different expression in the Greek text, however.) Also the reference to immortality is thought by these advocates to be more applicable to Christ.

Nevertheless, the great majority of commentators, with whom the writer concurs, understand the doxology to refer to the Father. The grammatical structure seems to distinguish Christ from the subject of *deixei*, and it is best to understand the Father as displaying Christ at the appearing. This harmonizes with the passages previously mentioned, where the season of the epiphany is in the Father's authority. Lest it be argued that the introduction of the Father into this context is awkward, it should be recognized that Paul often mentions one member of the Godhead and then exults with a doxology which broadens the original reference. A clear example is 1 Timothy 1:16-17. At that point he mentioned Christ and then embarked on a doxology honoring the invisible God. Furthermore, some of the descriptions in this doxology (all of which are nominative and belong to the subject of *deixei*) certainly apply more easily to the Father than to Christ. He is called the one "whom no one has seen nor is able to see." How can this refer to Christ? Yet it applies perfectly to the Father (John 1:18), and it was the eternal function of the Son to make known the Father (John 1:18), for from eternity Christ is the image of the invisible God (Col. 1:15). To argue that this is Christ in His essential deity seems to contradict the argument which these same men use concerning the "immortality" predicted of this one. It is averred that immortality refers to the body, and this is not applicable to the Father. But if it is only applicable to Christ, it must be applicable to Him in His incarnation, not in an essential deity which "no one has seen nor is able to see." The word "immortality" used is not *aphtharsia*, which signifies incorruptibility, but *athanasia* which means deathlessness, freedom from death. This being is the only one (*monos*) who possesses in Himself freedom from death. All others who obtain immortality must receive it from Him. To understand this of the Father agrees with John 5:26: "For as the Father hath life in himself, so hath he given to the Son to have life in himself." The use of the negative *athanasia* (with alpha privative), deathlessness, is equivalent to the positive term, absolute life. To say that *athanasia* is irrelevant when applied to the Father, because it is contrary to His nature to die anyway, is not a valid objection, for Hebrews 6:18 states that it is "impossible for God to lie," even though lying is also contrary to His nature anyway.

The first three designations in the doxology refer to God in His position as the supreme ruler of the universe, and of all lesser authorities. The next three characteristics denote God in His person, as the only deathless one (*athanasian*), the only completely holy one (*phōs oikōn aprositon*), and the only absolute Deity (*oudeis anthrōpōn oude idein dunatai*). To this one is ascribed praise in the conclusion of the doxology. To Him belongs all honor and all dominion eternally.

   C. *The minister is charged to perform a faithful ministry* (vv. 17-21a).

   1. This is accomplished by directing men toward spiritual goals.

> To the rich in the present age give command not to be exalted in mind, nor to have their hope set on the uncertainty of riches, but upon God who presents to us all things richly for enjoyment, to do good, to be rich in good works, to be generous, fellowshipping, storing up for themselves a good foundation toward that which is coming, in order that they may lay hold of that which is really life (vv. 17-19).

This advice is directed specifically toward those who

are already rich (not those who are desiring to be rich but may actually be poor, v. 9), for they are particularly subject to this error of a wrong goal. The persons Paul had in mind are legitimately rich. He gives no suggestion of avarice or dishonesty involved in the acquiring of the wealth. These persons have been entrusted by God with material wealth through some legitimate means. Now Paul challenges Timothy to warn them about the dangers of possessing wealth. Paul does not follow the communist line of denying personal property and wealth. He does not condemn rich men because they are rich, but he does warn them of the false trust which they may easily develop.

      a. Wealthy Christians should not be exalted in mind.

      Hupsēlophronein means to be highminded, proud, exalted in mind. Those who possess wealth in this present age (*en tōi nun aiōni*), as opposed to those who are materially poor, are often deluded into thinking that wealth is a mark of special divine favor. Yet all Scripture is of one voice in teaching that during the present age the wicked often are materially prosperous, whereas the righteous suffer and are poor. Consequently, if a Christian has riches, it cannot be considered as proof that he is more pleasing to God than his poorer Christian brothers. This passage indicates that Christianity in Ephesus had influenced some of the wealthy classes as well as the poor.

      b. Wealthy Christians should trust God, not riches.

      "The uncertainty of riches" (*ploutou adēlotēti*) is more emphatic and more accurate than the "uncertain riches" rendering of KJV. Spence explains this uncertainty which attaches itself to material wealth on two counts.[78] First, the duration of life itself, even for a day is uncertain, and wealth cannot be possessed after death. Second, the shifting circumstances of life, such as commercial depressions and war make wealth uncertain.

How foolish, then, to transfer one's trust from God to riches! Yet men show a preference for trusting a bank account rather than a God in heaven.

Paul reminds rich people that God is the one who has provided all things for us. No man possesses anything (*panta*) that God did not provide. Furthermore, God provided these blessings richly (*plousiōs*) for our enjoyment (*apolausin*). Here asceticism is branded a lie. God's blessings are not to be shunned, but used as God intended, and when this is done, the user receives a godly satisfaction. How foolish to transfer trust from God to riches, when God is the one who bestowed the riches!

    c. Wealthy Christians should be good stewards.

       Inasmuch as wealth itself is one of the "all things" which God has given richly, the rich man is then a steward of that which God has bestowed. In four infinitive phrases Paul shows how proper enjoyment of riches involves the using of them to bless others. If a rich man can share his wealth with others and find enjoyment in so doing, he is using his wealth as God intended. But if the thought of sharing is abhorrent to him, then he has fallen prey to the dangers Paul describes of having his hope on the possession of riches rather than on God.

Wealthy Christians are commanded to be continually working that which is intrinsically good (present infinitive *agathoergein*). They must seek to be rich, not just in material possessions, but in the multiplicity of attractive and worthwhile works (plural of *ergois kalois*) which their wealth enables them to perform. They must be generous toward others in need by giving over to them that which is good (*eu, meta, didōmi*), and are commanded to exhibit fellowship (*koinōnikous*), recognizing the brotherhood and mutual helpfulness that is shared by all believers.

    d. Wealthy Christians should be storing up treasure for eternity.

       Here is another of Scripture's paradoxes. Rich

men are told to store up treasure for the life to come by dispensing their treasures to others now. By using the material wealth God has given to bless others, the Christian is storing up (*apothēsaurizontas*) for himself a good foundation (*themelion kalon*) for the future (*eis to mellon*, "unto that which is coming"). By storing up this spiritual treasure through using wealth correctly, the Christian is laying hold on the true spiritual life which is genuine and lasting (*tēs ontōs zōēs*). Such spiritual activity is appropriating the real life.

   2. This is accomplished by guarding the deposit of the faith.

> O Timothy, guard the deposit, turning away from the profane, empty talkings and oppositions of the knowledge falsely named, which some professing missed the mark concerning the faith (vv. 20, 21a).

As Paul comes to the close of his letter, he gives in one sentence a summary of the contents of the entire epistle.

   a. What is to be guarded?

   Paul's expression is *tēn parathēkēn phulaxon*, guard the deposit. *Parathēkē* is a banking term, indicating a treasure entrusted to a bank for safekeeping. The word is peculiar to the Pastoral Epistles (occurring here; 2 Tim. 1:12, 14). In this instance it denotes that which is deposited with Timothy. In 2 Timothy 1:12 it denotes that which Paul has deposited with Christ (*tēn parathēkēn mou*), and in 2 Timothy 1:14 it again denotes that which was deposited with Timothy (*tēn kalēn parathēkēn*). In spite of the attractiveness of the attempt to understand *parathēkē* in the same sense in every case, being a reference to the gospel or the doctrine of the faith, such an understanding seems forced when applied to 2 Timothy 1:12. Context and construction must decide in what sense this very common figure (certainly not a technical theological term) is to be understood.

   Here Paul's meaning is clearly the gospel in its wider connotation, the true doctrine of Christian faith, as opposed to the heresy and worthless speculation of false men. Although the word *parathēkē* is not employed in the New Testament outside the Pastorals, the idea of the gospel as a sacred trust is found elsewhere in Paul's writings. "But as we were allowed of God to be put in trust with the gospel, even so we speak" (1 Thess. 2:4). The Christian faith is not an invention of men, but a treasure committed by God to men.

  b. How is it to be guarded?

   The positive action of guarding is explained by showing its negative aspects. The gospel is guarded by avoiding contamination with false teaching and false teachers.

   (1) By turning away from profane empty talkings.

   Ektrepomenos is a present participle, denoting a continual turning aside from these things. The minister should not allow himself to be drawn into arguments of this kind. *Bebēlous* signifies that which is of nonsacred character. *Kenophōnias* (from *kenos*, empty, and *phōnē*, voice) is plural and refers to empty talkings, arguments of no content, such as the affirmations of would-be law-teachers who understood not the things they were saying (1:7).

Paul does not tell Timothy to refute these things, but to turn away from them every time. There is no way to refute a myth or a fanciful fabrication, especially if the proponents themselves are incapable of thinking rationally (1:7). One is in danger of granting such errorists a measure of respectability by deigning to consider their schemes, and the uninformed may get the notion that their teaching does contain something after all, instead of seeing it for the empty talk which it is (*kenophōnia*). What must be done is to preach the truth positively, and the myths will be shown to be false.

   (2) By turning away from falsely-named knowledge.

There is nothing to fear in true knowledge. But when men parade their hypotheses and schemes as settled fact, particularly in the spiritual and religious realm, such knowledge is falsely named and must be shunned. This sort of knowledge which by its nature is the antithesis (*antitheseis*) of revealed religious truth is the counter affirmation of the enemies of God to the genuine spiritual knowledge revealed by God's Word. This falsely-named knowledge subjects God and His revelation to the mind of man.

Throughout the history of the church, there have been men who have claimed a superior knowledge, and have subjugated Scripture to their boasted intellect. Whether they be termed Gnostics or modern liberals, the attitude is the same. Inasmuch as *gnōseōs* (knowledge) is a common word and is easily explained in the context apart from any technical associations with second-century Gnosticism, any argument against Pauline authorship based on this reference must be rejected.

c. From whom is it to be guarded?

The danger to the gospel deposit lies in the subtleties of some (*tines*) who are professing this knowledge (*hēn epaggellomenoi*). These persons, apparently endeavoring to assume some prominence in the congregation (1:7), have missed the mark (*ēstochēsan*) concerning the true doctrine of the Christian faith (*peri tēn pistin*). By promoting false doctrine, they have been aiming in the wrong direction. They have not been advancing toward the true faith at all. This same verb was used to characterize the teachers of 1:6. Such men not only suffer spiritual loss themselves, but through mutilation of the gospel message they endanger others also.

Thus Paul recapitulates the content of his letter. Because of false men who are ever active in thwarting the gospel, Timothy and all ministers must be ever alert to safeguard the true message. This they can do by faithful preaching of its truth, and caring for the organization and needs of the church in the God-appointed way, so that the faith may be preserved in the hearts of believers and may be held forth to the world.

Conclusion (6:21b)

The grace with you (v. 21b).

This briefest of Pauline endings (same as Col. and 2 Tim.) desires the manifestation of divine favor upon his readers in whatever way it may be needed. The best reading is *humōn* (rather than *sou*, thee), and the plural is doubtless an indication that Paul expected this letter to be read to the entire church. Though the letter was a personal one to Timothy, it was official and not private, and thus the more inclusive *humōn* is easily understood. Every reader may include himself as one of the *humōn* if he has responded in faith to the sound doctrine proclaimed in Jesus by Paul, and has "guarded the deposit" of that truth in his heart as a sacred trust from all attempts of Satan and men to lead astray.

Notes

[1]James Hope Moulton and George Milligan, *The Vocabulary of the Greek Testament* (Grand Rapids: Eerdmans, 1949), p. 70.

[2]E.K. Simpson, *The Pastoral Epistles* (Grand Rapids: Eerdmans, 1954), p. 24.

[3]Patrick Fairbairn, *The Pastoral Epistles* (Edinburgh: T. and T. Clark, 1874), p. 74.

[4]Quoted by John Calvin, *Commentaries on the Epistles to Timothy, Titus, and Philemon*, trans. William Pringle (reprint ed., Grand Rapids: Eerdmans, 1948), p. 22.

[5]Richard Chenevix Trench, *Synonyms of the New Testament* (1948; reprint ed., Grand Rapids: Eerdmans, 1950), p. 181.

[6]Simpson, p. 29. Greek has been transliterated.

[7]William Kelly, *An Exposition of the Two Epistles to Timothy*, 3d ed. (London: C. A. Hammond, 1948), p. 15.

[8]Fairbairn, p. 90.

[9]Archibald Thomas Robertson, *Word Pictures in the New Testament* (New York: Harper and Brothers, 1931), 4:563.

[10]White, p. 98.

[11]Marvin R. Vincent, *Word Studies in the New Testament* (reprint ed., Grand Rapids: Eerdmans, reprinted 1946), 4:216.

[12]Moulton and Milligan, p. 218.

[13]Trench, p. 191.

[14]Simpson, p. 40.

[15]Vincent, p. 217. Greek has been transliterated.

[16]Joseph Henry Thayer, *A Greek English Lexicon of the New Testament* (New York: American Book Co., 1889), p. 286.

[17]Spence, p. 186.

[18]H. E. Dana and Julius R. Mantey, *A Manual Grammar of the Greek New Testament* (New York: Macmillan, 1946), p. 100.

[19]Moulton and Milligan, p. 46.

[20]Webster, as cited by Fairbairn, p. 121.

[21]Alfred Plummer, "The Pastoral Epistles," *The Expositor's Bible*, ed. W. Robertson Nicoll (reprint ed., Grand Rapids: Eerdmans, 1943), 6:410-11.

[22]Trench, pp. 333-34. Greek has been transliterated.

[23]Calvin, p. 65.

[24]John Chrysostom, as cited by Plummer, p. 412.

[25]R. C. H. Lenski, *The Interpretation of St. Paul's Epistles to the Colossians, to the Thessalonians, to Timothy, to Titus and to Philemon* (Columbus, Ohio: Wartburg, 1946), p. 560.

[26]Kenneth S. Wuest, *The Pastoral Epistles in the Greek New Testament* (Grand Rapids: Eerdmans, 1958), p. 48.

[27]Letha Scanzoni and Nancy Hardesty, *All We're Meant to Be* (Waco, Tex.: Word, 1974), pp. 70-71.

[28]Susan T. Foh, *Women and the Word of God* (Philadelphia: Presbyterian and Reformed, 1979), pp. 122-23.

[29]Paul K. Jewett calls this passage the "Magna Carta of Humanity." *Man as Male and Female* (Grand Rapids: Eerdmans, 1975), p. 142.

[30]Virginia Ramey Mollenkott, *Women, Men and the Bible* (Nashville: Abingdon, 1977), pp. 101-102.

[31]Mollenkott, pp. 91, 104; Scanzoni and Hardesty, pp. 70-72.

[32]Mollenkott, p. 104.

[33]Howard A. Snyder, "Woman's Place," *Light and Life*, 114, no. 2 (February 1981): 12.

[34]Jewett, p. 119.

[35]Jewett, pp. 60-61.

[36]H. A. Ironside, *Addresses on the First and Second Epistles of Timothy* (New York: Loizeaux Brothers, 1947), p. 72.

[37]Simpson, p. 48. Greek has been transliterated.

[38]Leo P. Foley, "The Pastoral Epistles," *A Commentary on the New Testament*, ed. by E. H. Donze *et al* (Kansas City, Mo.: Catholic Biblical Association, 1942), p. 574.

[39]White, p. 110.

[40]Apostolos Makrakis, *Interpretation of the Entire New Testament*, trans. Albert George Alexander (Chicago: Orthodox Christian Educational Soc., 1950), 2:1720.

[41]Spence, p. 188.

[42]Lewis C. Hohenstein, "She Shall be Saved through the Childbearing," mimeographed (Winona Lake, Ind.: Grace Theological Seminary, 1949), p. 46.

[43]Lenski, pp. 579-80.

[44]J. J. Van Oosterzee, "The Two Epistles of Paul to Timothy," trans. E. A. Washburn and E. Harwood, *A Commentary on the Holy Scripture*, ed. John Peter Lange, trans. Philip Schaff (New York: Scribner's 1915), 8:38.

[45]*Constitutions of the Holy Apostles, Ante-Nicene Fathers*, ed. by Alexander Roberts and James Donaldson (Grand Rapids: Wm. B. Eerdmans Pub. Co., reprinted 1951), 7:457.

[46]Plummer, p. 417.

[47]Lenski, p. 580.

[48]Calvin, p. 81.

[49]White, p. 114. Greek has been transliterated.

[50]Irwin Woodworth Raymond, *The Teaching of the Early Church on the Use of Wine and Strong Drink* (New York: Columbia U., 1927), p. 88.

[51]Charles R. Erdman, *The Pastoral Epistles of Paul* (Philadelphia: Westminster, 1928), p. 43.

[52]Charles J. Ellicott, *The Pastoral Epistles of St. Paul* (5th ed.; London: Longmans, Green, and Co., 1853), p. 48.

[53]This is the view of William Hendriksen, *The Pastoral Epistles* (Grand Rapids: Baker, 1957), p. 140; C. K. Barrett, *The Pastoral Epistles* (Oxford: Clarendon, 1963), p. 65.

[54]This is the view of Donald Guthrie, *The Pastoral Epistles*, in The Tyndale New Testament Commentaries series (Grand Rapids: Eerdmans, 1957), p. 89.

[55]This view is preferred by Ralph Earle, "1 Timothy," *The Expositor's Bible Commentary*, Frank E. Gaebelein, gen. ed., Volume 11 (Grand Rapids: Zondervan, 1978), p. 370; J.N.D. Kelly, *The Pastoral Epistles* in Black's New Testament Commentaries (London: Adam & Charles Black, 1963), pp. 90-91; H. P. Lidden, *Explanatory Analysis of St. Paul's First Epistle to Timothy* (Minneapolis, Minn.: Klock & Klock, 1897), p. 38.

[56]Simpson, p. 65.

[57]White, p. 121.

[58]Ellicott, p. 55. Greek has been transliterated.

[59]Warren E. Purdy, "The Meaning of the Phrase 'Saviour of All Men' in First Timothy 4:10," mimeographed (Winona Lake, Ind.: Grace Theological Seminary, 1954), pp. 33-48.

[60]*Ibid.*, p.48.

[61]White, p. 126.

[62]Archibald Thomas Robertson, *A Grammar of the Greek New Testament in the Light of Historical Research* (Nashville: Broadman, 1934), p. 854. Greek has been transliterated.

[63]James Hope Moulton, *A Grammar of New Testament Greek*, 3rd ed, (Edinburgh: T. and T. Clark, 1908), 1:125.

[64]Fairbairn, p. 189.

[65]Robertson, *Word Pictures*, 4:582.

[66]Herman A. Hoyt, "The Pastoral Epistles," mimeographed (Winona Lake, Ind.: Grace Theological Seminary, n.d.), p. 100.

[67]Ironside, p. 110.

[68]Wuest, p. 76.

[69]Calvin, p. 118.

[70]White, p. 131.

[71]Ironside, pp. 117-18.

[72]Plummer, p. 424.

[73]Fairbairn, p. 202.

[74]W. J. Conybeare and J. S. Howson, *The Life and Epistles of St. Paul* (1949; reprint ed., Grand Rapids: Eerdmans, 1951), p. 755.

[75]Fairbairn, pp. 217-18.

[76]Ellicott, p. 93.

[77]Simpson, p. 87.

[78]Spence, p. 214.

5

EXPOSITORY EXEGESIS AND TRANSLATION OF TITUS

INTRODUCTORY OBSERVATIONS

THE EPISTLE TO TITUS is likewise a pastoral letter and not a *mere* personal letter, because it was intended to convey through Titus a message to the church. It was written at approximately the same time as 1 Timothy, during a time of freedom from imprisonment. Because of a lack of sufficient chronological and geographical data, it is impossible to ascertain beyond all doubt whether 1 Timothy or Titus was written first. (See chapter 3 for discussion, and my opinion.) Most students place Titus shortly after 1 Timothy. Both letters were written before 2 Timothy, however.

Objections to Pauline authorship have followed the same lines as those directed against 1 Timothy. The reader is referred to my explanation and answers regarding 1 Timothy in chapter 3. No reason has been forthcoming to cause the careful student to reject the Pauline authorship of Titus. The historical testimony is strong and positive. The genuineness of the epistles to Timothy and Titus has been maintained throughout the history of the Christian church, and is championed today by recognized scholars in many lands.

Titus himself is mentioned in the New Testament only in 2 Corinthians, Galatians, 2 Timothy, and Titus. He was a pure Greek (Gal. 2:3), not part Jewish as Timothy was. Because of his close association with Paul for many years, he may have been a convert of the great apostle, but there is no scriptural statement of this fact. Titus accompanied Paul and Barnabas to Jerusalem on one occasion, and served as the successful test case in the matter of circumcision (Gal. 2). Since he was a pure Greek, he was not required to be circumcised, in spite of the strenuous attempts of legalistic Jews to force this rite upon gentile Christians. His name appears nine times in 2 Corinthians with references to the collection for the poor. Because of the difficulties of this task (i.e., collecting money from a divided church), it is a compliment to Titus' ability that he was chosen as Paul's envoy for this work. The name of Titus does not appear in Acts, of which Luke is the author, an omission which leads some to suggest he was Luke's brother.

Titus was left in Crete by Paul to carry out the organization of the work (Titus 1:5), apparently serving there in the same capacity as Timothy in Ephesus. He was Paul's representative. This was after Paul had visited Crete during his release from imprisonment. Paul had then gone on toward Nicopolis (Titus 3:12, in Greece). Somewhere en route, he wrote the epistle to Titus.

OUTLINE

The Greeting (1:1-4)

I. INSTRUCTION CONCERNING ADMINISTRATION OF THE CHURCH (1:5-16).

A. *The method of administration in the church was by the selection of elders* (vv. 5-9).

B. *The need for administration in the church was the presence of false teachers* (vv. 10-16).

II. INSTRUCTION CONCERNING CONDUCT AMONG CHURCH MEMBERS (2:1-15).
   A. *Conduct of the older men* (vv. 1-2).
   B. *Conduct of the older women* (v. 3).
   C. *Conduct of the young women* (vv. 4-5).
   D. *Conduct of the young men* (vv. 6-8).
   E. *Conduct of slaves* (vv. 9-10).
   F. *The basis of all Christian conduct* (vv. 11-15).
III. INSTRUCTION CONCERNING THE CONDUCT OF CHURCH MEMBERS IN THE WORLD (3:1-11).
   A. *The nature of proper conduct toward the world* (vv. 1-2).
   B. *The reason for proper conduct toward the world* (vv. 3-7).
   C. *The encouragement of proper conduct toward the world* (vv. 8-11).

Concluding References (3:12-15)

TRANSLATION AND EXEGESIS

Greeting (1:1-4)

The writer.

   Paul, slave of God and apostle of Jesus Christ in accord with the faith of God's elect ones and full knowledge of the truth which is in accord with godliness, upon the basis of hope of life eternal which God who does not lie promised before eternal times, but he made clear at its own seasons his word in a proclamation with which I myself was entrusted by order of our Saviour God . . . (vv. 1-3).

   The writer's *position* is given by two designations. He is God's slave and Christ's apostle. The expression "slave of God" is used at no other place by Paul (he usually says "slave of Jesus Christ"), but it is most unlikely that a forger would differ in so obvious a place. A slave (*doulos*) is "one who gives himself up wholly to another's will,"[1] not just a worker. This characteristic should be true of all

Christians. Since, however, there are various ranks among the bondservants of God, Paul adds the designation that he is Jesus Christ's apostle. This title should be understood in its narrowest sense as including the twelve plus Paul (see comments on 1 Tim. 1:1). In this capacity Paul was exercising the bond service, carrying out the commission Christ had given him.

The *standard* by which Paul's apostleship can be measured and evaluated is next given. It is in accord with (*kata*) or in harmony with the faith which God's elect possess. By the terms "faith" (*pistin*) and "full knowledge of the truth" (*epignōsin alētheias*), Paul shows that he refers to believers' personal faith in the revealed truths of salvation. Paul's ministry could be measured by this yardstick. Believers are responsible to test the spirits (1 John 4:1). Paul could be tested by comparing his preaching and teaching with the doctrine which the believers held. The full knowledge (*epignōsis*) of God's truth, which had produced godliness in the lives of the Cretan believers, would assent to all that Paul would say in this epistle. "He that knoweth God heareth us" (1 John 4:6).

Paul's *commission* is explained as the proclamation of God's promise of eternal life. Eternal life is here spoken of as a "hope" because it has many aspects as yet unrealized, even though it is a present possession of the believer. God, whose very nature is the absence of falsehood (*apseudēs*), promised eternal life before eternal times (*chronōn aiōniōn*). Salvation was purposed and settled before creation. Christ was the "Lamb slain from the foundation of the world" (Rev. 13:8). Of course, the promise was not made known to men until there were men created to receive it. The clear, public revelation (*ephanerōsen*) of God's promise was made at the fitting season (*kairois idiois*), that suitable time in God's program which He Himself had chosen (cf. Gal. 4:4, "when the fullness of the time was come"). It was the proclamation of this message (*logon*) that Christ the divine Word has come and provided redemption and eternal life which formed the content of Paul's commission. This commission Paul regarded as an authoritative command (*kat' epitagēn*, see 1 Tim. 1:1) from our Savior God. The designation "our Saviour God" occurs three times in 1 Timothy and three times in Titus, and is one of the distinctive marks of these Pastoral Epistles.

The addressee.

> To Titus, genuine child in accord with common faith: grace and peace from God the Father and Christ Jesus our Saviour (v. 4).

Paul in writing to Titus assigns him the same *position* employed of Timothy in the first epistle. (The reader is referred to the discussion of 1 Tim. 1:2.) As measured by the common faith held by all Christians, Titus is a genuine child of God.

The *blessing* for Titus is also similar to the one given to Timothy (1:2), with the omission of "mercy" (although it is found as an addition in some inferior texts). Paul states that these blessings will proceed from the Father and Christ Jesus. It is interesting to note that the title "our Saviour" is applied in verse 4 to Christ, while in verse 3 it was given to the Father. Both the Father and the Son (and the Spirit also) are united in the work of saving men.

I. INSTRUCTION CONCERNING ADMINISTRATION OF THE CHURCH (1:5-16).

    A. *The method of administration in the church was by the selection of elders* (vv. 5-9).

    1. Command.

> For this cause I left you behind in Crete, that you might further put in order the things which are lacking, and might establish in each city, elders, as I directed you . . . (v. 5).

Although Paul touched at the Mediterranean island of Crete on his voyage to Rome (Acts 27:7-13), he did not preach there, nor is there record of any believers who came to visit with Paul at that time. (Cretans were in Jerusalem on the Day of Pentecost, however, Acts 2:11.) The visit of Paul to Crete, when he left Titus behind to finish the organization, must have occurred after a release from his Roman imprisonment (see chapter 3).

The command now given to Titus in writing was to put in order the administrative affairs of the church on the island. Paul had begun this work personally, and now Titus is urged to carry it further (prefix epi, "in addition," attached to verb "put in order").

To carry out this directive Titus must arrange for the selection of elders. The verb kathistēmi means to "set down, establish, arrange." It does not mean "ordain" in the sense of laying on hands, although this was undoubtedly done. This verb does not tell how the selection was to be made. The method of such choices is shown in such passages as Acts 14:23 and 2 Corinthians 8:19 to be by congregational election.

Elders (presbuterous) are synonymous with overseers or bishops (v. 7). The former term connotes their dignity, and the latter their function (see comments on 1 Tim. 3:1).

2. Qualifications.

The reader should compare 1 Timothy 3:1-7, where similar qualifications are listed for overseers at Ephesus. An interesting difference is the absence of any disqualification of novices at Crete (cf. 1 Tim. 3:6). Apparently in a new work such as Crete, it might have been necessary to use recent converts in places of leadership. Such is not to be the general policy, however, and was not necessary in the established work at Ephesus.

a. General qualification.

If anyone is unaccused . . . for it is necessary for the overseer to be unaccused as God's steward . . . (vv. 6-7).

The adjective "unaccused" (*anegklētos*) is derived from *kaleō* (call), *en* (in), and the alpha privative (*not*), and means one who is not called in question or called to account. The gender of the terms in this passage is masculine, showing that the overseer must be a male who cannot be successfully accused on any of these important matters. *Anegklētos* is used to describe deacons in 1 Timothy 3:10. The reason for such a high standard is the fact that overseers are stewards of God's property. The parable of the unjust steward comes to mind here (Luke 16:1-13).

    b. Family qualifications.

    . . . husband of one wife, having believing children not involved in accusation of dissoluteness or uncontrolled (v. 6).

    (1) Husband of one wife (see comments on 1 Tim. 3:2).

    (2) Having believing children (*tekna echōn pista*).

Children who were still pagans would be a great handicap to an elder. In that day when overseers were selected, not from among seminary graduates of which there were none, but from adult converts, this qualification would indicate that the candidate was a careful Christian.

    (3) Having children who are not unruly.

It is possible for one's children to be professed Christians but still be a source of embarrassment to their fathers because of unrighteous lives. "Dissoluteness" is *asōtia* (from *sōzō*, to save, and alpha privative), and designates the character of an abandoned man, one that cannot be saved. No such accusation should be possible against the overseer's child. The offspring should also be properly controlled by his parents, not unruly and insubordinate. The Greek term describes one who is not brought under subjection, *anupotakta*). The case of the wayward "preacher's boy" is all too frequently occurring.

    c. Personality qualifications.

> . . . not self-pleasing, not soon angry, not beside wine, not a striker, not shamefully greedy of gain, but hospitable, a lover of goodness . . . (vv. 7*b*-8*a*).

    (1) Not self-pleasing (*mē authadē*).

    This adjective is derived from *hēdomai*, enjoy oneself, take pleasure, and *autos*, self. Thus comes the meaning of self-pleasing, self-willed, arrogant. Here is the headstrong, stubborn man who demands his own way without regard for others.

    (2) Not soon angry (*mē orgilon*).

    Orgilon appears only here in the New Testament, although the cognates *orgē* (wrath) and *orgizō* (provoke, be angry) are frequent. The adjective means irascible, prone to anger.

    (3) Not beside wine (see comments on 1 Tim. 3:3).

    (4) Not a striker (see comments on 1 Tim. 3:3).

    (5) Not shamefully greedy of gain.

    (See comments on 1 Tim. 3:8, where the qualification is demanded of deacons.)

    (6) Hospitable (see comments on 1 Tim. 3:2).

    (7) A lover of goodness (*philagathon*).

    This term is closely connected in form and thought to the preceding one. Literally, "hospitable" is "a lover of strangers." The next term enlarges the idea to include devotion to all that is good and beneficial. The overseer should be an ally and an advocate of everything worth while.

    d. Mental qualification.

> . . . sound-minded . . . (v. 8*b*).

    (See comments on 1 Timothy 3:2.)

    e. Spiritual and moral qualifications.

> . . . righteous, holy, self-controlled, holding firmly to the faithful word in accord with the doctrine, in order that he may be able both to exhort in the teaching

which is healthful and to refute those contradicting (vv. 8c-9).

(1) Righteous (*dikaion*)

This term and the one following are similar, but have a different emphasis. "Righteous" or "just" refers to conduct which meets the approval of God. The term is a legal one, and here refers to the verdict as pronounced by the divine judge.

(2) Holy (*hosion*).

Hosios means holy in the sense of unpolluted. Conduct which is true to one's moral and religious obligations is denoted by this word. Lenski defines it as "conduct which observes the true and established ordinances of the Lord."[2]

(3) Self-controlled (*egkratē*).

The root of *egkratē* is *krateō*, to hold, seize, and *en*, in. The adjective means that which is held in check, restrained. It was the usual Greek term for self-control, particularly regarding sensual appetites.

(4) Holding firmly to the Word.

The overseer of the congregation must cling to the Word which is characterized as faithful, trustworthy, or reliable (*pistou*). This designation of God's Word was used elsewhere by Paul (1 Tim. 1:15; 3:1; 4:9; 2 Tim. 2:11; Titus 3:8). In these other uses it was a kind of formula.

The phrase *kata tēn didachēn* has been translated in the KJV "as he hath been taught," thus meaning that the elder must hold on to the teaching which was imparted to him. Others have suggested the meaning that he should hold to the "faithful word in his teaching" (that is, in his own teaching ministry). The Greek text says, "in accord with the doctrine." The elder must hold to God's Word which is in accordance with the recognized body of Christian truth taught by the apostles (cf. Acts 2:42).

Two reasons are given for the elder's adherence to God's Word. These reasons should be considered as an explanation of the requirement "able to teach," laid down for overseers (1 Tim. 3:2). He must be able to encourage and exhort (*parakalein*) believers in the healthful (*hugiainō*) teaching of true doctrine. This important function of his ministry will do much to protect his people from the inroads of error and false teachers. He must also be equally able to refute (*elegchein*) those who oppose sound doctrine with the diseased teachings of legalism and other error. The durative action of both infinitives (exhort and refute) suggests that these are continuing functions, never to be laid aside. The minister must always promote the truth and ward off error.

    B. *The need for administration in the church was the presence of false teachers* (vv. 10-16).

Mention of the elder's responsibility to refute opponents provides a transition to the discussion of false teachers.

    1. The nature of these false teachers.

> For there are many uncontrolled ones, vain talkers and mind-deceivers, especially those out of the circumcision, whom it is necessary to stop the mouth . . . (vv. 10-11*a*).

They are characterized as unruly or uncontrolled (*anupotaktoi*), not allowing themselves to be placed under any authority. (The same word is used in v. 6 of unruly children.) This term suggests that the false teachers were at least professing Christians, because it would be unlikely to call unbelievers "uncontrolled" since the church has no claim on their obedience. Vain talkers (*mataiologoi*) are those whose talk does not accomplish anything. It is useless and futile. Mind-deceivers (*phrenapatai*) is the characterization of these errorists from the aspect of their result or at least their purpose. While such descriptions fit all types of false teachers, they were especially applicable in Crete to those of Jewish background ("of the circumcision"). These are the ones who must be silenced, as effectively as by putting a gag into the mouth and thus preventing speech (*epistomizein*).

2. The deeds of these false teachers.

... ones who upset whole houses, teaching things which they must not, for the sake of shameful gain. Some one of them said, a prophet of their own:
Cretans always liars, evil beasts, lazy bellies. This testimony is true (vv. 11b-12).

a. They upset whole houses.

Entire families were in upheaval and faith was endangered by these teachers. (Cf. 2 Tim. 3:6, for a similar description.)

b. They were teaching for shameful profit.

The shameful gain (*aischrou kerdous*) is the motive which elders must successfully shun (v. 7). A great many religious deceivers would stop if there were no financial profit involved in their deeds.

c. They were lying.

Paul reinforces his charge by appealing to one of the well-known Cretan poets. Epimenides (born *c*. 600 B.C.) was acclaimed by his countrymen as a prophet because of his unusual powers. Vincent states:

A legend relates that, going by his father's order in search of a sheep, he lay down in a cave, where he fell asleep and slept for fifty years. He then appeared with long hair and a flowing beard, and with an astonishing knowledge of medicine and natural history. It was said that he had the power of sending his soul out of his body and recalling it at pleasure, and that he had familiar intercourse with the gods and possessed the power of prophecy. . . . He is said to have lived to the age of 157 years, and divine honors were paid to him by the Cretans after his death.[3]

The fact that this poem refers to Cretans does not contradict Paul's statement that the opponents of the gospel were "of the circumcision," for many of the Cretans were Jews (cf. Acts 2:11). Paul's use of Epimenides placed his

Cretan readers in a dilemma. They could either agree to the statement and admit their baseness, or deny its truth and thus repudiate their chosen prophet and revered forefather. Paul says the statement is true. The immorality of Crete was well known. "To play the Cretan" meant "to lie" (krētizein). Epimenides also stated that the absence of wild beasts from Crete was supplied by its human inhabitants.

    3. The rebuke of these false teachers.

> For which cause rebuke them sharply, in order that they may be healthy in the faith, not holding to Jewish myths and commandments of men turning themselves away from the truth. All things are clean to the clean; but to the polluted and unbelieving nothing is clean, but even their mind and conscience has been polluted. God they are professing to know, but by their works they are denying, being abominable and unpersuaded, and for every good work discredited (vv. 13-16).

    a. They must be sharply rebuked for the purpose of restoring them to sound doctrine.

Because of the presence of unruly Jewish elements at work among a people, admitted even by its poet to be of low moral caliber, Titus is to rebuke the false teachers. This rebuke is to be sharp and severe (apotomōs from apo, off, from, and temnō, cut as with a knife). The purpose, however, is restorative, not vindictive. Healthful doctrine is the goal of the apostle. Some broaden the scope of "they" (subject of the verb "be healthy") to include not just the false teachers, but the victims of their teaching as well.

    b. They must be warned against following Jewish myths and commandments of men who turn away from the truth.

Verse 14 indicates that these erroneous doctrines were Jewish in origin (v. 10 also). First Timothy 1:4-11 should be compared to this passage. Both groups promulgated myths (muthois), and were apparently endeavoring to force the keeping of the Mosaic Law together with fanciful additions upon the many Christian converts in Ephesus and Crete. Such men are in the process of turning away from (present participle *apostrephomenōn* stresses progressive action) the truth which God revealed.

    c. They must be warned that such false teaching gives evidence of a polluted mind and conscience.

    Verse 15 takes us deeper into the condition of these false teachers. Jewish legalists made distinctions between clean and unclean, often going far beyond what the Old Testament had required. Jesus taught that even with such distinctions, it was not the physical food itself which was defiling (Matt. 15:11, 17-20). Furthermore, the distinctions between clean and unclean meats of Jewish ceremonialism were ended by God Himself, as announced to Peter on the housetop in Joppa (Acts 10:15). Consequently, to those who have been cleansed (*tois katharois*) by the blood of Christ, no such discriminatory maxim as proclaimed by the legalist can apply. Obviously this is not license for Christians to indulge in all sorts of sensual excesses. First Timothy 4:4-5 (see comments) provides the same teaching with the effective safeguard.

    To unbelievers, however, nothing is clean because their sinful lives, thoughts, and motives, which are at cross-purposes with God, will infect even that which is intrinsically pure. Good food will be used to gain strength for evil deeds. Such persons are defiled in their intellectual (*nous*, mind) and moral (*suneidēsis*, conscience) nature so that their decisions and attitudes are no longer reliable guides. Only the light of the gospel and the regeneration of the Spirit can bring such persons into real purity.

    d. They must be warned that the profession to know God may be challenged by conduct which denies Him.

    Verse 16 shows the close relationship in Paul's theology between faith and works. Paul and James are not in conflict. A life of deeds which contradicts the profession of the lips is clearly sketched for what it is. Such persons are abominable (*bdeluktoi*, disgusting, detestable) and unpersuaded (*apeitheis*) to the teaching based on God's Word. As far as usefulness to anything good is concerned, they have been tested and found to be false, unfit, useless (*adokimoi*, disapproved by test).

II. Instruction Concerning Conduct among Church Members (2:1-15).

Titus has been warned in the concluding verses of chapter 1 to resist false teachers and their doctrines, and to maintain the healthful teaching of the gospel. This instruction must be applied by Titus to the individual groups under his pastoral care.

A. *Conduct of the older men* (vv. 1-2).

> But as for you, continue speaking the things which are becoming to the healthful teaching [that] older men be sober, dignified, sound-minded, healthy in the faith, the love, the patience (vv. 1-2).

The opening clause of verse 1 introduces the entire section which follows. The present imperative *lalei* (continue speaking) stresses continuing action, and hence encourages Titus to maintain the course on which he has embarked. Just as he has been proclaiming sound doctrine, so he is to encourage these practical virtues which are consistent with the gospel truths.

These admonitions are directed to the aged men in the church (not the official "elders"). "Sober" (*nēphalious*) means abstaining entirely from wine. From this meaning came the usage as temperate, sober in judgment. The latter meaning could include the former. This is the same word used of overseers and deaconesses in 1 Timothy 3:2, 11. "Dignified" (*semnous*) was used of both deacons and deaconesses (1 Tim. 3:8, 11). Frivolity in an older man is unbecoming, especially to one who has matured in the Christian life as well. The description "sound-minded" (*sōphronas*) was also employed of overseers (1 Tim. 3:2). This involves complete mastery of oneself, the curbing of desires and impulses, a sound and balanced judgment.

The word "healthy" (*hugiainontas*) is a participle from *hugiainō*, to be sound or healthy, and is a frequently used word in the Pastoral Epistles. Healthy Christian lives are the result of healthful doctrine (v. 1). The three areas of the Christian's life where his health is to be clearly evident are faith, love, and patience. Each term has the definite article. Hence it is "the faith" (that is, Christian truth), "the love" (which is the Christian's duty, John 13:34), and "the patience" (which the Christian is to display on earth while waiting for his Lord, James 5:7-8).

The above-mentioned virtues should be cultivated by all Christians, but older men especially need to manifest them. Such men are naturally looked to as leaders in the church, whether or not they may hold office, and their example should give no cause for stumbling.

B. *Conduct of the older women* (v. 3).

> . . . older women likewise reverent in demeanor, not slanderous, nor enslaved by much wine, teachers of good . . . (v. 3).

Healthful doctrine should manifest itself in certain distinctive ways among the older women of the congregation. *Katastēma* (demeanor) expresses a "dignified carriage, such as becomes an elderly matron."[4] "Reverent" (*hieroprepeis*) literally means "befitting that which is sacred to God" (from *prepei* and *hieros*). The mature Christian woman should always exhibit in her manner a recognition of the sacredness of every aspect of life to the child of God. The phrase "not slanderous" was used of deaconesses (1 Tim. 3:11, see comments). The danger of unguarded speech by elderly women with time on their hands is obvious. Calvin stated the danger in severe terms: "Talkativeness is a disease of women, and it is increased by old age."[5] Wine was not absolutely forbidden, since in that day and region it was the common beverage. But its dangers were noted (see comments on 1 Tim. 3:8). On the positive side, older women were to be teachers of good (*kalodidaskalous*). This teaching was not to be public or official within the church (1 Tim. 2:12), but its scope is outlined in the following clauses.

C. *Conduct of the young women* (vv. 4-5).

> . . . in order that they may train the young women to be husband-lovers, children-lovers, sound-minded, pure, home-workers, good, being subject to their own husbands, in order that the word of God may not be blasphemed (vv. 4-5).

This series of admonitions to young women is to be called to their attention particularly by the older women in the church. Of course, the pastor will also deal with these matters, but propriety will keep a young minister from becoming too specific and personal in his dealings with young women. Christian women who are older are admirably suited for this task. By example and by word they may accomplish much. The verb "to train" (*sōphronizōsin*) means to restore one to his senses, make sound-minded, train, and is a cognate of the adjective translated "sound-minded" in verse 5. In verse 4 construction of the sentence demands that the rendering "to train" be used.

The list of virtues describes a young wife whose traits would make her ideal in any age. The characteristics of devotion to their husbands and to their children are natural emotions, but many times depraved human nature succeeds in perverting such normal love. "Sound-minded" (*sōphronas*) was also used of older women (v. 2). *Hagnas* (pure) in this passage carries the idea of being "chaste." "Homeworkers" (*oikourgous*) describes the active housewife, whose labors are beyond measure and whose efforts will bless the lives of her children and husband in countless ways. Such a wife is to be distinguished from the busybody whose idleness is a curse to her and all her acquaintances (cf. 1 Tim. 5:13). *Agathas* (good) is rendered "kind" by some, but there does not seem to be any strong reason why the more general idea should not be understood. She should be doing that which is good and beneficial to others, particularly in her own home.

The final responsibility laid upon young women is to be subject to their own husbands. The participle may be understood as middle voice, and rendered "subjecting yourselves," thus emphasizing the woman's responsibility in the matter. Paul believed the husband should be the head of the wife, but wherever Christianity and Paul's teachings have gone, womanhood has been exalted. Here Paul provides a spiritual motive for such action on women's part. The danger that the Word of God may be blasphemed because of an unruly wife is mentioned. If the husband were an unbeliever, he would often blame the gospel (unfairly, perhaps) for causing it. The world usually judges religion, not by its doctrines, but by its effects on its adherents. The gospel ought to make a woman a better wife.

D. *Conduct of the young men* (vv. 6-8).

> The younger men likewise exhort to be sound-minded, concerning all things showing yourself a model of good works, incorruptness in the teaching, dignity, healthy speech not to be condemned, in order that he who is opposed may be shamed, having nothing bad to say about us (vv. 6-8).

The comparatively young age of Titus made it inadvisable for him to counsel the young women too personally, but this factor was in his favor for teaching the younger men. (Of course, Titus must have been nearing forty years of age at this time.)

Young men are to be encouraged to be sound-minded (*sōphronein*). Sound-mindedness is an important scriptural virtue, expected of all ages and ranks of Christians (1:8; 2:2, 5; etc.). It is a mark of spiritual maturity and should be the goal of the young.

Titus can do much in his ministry by presenting himself as an example for his people (and particularly the young men) to follow. The phrase "concerning all things" (*peri panta*) is attached to the previous clause by some, but I think it is more likely used here with what follows. The minister (in this instance, Titus) is to continually be offering himself (present participle emphasizes progressive action) a pattern or model (*tupon*) of good works. Young men demand heroes to follow. The minister should be a worthy object for their imitation (see 1 Cor. 4:16; 11:1).

The minister should also continually be holding before (*parechomenos*, from *echō*, hold, and *para*, alongside) the young men incorruptness in the teaching of God's Word. The doctrine he presents should have no taint of heresy or impurity. The manner of presenting doctrine, as well as all other phases of his ministry, should be done with dignity (*semnotēta*). Much can be done toward attracting men to the gospel and encouraging their spiritual growth by the manner of the pastor's conduct. "Dignity" and "dignified" are favorite words in the Pastorals, occurring six times in 1 Timothy and Titus, and only once elsewhere (Phil. 4:8, also a Pauline use). ("Sincerity," KJV, is not found in the best manuscripts.)

The thought of healthy teaching is widened at the close of this sentence to include all speech (*logon*) on the part of Titus. All his conversation should be such that nothing frivolous or unsound can be discovered in it. *Akatagnōston* is etymologically "not known against," and suggests a courtroom where the judge cannot gain knowledge of any kind of flaw. For such persons the plaintiff has no case.

E. *Conduct of slaves* (vv. 9-10).

Slaves to be subjecting themselves to their own masters in all things, to be well-pleasing, not contradicting, not embezzling, but displaying all good faith, in order that they may adorn the teaching of our Saviour God in all things (vv. 9-10).

1. They should be voluntarily submissive to their masters.

Since subjection to masters was understood as part of the legal system of the day, Paul's command to be "subject to masters" must refer to voluntary submissiveness by those already slaves. That voluntary subjection (*hupotassesthai* may be middle voice here) must not be accompanied by sullenness, but eagerness, a striving to please (*euarestous*).

It is generally believed by historians that slaves outnumbered free men in the Roman Empire during the first century. Hence a great percentage of early converts, particularly in the larger cities, must have been of this class. Many of these slaves were well-educated, holding responsible positions for their masters. Yet Paul did not advocate revolution to rectify the situation. Spence states it well:

> Indeed, the repeated warnings to this unfortunate and oppressed class (see Eph. 6:5; Col. 3:22; I Tim. 6:1) tell us that among the difficulties which Christianity had to surmount in its early years was the hard task of persuading "the slave" that the divine Master who promised him a home . . . among the many mansions of His Father, meant not that the existing relations of society should be then changed, or its complex framework disturbed.[6]

Nevertheless, the gospel that Paul preached did eventually bring about the abolition of slavery in much of the world, by proclaiming the worth of individual men, and the principle of brotherly love.

2. They should avoid the common faults of slaves.

Two of the most common are mentioned. Contradicting (*antilegontas*) involves arguing or disputing the master's commands, and may include conduct which thwarts the master's desires. Embezzling denotes keeping a portion apart for oneself (the root of *nosphizomenous* is *nosphi*, apart, aside). This was the usual word for petty theft.

Such pilfering was a common vice of slaves, since there was abundant opportunity. The Christian slave, on the contrary, must display good faith (*pistin agathēn*) in all relationships (*pasan*) with his master. (Ananias and Sapphira were guilty of embezzlement, as the use of the same word in Acts 5:1 indicates.)

    3. They should seek to adorn Christian teaching by all their actions.

It is interesting that when Paul speaks of the conduct of slaves, his purpose is not merely the negative one that the gospel might not be blasphemed (v. 5), but the positive one that they might adorn (*kosmōsin*) Christian teaching. Slaves who would live according to these instructions would reflect honor upon the Christian faith which they profess. As a beautiful picture may be enhanced by an appropriate frame, so we (whether slaves, employees, or in other positions) make Christian teaching attractive if we exhibit its power and truth in our lives. It is the glory of the gospel which can so transform lives that even those of the lowest social order can adorn God's truth.

The reader should consult 1 Timothy 6:1-2 for additional Pauline teaching concerning slaves.

F. *The basis of all Christian conduct.*

All of the previously mentioned transformations of life are the product of the gospel, which Paul summarizes here. Verses 11-15 provide one of the great summaries of Christian truth. Christian conduct is shown to have a threefold basis.

> For there has appeared the grace of God, saving for all men, instructing us that having denied the ungodliness and the worldly desires, we should live soundmindedly and righteously and godly in the present age . . . (vv. 11-12).

1. The grace of God which brought salvation.

Conduct which accords with Paul's high standard is the fruit of salvation through God's grace. "Has appeared" (*epephanē*) points to a past act (aorist indicative) and literally means "became visible," "came to light," "became clearly known." Our word "epiphany" is a derivative. Thus the epiphany here referred to was Christ's first coming, which accomplished our redemption. This coming of Christ was an act of pure grace on God's part, in no sense merited by men. It was also sufficient for all men. (Note the coupling of the phrase "saving for all men" with "grace" rather than with "appeared" as in KJV.) God is the Savior of all men, although His blessings are limited chiefly to physical provision during this life for unbelievers. His saving work includes spiritual salvation for believers and is eternal in duration. (See comments on 1 Tim. 4:10.)

2. The divine teaching for the present age.

The past work of Christ in making visible our redemption at Calvary can never be overemphasized. However, to neglect our present responsibility is to dishonor the efficacy of what Christ did. The grace of God which sent Christ also provided us instruction. *Paideuō* originally meant "to train children," "to chasten or discipline," and then came to mean "educate," "train," "instruct." This instruction is for believers in this period of time before Christ returns (literally, "in the now age").

Negative instruction is named first. Believers must deny or renounce ungodliness. *Asebeian* is just the opposite of *eusebeia* (godliness, 1:1), and thus means a lack of reverence toward God. Believers must also renounce those desires (*epithumias*) of life which rise no higher than this world. Such desires belong to a realm which is at variance with God, and are in Satan's domain (1 John 5:19).

Positive instruction urges believers to live in a sound-minded manner (*sōphronōs*). Various forms of this word are used in verses 2, 4-6 of this chapter. It describes a mind which has been set in proper balance, having gained mastery over itself through salvation which frees from the shackles of sin. Believers need to live righteously (*dikaiōs*). Their conduct in this life among their neighbors should always be such as evokes God's approval. "Righteous" seems always to include the forensic sense in the New Testament. Paul's third adverb is *eusebōs*, in a godly manner. Christian conduct should manifest reverence toward God who provided salvation.

3. The blessed hope of the second coming.

> . . . looking for the blessed hope and appearing of the glory of our great God and Saviour Christ Jesus, who gave himself in our behalf in order that he might ransom us from all lawlessness and might cleanse for Himself a people for his own possession, zealots of good works. These things continue speaking and exhorting and refuting with all authority; let no one despise you (vv. 13-15).

The coming of Christ to claim His church, and vindicate her by a glorious display, provides motive and stimulus for Christian conduct. The use of the article *tēn* with "blessed hope" and its absence from the term "appearing" (which is in the same case as "hope" and is joined to it by *kai*, and) indicates that the blessed hope and appearing of the glory are one event. Various phases of Christ's second coming are not distinguished here. Rather, Paul is looking to the culmination of salvation, which will occur when Christ and Christian faith are finally vindicated by the visible display of glory evident to all the world. *Epiphaneia* was often used by the Greeks of intervention by their deities into human affairs.

This epiphany will be the second epiphany of Christ described in these verses (see v. 11). Some have understood both the Father ("the great God") and Christ ("our Saviour") to be named here. However, following the same principle regarding the Greek definite article, as in the case of "blessed hope and appearing," it is seen that only one Person is in view. Jesus Christ is our great God and Savior. The same phrase was often used in the papyri and by the Greek Fathers to refer to Christ. This is certainly the thought of the context, for it was Christ who gave Himself for our redemption (v. 14). Furthermore, the coming of Christ in a display of glory is taught elsewhere in Scripture, but the term "epiphany" is never used of the Father. For a summary of arguments in support of both views, the reader should consult Vincent on this passage.

The return of Christ becomes an even greater stimulus for proper conduct when we realize what He has done for us. He paid the ransom (*lutrōsētai*) to rescue sinners from the slavery of sin. "Lawlessness" (*anomias*) is the very essence of sin, being rebellion against the law of God (1 John 3:4, "sin is lawlessness"). Positively, Christ desired a people that would be uniquely His. *Periousion* is derived from a root meaning "to be over and above," and acquired the meaning "abundance," "property," "wealth," "that which belongs to one's possessions." A similar expression is used in the Old Testament to describe God's purposes for Israel (Exod. 19:5; Psalm 135:4; see also 1 Peter 2:9). Our prospects of being with the one who has granted us such honor should certainly move us to be zealots of good works. (I have translated the singular noun *zēlōtēn* as a plural, because it is in apposition with the collective "people," a singular noun in Greek, but considered plural in this instance in English idiom.)

These directives for Christian conduct need to be continually urged upon believers. Inconsistent behavior must be pointed out and false principles refuted. Every form of authority should be employed in order to command the assent of believers to their responsibility. No one must be permitted to disregard the minister in these practical matters.

III. INSTRUCTION CONCERNING THE CONDUCT OF CHURCH MEMBERS IN THE WORLD (3:1-11).

This section of the epistle treats of those relationships which Christians bear to the world outside. In all such discussions, Paul shows the close association of doctrine and life.

   A. *The nature of proper conduct toward the world* (vv. 1-2).

> Continue reminding them to be subjecting themselves to rulerships, to authorities, to be obedient, toward every good work to be ready, to blaspheme no one, to be nonfighting, gentle, displaying all meekness toward all men (vv. 1-2).

   1. The Christian should fulfill his obligations toward civil government.

Verse 1 outlines the duty to government. There should be willing *subjection* to rulers and authorities. Since all citizens are legally subject to the state, the infinitive *hupotassesthai* must be middle voice ("subjecting yourselves") and a reference to willingness (instead of the passive "be subject"). Christians must not let the sinful personal lives of rulers influence their submission. Governmental authority must be recognized as God-given (Rom. 13). Submission will be made more palatable if Christians remember to pray for rulers (1 Tim. 2:2).

Believers should give *obedience* to their government. *Peitharcheō* means "to obey one in authority," and denotes in this context the general principle of obedience to government. Of course, this principle is not absolute. We are not to obey in cases that are morally wrong (see Acts 5:29). In such instances Christians should quietly disobey and be obedient to the consequences. As a rule, however, civil authority operates to restrain evil and encourage good. Even early persecutions were probably done on legal grounds (charge of treason). Obedience to government obligates believers to observe all civil laws, from traffic regulations to payment of taxes.

Christians should be in *readiness for every good work*. In this context, there can certainly be no limitation of this phrase to purely Christian affairs. The believer dare not hold himself aloof from the world about him. He must use his influence for good, and thus will commend his gospel to governments and the world at large. Historians record that the Cretans were noted for their rebellious spirit. Christianity was not to be a tool for political agitation.

    2. The Christian should fulfill his obligation toward fellow citizens.

Verse 2 extends the scope to include all men outside the church. No Christian should revile another person. *Blasphēmein* means to revile, heap curses upon, speak reproachfully of, blaspheme. Often the term is used with reference toward God, but here it is to men. Our desire should always be to influence men for good and toward God. Another negative term follows: Christians should be nonfighting (*amachous*, see 1 Tim. 3:3). Those who are quarrelsome and contentious with their neighbors are poor citizens and poor witnesses for Christ.

Christians have the positive duty to be gentle (*epieikeis*, see 1 Tim. 3:3) and meek (*prautēta*). The two terms are similar, but Lenski distinguishes the former as referring to outward conduct which yields our rights to the other person, and the latter as the inward virtue which produces such conduct.[7] Retaliation is never to be the Christian response to unrighteous conduct.

  B. *The reason for proper conduct toward the world* (vv. 3-7).
    1. The remembering of our former condition as a part of the world.

> For even we ourselves were formerly senseless, disobedient, deceived, slaving for desires and pleasures of various kinds, living in malice and envy, detestable, hating one another (v. 3).

The first of Paul's two reasons is a reminder of our previous unconverted state. When we remember what we once were, we will be less likely to revile unbelievers. Seven characteristics are indicated. Before salvation we were without understanding (*anoētoi*). The unsaved person is unable to perceive God's truth because his intelli-

gence in spiritual matters is darkened (Eph. 4:18). Consequently, sinners are disobedient (*apeitheis*) to the revealed will of God, and are deceived (*planōmenoi*), being
caused to wander from the true course of God's will because they have followed their own unaided intellect.

Such a course of action inevitably involves sinners in a
continual slaving (*douleuontes*) for various desires and
pleasures. "Whosoever committeth sin is the slave of sin"
(John 8:34). Desires and pleasures which belong solely to
this life have no eternal value, and only enslave their
victims. Only by Christ's atoning work can sin's bonds be
broken and the sinner set free. Those whose efforts are a
continual search for pleasure and satisfaction invariably
lead lives of malice (*kakiāi*) and envy (*phthonōi*). Full
satisfaction is never reached; one pleasure is never
enough. Life becomes a mad race to keep up with one's
associates, with the inevitable undercurrents of jealousy
and hard feelings. As such a course progresses, the sinner
becomes detestable (*stugētoi*) to those who know him,
and certainly is to God, and the outcome is a society of
mutual distrust, persons hating one another (*misountes
allēlous*). Paul says: "Before you revile your pagan neighbor, pause for a moment's reflection on your own personal history."

2. The realizing of our present condition as the unmerited blessing of God.

> But when the kindness and the love for man of our
> Saviour God appeared, not out of works in the realm of
> righteousness which we did, but in accord with his
> mercy he saved us through washing of regeneration and
> renewing of the Holy Spirit, whom he poured out upon
> us richly through Jesus Christ our Saviour, in order that
> we having been justified by that grace might become
> heirs in accord with hope of life eternal (vv. 4-7).

This second of Paul's reasons for proper conduct centers upon an evaluation of the believer's present situation. The only explanation of our better spiritual and

moral state is the active intervention of God Himself. The cause was not in us. The following verses present a typically Pauline summary of Christian truth.

a. The realization of the love of God for men.

Four expressions describe God's love. *Chrēstotēs* denotes kindness, benevolence, benignity, a disposition to bless. *Philanthrōpia* (root of the English "philanthropy") means love for mankind. It is used here of God's love for man, and in Acts 28:2 of men's love for other men. In the Titus passage, *philanthrōpia* seems to specify the particular display of God's attribute of kindness: namely His special love for mankind. This love of our Savior God for men came to public view (*epephanē*) when He sent Christ to save us (Rom. 5:8).

God's mercy (*eleos*) was also an indication of His love. Mercy is the withholding of what is due. Consequently, our present condition of new life is not due to any deeds which we performed in the realm of righteousness. The product of our lives could bring only the verdict of guilty when tried by the demands of God and His law. Mercy, however, withheld the punishment which was due, and grace (*chariti*, v. 7) bestowed God's favor on undeserving men.

b. The realization of the gift of salvation.

The aorist *esōsen* (he saved) points to a past act of saving. God saved us by the giving of Christ at Calvary. This act need never be repeated; it was done once for all. Its efficacy is appropriated by believers. The channel whereby salvation reaches us is expressed by two phrases. "Through washing of regeneration" (*dia loutrou paliggenesias*) signifies that cleansing of the believer from the guilt of sin which makes regeneration possible. "Renewing of the Holy Spirit" (*anakainōseōs pneumatos hagiou*) describes the impartation of eternal life in the person of the indwelling Holy Spirit.

The reference to "washing" is explained by many as baptism, and thus the ceremony is made essential to salvation (although not all who teach this would explain its relation to salvation in exactly the same terms). However, the idea of washing with physical water is certainly not demanded by this phrase. "Washing" is *loutrou*, and does not refer to the material apparatus of washing, as is suggested by the translation "laver" (ASV margin). Another Greek word (*loutēr*) would have been expected for "laver." Simpson states:

> The version *laver* lacks corroboration, except in patristic treaties, colored by the dogma of baptismal regeneration and the LXX term thus translated is *loutēr*, which undoubtedly signifies a bathing-tub. . . . It is chiefly in the plural that the word means *baths*. For the active sense of washing there is abundant evidence throughout Greek literature.[8]

There are other scriptural references which pair the ideas of water and the Spirit as imparting our salvation, and to them we turn for aid in understanding verse 5. John 3:5 makes new birth dependent upon water and the Spirit. First Peter 1:23 makes new birth resultant upon the Word of God and the Spirit ("seed"). Here the water would seem symbolic of God's Word. Ephesians 5:26 supports this symbolic identification: "That he might sanctify it, having cleansed by the washing [*loutrōi*] of the water in the word" (Greek). Hence the washing which secures regeneration is that cleansing bath of justification, whereby the effects of Christ's death are applied to our sinful hearts. This is done through the instrumentality of the Word of God, which reveals man's sin and God's provision.

Renewing is *anakainōseōs*, and refers to something which is entirely new in kind (root *kainos*), not merely new in time (*neos*, young, recent). The impartation of the Holy Spirit makes us new creatures, in contrast to the old condition of life. The Spirit has been bestowed through Christ, who also is called "our Saviour" here. Thus all Persons of the Trinity are involved in the salvation of sinners. The washing and the making new are the two basic elements of our regeneration, both of which are the work of God.

      c. The realization of our Christian possessions.

         (1) We have been justified.

      Dikaiōthentes is a word from the courtroom, and means "having been pronounced guiltless." The grace of God displayed at Calvary provided in Christ a substitute for the punishment of sinful men. As a result, the believer who claims this God-provided substitute is released from all guilt. The crushing burden of sin is now removed.

         (2) We are heirs.

      Furthermore, because of justification, we become heirs, in line for an inheritance. Full possession of the inheritance has not been experienced as yet, but it is safely reserved for us, awaiting the time when Christ shall come and even our bodies will be glorified (see 1 Peter 1:3-5).

         (3) We have the hope of eternal life.

      It seems likely that the genitive "eternal life" is subjective and the phrase should be rendered "eternal life's hope." Eternal life is already the possession of believers. When men who were dead in sin, without God and without hope, were born again, the eternal life which they acquired brought to them a hope which transformed their existence. The blessed realities that await the believer in the life to come, and the assurance of God's care and providence in the present combine to give a hopefulness to life which is founded upon real knowledge of God's purposes for His children.

    C. *The encouragement of proper conduct toward the world* (vv. 8-11).

    1. Proper conduct is achieved by the continual affirmation of profitable things.

      Faithful is the word, and concerning these things I wish you to be affirming, that the ones having believed

God might take thought to take the lead in good works.
These things are good and profitable for men (v. 8).

Here occurs the fifth use of the formula, "faithful is the word," in the Pastoral Epistles. In this instance it refers to the preceding summary of truth (vv. 4-7), and uses it as a basis for the exhortation to follow. These sublime truths are to be stoutly maintained and urged (*diabebaiousthai*) upon believers. Orthodox preachers of the gospel must be no less forceful in their presentation of truth than are the errorists in their falsehoods (same word is used of false teachers in 1 Tim. 1:7). By affirming the truths of the gospel and directing the minds of believers to them, God's minister has laid the foundation for Christian conduct. In Paul's teaching, faith must come first; works flow from it. We must be careful to maintain the proper order.

Persons who have put their faith in our Savior God are expected to take the lead in good works. *Proistasthai* means to stand before, preside, superintend, take the lead. (The ASV margin, "profess honest occupations" seems to be unwarranted, since all other uses of this verb in the New Testament are with the usual sense.) Christian faith is intended to change human lives. Christians are to be lights in the world. They should be in the forefront in good works, not dragging their feet while others take the lead. Of course, good works must be the fruit of faith, not a substitute for it.

2. Proper conduct is achieved by the avoidance of unprofitable things.

But foolish questionings and genealogies and strife and battles about the law be shunning; for they are unprofitable and vain. A heretical man after one and a second admonition be disdaining, knowing that such a one has been turned aside and is sinning, being self-condemned (vv. 9-11).

a. The minister should shun foolish questionings and genealogies.

"Questionings" and "genealogies" are referred to in 1 Timothy 1:4, indicating that the same sort of problems existed in Crete as in Ephesus (see comments). Here both are termed *mōras* (root of our word "moronic"), foolish, stupid, silly. They were apparently Jewish (Titus 1:14), with the genealogical tables of the Pentateuch expanded and interwoven with fanciful tales. Titus is not even to investigate them, for they are of no value and utterly useless (*mataioi*) for the production of Christian virtues.

b. The minister should shun strife and battles about the law.

The chief characteristic of these would-be Law-teachers who so threatened the church was their ignorant but vocal affirmations, and parade of pseudo-knowledge (see 1 Tim. 1:3-11). Their application of the Mosaic Law to the wrong persons was strongly attacked by Paul. Although Titus must never compromise the truth, he must not descend to the level of bickering and fighting. Such a situation is likely to grant a sort of standing to the false teacher, and confuse the unlearned. Fightings disturb those who are not well-grounded in the faith, and do not produce purer conduct in older Christians.

c. The minister should disdain the heretical person.

(1) What is a heretical person?

The term *hairetikos* is based on a root meaning "choice." In the literal and original sense, a heretic was one who makes a choice which pleases him, independent of other considerations. In the realm of doctrine, a heretic came to denote one who chose to follow doctrine contrary to that of the church. From this basis arose the meaning of one who caused dissension and division, gathering around himself others of like persuasion and thus causing schism in the church. This latter idea is clearly found in New Testament usage (1 Cor. 11:18-19). Hence Paul in the letter to Titus means by this term the

person or persons whose actions are divisive because
they are contrary to the teaching of God's Word.

(2) How must one deal with the heretical person?

The first obligation is to admonish the one at
fault, pointing out the error of his action or of his doctrine. If one admonition is not effective, a second should
be given. However, if the truth is clearly shown to him
and the warnings are disregarded, further remonstrance is
a waste of time and merely gives the offender undeserved
publicity. The minister should then disdain (*paraitou*),
beg off, decline, or refuse to have further dealings with
the heretical person. Paul, of course, is giving principles
here, rather than legislating for every case. In some cases
excommunication may be called for, if the doctrinal
variance is basic to Christian faith. Each case must be
separately considered.

(3) What is the explanation for such persons?

The heretical man is first explained as having
been turned aside. The passive voice suggests a cause
outside the offender, most likely Satan or his demons (see
1 Tim. 4:1-2). He has been caused to turn away from true
doctrine and proper conduct. He is also guilty of a course
of sinning (*hamartanei*, present tense) against the light of
God's Word which was presented to him in the admonitions just given. *Hamartanei* is the common word for sinning, and denotes sin as a missing of the mark, a failure to
fulfill God's demands. Such action does not need a judge
to pronounce guilt. By deliberately rejecting the admonition of God's Word and continuing to sin against the light,
the heretical man condemns himself (*autokatakritos*) by
his persistence in his chosen course.

Concluding References (3:12-15)

Whenever I shall send Artemas to you or Tychicus,
be diligent to come to me unto Nicopolis, for there I
have decided to spend the winter. Zenas the lawyer

and Apollos send forth diligently, that nothing be lacking to them. And let ours also learn to take the lead in good works for the necessary uses, in order that they may not be unfruitful (vv. 12-14).

Titus. A number of brief, personal notes bring the letter to its close. The first note directs Titus to meet Paul for the winter at Nicopolis. Zahn lists nine cities of this name,[9] but the most famous and the most likely from geographical considerations was Nicopolis in Epirus (a part of Achaia). Paul himself had not yet reached Nicopolis, but after careful planning had come to the settled resolve (perfect tense of *krinō*) that this was the most suitable place in view of his itinerary.

Artemas or Tychicus. One of these men was being sent apparently to take the place of Titus in Crete while he left to join Paul. Since this is the only scriptural mention of Artemas, our knowledge of him is limited to the conclusion that he was one of Paul's trusted assistants, on a par with Tychicus. Tychicus was from the province of Asia (Acts 20:4), and accompanied Paul on his third journey. He had been sent by Paul on missions to churches at Ephesus (Eph. 6:21) and Colosse (Col. 4:7). On a subsequent occasion he would be sent to Ephesus again, probably as a replacement for Timothy and as the bearer of the second epistle to Timothy (2 Tim. 4:12).

Zenas and Apollos. These two men are to be received by Titus and outfitted for the continuation of their journey. It is very likely that they would be bearers of this letter. *Propempson* means "send forward on a journey" with supplies, funds, or whatever else is needed. It also implied escorting the traveler part of the way. Titus is to care for this matter diligently (*spoudaiōs*, earnestly, with haste). It is not known whether the designation "lawyer" marks Zenas as a converted Roman jurist or an ex-rabbi (teacher of Mosaic Law), since Zenas is not mentioned elsewhere. Apollos is the well-known Christian preacher who first appeared in Ephesus (Acts 18:24) and was theologically oriented by Aquila and Priscilla. Passing over to Corinth, he exercised a great ministry in that city (Acts 19:1; 1 Cor. 1:12; 3:4-6, 22; 4:6; 16:12). Paul had no ill feelings toward Apollos, in spite of factious brethren at Corinth who considered them as rivals, and they appear at this point as close associates in the work of Christ.

The Cretan believers. The church in Crete is to take the lead (same word as in 3:8) in good works. Their Christian faith is to find outlet in daily life. These good works are to be performed not as mere exercises, but for necessary uses (*anagkaias chreias*). The outfitting of Zenas and Apollos would provide one occasion (Titus personally would not have sufficient financial resources to care for all that was involved). By grasping such opportunities for doing good as lie all about us, we enable the Spirit of God to make our lives fruitful, productive of the virtues which God desires in believers (see Gal. 5:22-23).

The Final Greeting.

> All those with me greet thee. Greet those who love us in faith.
>
> The grace with you all (v. 15).

Paul's associates join with him in sending greetings to Titus (*se*). Titus in turn is to relay this greeting to all the church which loved and respected the great apostle. The final blessing which desired "the grace," that favor of God so precious and so necessary for Christian life and growth, is shorter than some of Paul's benedictions (cf. 2 Thess. 3:18). However, it is very similar to 1 and 2 Timothy, and all have the same thought, whether expressed in longer or shorter form. Paul was free to vary it as he chose. A forger would be pressed to keep rigidly to one form.

The plural *humōn* shows that Paul had the whole church in mind, not just Titus alone. The grace which he desired to be "with you all" was intended to bless the lives of Titus and every other believer who should come under the influence of this letter. Believers everywhere and in every age have come to see that a knowledge of "our Saviour God" and an ensuing life of godliness are the results of "the grace" of God bestowed upon them.

NOTES

[1]Thayer, p. 158.
[2]Lenski, pp. 898-99.
[3]Vincent, pp. 336-37.
[4]Simpson, p. 103.
[5]Calvin, p. 311.
[6]Spence, p. 257.
[7]Lenski, p. 982.
[8]Simpson, p. 114.
[9]Zahn, pp. 53-54.

6

EXPOSITORY EXEGESIS AND TRANSLATION OF 2 TIMOTHY

INTRODUCTORY OBSERVATIONS

SECOND TIMOTHY is the last of Paul's letters, and was written from a prison in Rome during the years A.D. 64-68. As explained in detail in chapter 3, Paul apparently was released from his first detention. After the burning of Rome in July, A.D. 64, Nero, to stop criticism of himself, blamed the Christians, and Christianity was made an illegal religion. Sometime thereafter, Paul was apprehended and faced certain death.

Timothy himself was in Ephesus when the letter was written, just as was the case regarding 1 Timothy. This fact seems assured from a number of incidental notices. He is asked to greet the household of Onesiphorus, who was from Ephesus (4:19; cf. 1:16, 18). Timothy is urged to come to Paul by way of Troas, which was the usual way to travel from Ephesus to Rome (4:13). And Tychicus was being sent to Ephesus, the implication being that he would take the place of Timothy there (4:11-12).

This final letter to Timothy is more personal and less official than the other Pastorals. It abounds with those intimate references which close friends may share (1:4-6;

3:14-15), and the emotional element, though always controlled, is warmly human (4:6-9, 16-17). However, the epistle does have an official aspect, for Paul evidences concern about the church, as well as about Timothy and himself. Such passages, as 2:2; chapter 3; and the plural "you" in 4:22, indicate that Paul's purpose included all the church.

The tone of this epistle, a remarkable blending of gloom and joy, can be accounted for by several factors. The shadow of impending death certainly gives reason for solemnity (4:6). Furthermore, Paul is almost alone at this time, his only companion being Luke (4:11). The circumstances involved in the absence of some companions was most discouraging (4:10, 16). Also, his anxiety about the churches was sufficient to cause the shepherd heart of the great apostle to be somewhat subdued (chap. 3). But greater than all of this was his unflinching faith that God was still sovereign, and that the privilege of serving Him was worth any sacrifice (3:11, 4:1, 8, 17-18).

The immediate purpose of the letter was to summon Timothy (4:9, 11, 13, 21). As it unfolds it contains the last recorded instructions of Paul to his most intimate disciple, and through him to the church. Thus it becomes an even more precious document to Christians. Since Paul knew beyond reasonable doubt what lay just ahead (4:6), his words are most significant. In view of the experiences of his life, we want to know whether he regarded Christian faith as worth the sacrifice. What does he think about the importance of doctrinal issues now? What characteristics does he foresee in the church of the future? How does he face death? We shall seriously reflect upon his opinions in 2 Timothy.

OUTLINE

The Greeting (1:1-5)

I. CHARGE TO BE UNASHAMED OF THE TESTIMONY OF CHRIST (1:6-18).

A. Timothy must not be ashamed (vv. 6-11).
B. Paul was not ashamed (vv. 12-14).
C. Onesiphorus was not ashamed (vv. 15-18).

II. CHARGE TO BE STRONG IN THE SERVICE OF CHRIST (2:1-26).
A. The minister as a child (vv. 1-2).
B. The minister as a soldier (vv. 3-4).
C. The minister as an athlete (v. 5).
D. The minister as a farmer (vv. 6-13).
E. The minister as a workman (vv. 14-19).
F. The minister as a utensil (vv. 20-23).
G. The minister as a bond servant (vv. 24-26)

III. CHARGE TO WITHSTAND THE APOSTASY FROM CHRIST (3:1-17).
A. The coming of the apostasy (vv. 1-9).
B. The withstanding of apostasy (vv. 10-17).

IV. CHARGE TO PREACH THE WORD AS THE MINISTER OF CHRIST (4:1-8).
A. The nature of the charge (v. 1).
B. The content of the charge (v. 2).
C. The reason for the charge (vv. 3-4).
D. The continuation of the charge (v. 5).
E. The encouragement toward the charge (vv. 6-8).

Concluding References (4:9-22)

A. Timothy is instructed to come to Paul quickly (vv. 9-13, 21a).
B. Timothy is warned against Alexander the coppersmith (vv. 14-15).
C. Timothy is informed of Paul's first defense (vv. 16-18).
D. Greetings are sent to Paul's friends (v. 19).
E. Paul's fellow workers are indicated (v. 20).
F. Greetings are sent from Paul's companions (v. 21b).
G. Benediction (v. 22).

TRANSLATION AND EXEGESIS

The Greeting (1:1-5)

The writer.

> Paul, apostle of Christ Jesus through the will of God in accord with the promise of life which is in Christ Jesus . . . (v. 1).

His *position* is apostle of Christ Jesus, the same as claimed in 1 Timothy 1:1. Timothy had no doubts about Paul's position and authority, but this letter was official as well as personal and thus the full title was in order. Paul's apostleship was a responsibility which he exercised through the will of God (*dia thelēmatos theou*). The will of God which had constituted him an apostle also was leading him at the time of writing as a doomed prisoner in Rome to the end of his earthly career. Yet Paul had no misgivings about the will of God for his life. Just because suffering enters one's life, it is no indication that the individual is out of God's will. Though most Christians admit this academically, do we really believe it? How wonderful to walk so close to God that His will for our lives is crystal clear! Then the worst of human suffering can be borne with a cheerful spirit.

The *standard* by which Paul's ministry can be measured and evaluated is given in the phrase "in accord with the promise of life" (*kat' epaggelian zōēs*). God who gave men life in Christ is the one who set up the apostles to testify of this life. The promise of eternal life made apostles needed to announce the message. Therefore, Paul's apostleship is explained on the basis of God's promise of life. (In translation, "the" is supplied with "promise" because the following attributive phrase with *tēs* shows that the entire idea is most definite.)

The addressee.

> To Timothy, beloved child: grace, mercy, peace, from God the Father and Christ Jesus our Lord (v. 2).

Timothy's *position* is that of a beloved child (*agapētōi teknōi*). The greeting (in 1 Tim. 1:1) emphasized the genuineness of his spiritual birth. Here the connotation is the affection which bound Paul and Timothy together. Of course, Paul still regarded Timothy as a genuine believer (cf. v. 5).

The *blessing* pronounced upon Timothy consisted of grace, mercy, and peace. These are the same terms used in the first epistle, and these two instances are the only ones where this exact blessing is employed by Paul. (In Titus 1:4, "mercy" is omitted in the best manuscripts.) These three terms summarize all that Paul could possibly wish for Timothy, for time and eternity.

The *thanksgiving*.

> Gratitude have I to God, whom I serve from [my] ancestors in a pure conscience, as without ceasing I have the remembrance concerning you in my prayers night and day, longing to see you, remembering your tears, in order that I may be filled with joy, having received a reminder of the unhypocritical faith in you, which dwelled first in your grandmother Lois and your mother Eunice, and I am convinced that also in you (vv. 3-5).

Paul's gratitude to God on this occasion is evoked by the blessed memories he has of others whose lives meant much to him. Note the repeated use of "remembrance," "remembering," and "reminder" in this sentence.

He is thankful for *his own godly ancestry*. The God whom he now serves (*latreuō*, present tense) is the same God in whom he had been taught to trust by his forebears (*progonōn*). Though his parents had not taught him to be a Christian, they had reared him in the ancestral faith in the true God. For years he had misunderstood many things and had persecuted the church, but when he became a Christian, he did not need to abandon his God. In fact Paul argued most clearly that Christian faith was the fulfillment of "the promise made of God unto our fathers"

(Acts 26:6). Now he was active in serving the ancestral God in the proper way, and with a conscience not condemning because his life was pure.

The relating of Paul's faith to the historic faith of Israel is particularly significant in view of the fact that he was probably facing execution for teaching an illegal religion, when actually he worshiped the God of his fathers, the God of Israel.

Paul is also thankful for *his remembrance of Timothy*. These precious memories cause him to pray unceasingly for his younger associate. When Paul prayed to express his needs (*deēsesin*) to God, those needs included entreaties for Timothy. Each Christian should feel a need for the well-being of every other Christian, since all are members of one body.

Paul's remembrance of Timothy centers on three themes. He has remembrance of Timothy's tears. Evidently these were the tears shed at their last parting, since joy is anticipated if they should meet again. In that society emotions were more freely expressed among men (Acts 20:37).

Further, he has remembrance of Timothy's unhypocritical faith (*anupokritou pisteōs*). Such faith is genuinely from the heart, not mere lip-faith. The use of an aorist participle, "having received a reminder" (*hupomnēsin labōn*), may indicate that something specific had occurred which reminded Paul of Timothy's faith. What a tribute to the godliness of Timothy that the incident which brought him forcibly to Paul's attention was a Christian virtue! Are we sufficiently outstanding in Christian graces that a virtue displayed by another will serve to remind onlookers of us? So often, it is the faults of Christians which serve as reminders to others.

Finally, he has remembrance of Timothy's godly ancestry. This genuine faith which Timothy possessed was first the possession of his grandmother Lois and mother Eunice. Some interpret this as a statement that Lois and

Eunice became Christians before Timothy. King suggests that Lois may have been at Pentecost or had heard Paul before he came to Lystra (Lystra was not far from Tarsus), and led her family to Christ.[1] Acts 16:1 merely says that Timothy and his mother were already believers when Paul visited Lystra the second time. In view of the preceding verses in 2 Timothy, where Paul traces his belief in God to his ancestral heritage, it seems most logical to understand this reference in the same light. Lois and Eunice were godly Jewesses who reared young Timothy in the Old Testament (2 Tim. 3:15) and true faith in the God of Israel. Paul and Barnabas advanced this faith to the receiving of Christ as the Messiah. Paul is grateful for the genuine faith of this godly family, and he is convinced that Timothy is a worthy example of this faith (perfect passive form *pepeismai* means "be convinced").[2]

I. CHARGE TO BE UNASHAMED OF THE TESTIMONY OF CHRIST (1:6-18).

The theme of this section is indicated by the repetition of the phrase "not ashamed" (vv. 8, 12, 16).

A. *Timothy must not be ashamed* (vv. 6-11).

1. Timothy may avoid being ashamed by rekindling the gift which God had given him.

For which cause I remind you to continue rekindling the gift of God which is in you through the laying on of my hands. For God gave not to us a spirit of cowardice, but of power and love and sound-mindedness (vv. 6-7).

The *nature* of Timothy's gift is suggested by its designation as a *charisma*, which term is used by Paul to denote that special bestowal by God for service. (See 1 Cor. 12–14 for a fuller discussion.) God never calls men to service without equipping them. Although the description of Timothy's specific spiritual gift is not given, the manner in which he is told to exercise it points to pastoral and administrative ability as his God-given responsibility. This function is to be fulfilled not with an attitude of cowardice (*deilias*), even though the pressures against Timothy at this time when Christianity was being ardently persecuted by the state can scarcely be imagined by most Americans. Rather, God has infused into His servants equipment for the task. Those who are submissive to the Spirit's control find there is power (*dunameōs*) sufficient to defeat the evil one, to win others, and to do all that God expects. God's gift must also be exercised in love (*agapēs*), without the harshness that power alone might evoke. Finally, power and love are to be exercised with the wisdom and good judgment (*sōphronismou*) which the Spirit of wisdom produces to safeguard the believer from fanaticism. Would not the operation of the church be smoother if every Christian used his gift in the manner outlined here?

The *reception* of Timothy's gift occurred at the time hands were laid upon him. First Timothy 4:14 should be read here (see comments). Paul evidently was associated with the elders in the ordination of Timothy. At the time that Timothy was formally set apart for special service, the spiritual gift was bestowed. First Timothy 4:14 tells us that prophecy was uttered on that occasion, no doubt to inform him and others of the gift. One must not conclude that the laying on of hands actually produced the gift, since 1 Timothy 4:14 shows it was only an accompanying circumstance (*meta*). Though the ordination ceremony may be chiefly a recognition of spiritual gifts which the candidate already shows evidence of possessing, still the Holy Spirit at such a time may grant additional enablement.

The *responsibility* of Timothy toward this gift is dramatically stated by the words, "Continue rekindling" (*anazōpurein*). This present infinitive emphasizes the continual stirring up into flame which is necessary. Just as a fire must be constantly stirred up lest it die out, so Timothy and all Christians must be constantly at work exercising the gifts which God has bestowed. There is no intimation here that Timothy had been failing. Rather, he is told to continue doing what he has been doing, for soon Paul will be removed from the scene and Timothy will be no longer an assistant but the head in Ephesus.

2. Timothy may avoid being ashamed by relying on the grace of God who has provided the gospel.

> Therefore, be not ashamed of the testimony for our Lord nor of me his prisoner, but suffer hardship along with me for the gospel in accord with the power of God who saved us and called [to] a holy calling, not in accord with our works but in accord with his own purpose and grace, which was given to us in Christ Jesus before eternal times, but was manifested now through the appearing of our Saviour Christ Jesus, when he rendered death ineffective and brought to light life and incorruption through the gospel, for which I myself was appointed herald and apostle and teacher (vv. 8-11).

The mode of expression in the phrase "be not ashamed" (aorist subjunctive) offers clear evidence that Timothy was not at fault along this line. The connotation is, "Don't start being ashamed," rather than, "Stop being ashamed" (for which the present imperative would be necessary). The alternative of being ashamed was to suffer hardship for the gospel. If a Christian leader in those troubled times gave his testimony for Christ, the almost certain aftermath would be personal suffering of some sort. Paul urges Timothy to join him in suffering these evils (sugkakopathēson). The cause in which they were engaged, the proclamation of the gospel, made every sacrifice worthwhile. It even prompted Paul to regard himself no longer as Nero's prisoner but the Lord's.

Such suffering is in accordance with (kata) the power of God. Just as the Israelites looked for encouragement in time of stress to their deliverance from Egypt, as the great historic display of Jehovah's power, so Christians ought to realize that any suffering they are called upon to experience for the sake of the gospel is in harmony with the power of Almighty God. His supreme display of power and wisdom and love occurred in providing salvation. Thus any suffering at the hands of wicked men because of the gospel should not alarm us, but rather cause us to see more clearly whose side we are on. There is also the suggestion here that the power of God which saved men will also strengthen and protect His witnesses.

The power of God which has saved believers and called them to a holy life is the product of His purpose and grace. Thus the grace of God is shown to be fundamental in salvation. No human works had any part to play. Salvation is rooted entirely in His purpose and grace. It is His inexplicable favor to undeserving sinners. Nor was salvation an afterthought of God. "Before eternal times" marks the formation of God's plan. The unveiling of God's grace occurred with the sending of Jesus Christ. Here the "appearing" (*epiphaneias*) of Christ is a reference to the incarnation, and includes all aspects of his coming—life, death, resurrection, exaltation.

Verse 10 closes with two circumstantial participles (no articles) which are rendered by temporal clauses. At Christ's appearing (and specifically His resurrection), He rendered death ineffective (*katargēsantos*). By paying the penalty (death) for sin, Christ removed its claim on believers. Now spiritual death can be replaced with spiritual life (eternal), and even physical death must eventually yield its victims. Though physical death is an experience still shared by believers, Christ removed its sting, for that which made it terrifying was the consciousness that it was the result of sin (1 Cor. 15:56). Now for Christians, death is the gateway to His presence (2 Cor. 5:6-8).

Paul's encouragement, therefore, is to remember the grace of God when facing hardship for the gospel. As Christians gain a clearer understanding of all that God has done for sinners, no sacrifice of ours can compare with

His. Consequently, the favor of God which saved us can also be relied upon to strengthen us and preserve us for the purpose He intended. Verse 11 adds Paul's own calm and steadfast testimony to the grace of God and the privilege of suffering for Him. Paul felt honored and grateful for the ministry God had given him. He felt no shame in suffering for the Gospel.

B. *Paul was not ashamed* (vv. 12-14).

> For which cause I also suffer these things, but I am not ashamed, for I know whom I have believed, and I am convinced that he is able to guard my deposit unto that day. Hold as a model of healthy words those which you heard from me in faith and love which is in Christ Jesus. The good deposit guard through the Holy Spirit who is dwelling in us (vv. 12-14).

As Paul developed the theme of being unashamed of Christ and the gospel, he set forth this personal testimony as an example and encouragement to Timothy. Verse 11 provided the transition.

1. Paul was not ashamed in his sufferings because he trusted Christ.

He knew with a settled assurance (*oida*) the one who was the object of his faith. This knowledge was sufficient to be absolutely convincing (*pepeismai*, see v. 5). The sufferings he was undergoing at present could not shake his faith in the certainty of his eternal future. He was convinced that Christ was able to keep his deposit.

The explanation of the phrase "my deposit" (*tēn parathēkēn mou*) has been in question from earliest times. Does it mean that which Paul has deposited with Christ (KJV), or that which Christ has deposited with Paul (ASV margin)? The latter view is largely an attempt to bring the "deposit" here into conformity with the "deposit" of verse 14 and 1 Timothy 6:20. In both those passages, the reference is to the gospel which is the responsibility of Timothy to guard from error or adulteration. Thus Paul is understood to say that even though his life was about ended, he was confident that Christ would preserve the gospel and place it in other hands so that the work would not be hindered.

The other view treats "my deposit" as Paul's commitment to Christ (just as a depositor at a bank may refer to his savings account as "my deposit," but the banker to whom the money is entrusted would not be likely to use the pronoun "my"). The contents of this deposit are variously explained as his reward, soul, final salvation, daily walk, and ministry. Thus Paul had no fears about the present, being assured that his entire cause was in the hands of his Savior. I believe this traditional view seems most likely, in spite of the attractions of the other. The use of "my" distinguishes this deposit from the others. Furthermore, Alford's argument that since the guarding of the deposit (v. 14) is said of the subject of the sentence (Timothy), as keeping a treasure entrusted to him, so the same principle applied here would refer this guarding to God as keeping a treasure entrusted to him, is a good one.[3]

The vindication of Christian suffering will occur at "that day" when Christ appears and the true nature of believers is manifested to the world. At this period are the events of resurrection, judgment, and reward.

2. Paul was not ashamed because he had held to sound doctrine, the pattern of which he was passing on to Timothy.

The ministry of the great apostle was a proclamation of the good news of salvation. This he had done by preaching, teaching, and writing, as well as by consistent Christian living. Now Paul was leaving the earthly scene. There remained the possibility that others coming later might alter or destroy the truth as Paul had taught it. Hence Paul cautions Timothy to remain true to the life-giving words from God Himself which he had learned from the lips and pen of the inspired apostle. These apostolic utterances were given in Christian faith and love;

there were no ulterior motives. Timothy must regard them as a model or pattern to be carefully copied. The modern idea of reinterpreting Christianity for the man of today, by setting Christian principles in new forms or molds, is at variance with Paul's injunction. The gospel proceeded from God to man. Hence man is not at liberty to change the meaning or the forms or the words in which God gave it through His chosen apostles.

   3. Therefore, Timothy is encouraged to guard the gospel message which was entrusted to him.

In verse 14 the gospel is called "the good deposit," and must be guarded as a banker guards the money left with him. To guard (*phulaxon*) involves protection against loss, destruction, or change. The message proclaimed by Paul and the other apostles is not to be changed, enlarged, or condensed, but preserved intact and used as God commanded. Such a responsibility can be fulfilled through (*dia*) divine assistance. The Holy Spirit who continually resides (present tense, *enoikountos*) in believers gives the ability.

   C. *Onesiphorus was not ashamed* (vv. 15-18).

> You know this, that all those in Asia turned away from me, of whom are Phygelus and Hermogenes. May the Lord grant mercy to the house of Onesiphorus, because he frequently refreshed me and was not ashamed of my chain, but when he was in Rome he diligently sought me and found—may the Lord grant to him to find mercy from the Lord in that day—and how many things he ministered in Ephesus, you yourself know better (vv. 15-18).

   1. All in Asia, who could have helped Paul, were ashamed and had turned away from him.

More encouragement is offered by way of contrasting examples. In Paul's hour of great need during the opening stages of his trial, evidently all persons of influence in Asia (the Roman province of which Ephesus was the capital) who had been asked to vouch for the apostle had refused to exert themselves on his behalf. The verb *apestraphēsan* points to an act of repudiation (aorist passive means "to repudiate"). Phygelus and Hermogenes, known to us only by this sad defection, were prominent in this refusal. They were apparently known to Timothy. The "all" (*pantes*) must be restricted in some such manner as suggested above. Obviously it must refer only to those who were in some position to help but refused to do so. Those who were his ministerial associates (such as Timothy) were themselves suspected and thus not of any use as witnesses.

    2. One from Ephesus was not ashamed and had associated himself with Paul.

    Onesiphorus is mentioned again in 4:19. He was a friend whose ministrations were not contingent upon favorable circumstances. On frequent occasions he brought refreshment to Paul. That refreshment doubtless included spiritual solace and physical comforts whenever possible. How much that must have meant to a man in a dungeon! Onesiphorus did not allow the dangers connected with Paul's case to frighten or embarrass him. His loyalty to Christ and the gospel included loyalty to Christ's suffering, manacled servant. When Onesiphorus arrived in Rome he persistently made search for Paul. It cost him much difficulty to find him. The ease of access which accompanied the first imprisonment was now gone (Acts 28:30-31). There may have been much "red tape" to go through. In all of this, Onesiphorus revealed that his prior kindnesses in happier days at Ephesus were displays of true Christian friendship, unaltered by circumstances. Timothy, being in Ephesus, knew by experience (*ginōskeis*, not merely by report [*oidas*, v. 15]), what Onesiphorus had done for Paul, even better (*beltion*) than Paul himself, for he was on the scene and could understand the full import of his deeds.

    The blessing which Paul asks for Onesiphorus and his house is mercy. Just as his benefactor had shown mercy to him, so he asks a like recompense for him (cf. Matt. 5:7). Paul knew that he would never again be free and in a position to reciprocate such kindness; consequently, he commits the responsibility to the Lord that these mercies might not go unrewarded. At the judgment seat of Christ there will be the ultimate recognition of the value of Christian living. (The rather awkward repetition of "Lord" [v. 18] is explained as follows: The first use is part of such a common formula that its recurrence was not noticed by the writer or reader.)

Romanists and many others have concluded from this passage that Onesiphorus was dead, and this reference has been used in support of the unscriptural doctrine of prayer for the dead. The request for "mercy," the mention of "that day" rather than some present blessing, and the references in 1:16 and 4:19 to his house apart from the man himself are supposed to demand this viewpoint. I must confess that I am unconvinced by these reasons, and I believe that such a view is not the most obvious meaning of Paul's words. The reason for requesting mercy for Onesiphorus in that day of Christ's return has been explained above. (Mercy was also requested for his household. Does this mean they were all dead?) The most likely reason his house alone is mentioned (1:16; 4:19) is that Paul knew that Onesiphorus had not yet returned home to Ephesus.

II. CHARGE TO BE STRONG IN THE SERVICE OF CHRIST (2:1-26).

The believer in general and the minister in particular are presented in seven pictures. This chapter is a good one for young people's talks, lending itself to much imagery and illustration. Every believer has a ministry to perform for Christ, and the strength comes from God's grace.

A. *The minister as a child* (vv. 1-2).

You, therefore, my child, continue growing strong in the grace which is in Christ Jesus, and the things which you heard from me through many witnesses, these things deposit with faithful men who shall be competent to teach others also (vv. 1-2).

1. A child possesses the nature of his parents.

The word "child" (teknon, not KJV "son") is derived from a verb meaning to give birth, bear a child, and denotes a relationship of nature. As used here by Paul, it was also a term of endearment. "My child" shows that Timothy's nature was the result of his relationship to Paul. Obviously the reference is to his spiritual nature, produced in Timothy by the gospel message, "the things which you heard from me." Because of the gospel, including the further explanation of it by Paul in subsequent years, Timothy was reborn as a child of God, and as Paul's child in the faith.

2. A child grows stronger with the passing of time.

The use of the present imperative endunamou emphasizes the progress expected in this strengthening. It is not accomplished all at once. Growth is the normal action of a child, and should characterize life in the spiritual realm as well. Physically, children grow by making use of every aid in the realm of food, rest, exercise, and hygiene. Spiritually, we grow by using God's means in the realm of (en) grace provided in Christ. This inexhaustible supply of God's favor made available in Christ is abundant to strengthen, sustain, and cause spiritual growth and health for the child of God.

3. A child receives instruction from his father.

One of the necessities of childhood is parental guidance. So Timothy, as Paul's spiritual offspring, is given that helpful instruction which will enable him to carry out successfully the responsibilities of the Christian life. Paul's instruction is: Deposit as a sacred trust those gospel truths which you learned from me into the care of trustworthy men. They in turn will hand them on to others. The gospel Timothy had learned from Paul was not some private message, given by Paul to Timothy. It was the same gospel which Paul had proclaimed everywhere, and many, many hearers could vouch for the message. There is no need to restrict the reference to the time of Timothy's ordination or baptism. The aorist form "heard" (ēkousas) may be understood as constative, gathering into one all that Timothy had heard from Paul during many years of association.

This is the only true apostolic succession: the faithful proclamation of the apostles' teaching without addition or alteration. Every believer should be concerned about telling the gospel to others. However, this passage is particularly applicable to ministers. Every such servant of God, while not neglecting the whole congregation, should endeavor to develop leaders who will be qualified and competent to carry the gospel effectively to others. This is how the gospel reached us. It is our responsibility to future generations.

B. *The minister as a soldier* (vv. 3-4).

Suffer hardship along with me as a good soldier of Christ Jesus. No one serving as a soldier entangles himself in the affairs of life, in order that he may please the one who enlisted [him] (vv. 3-4).

1. A good soldier endures hardship.

Christian life is a warfare. The figure is frequently used in the epistles. Remember, Paul is not talking about fighting to obtain salvation, but as Christ's servant. A good soldier does not abandon his weapons and flee. So God's good soldier must regard hardship as inevitable in a world that is hostile to God. Paul bravely endured the difficulties in his path. He challenges us to join him.

2. A good soldier does not entangle himself with the affairs of life.

Arndt and Gingrich translate the phrase, "become entangled in civilian pursuits."[4] The recruit is given a brief length of time to get his affairs in order. He must dispose of business commitments, or make arrangements to leave them in other hands during his absence. The reason is that he must be free to devote all his time, thought, and energy to the work of the military. He need not concern himself with earning a living, for all such needs are supplied by his enlistment. Certainly Christ's soldier must be no less devoted to the service of his Commander. Jesus taught the necessity of removing all entanglements (Luke 9:57-62), and Scripture promises the supply of every need (Phil. 4:19). Anything which hinders service for Christ must be removed. (Of course, Paul himself plied his trade of tentmaking from time to time, but it was a furtherance to his ministry, not an entanglement.)

3. A good soldier seeks to please his commander.

When interests are divided, service is curtailed and the commander is displeased. The Christian has enlisted for life in the service of Christ, and is bound to his commander not only by duty and loyalty but by the stronger cord of love.

C. *The minister as an athlete* (v. 5).

> And also if someone competes in an athletic contest, he
> is not crowned unless he competes lawfully (v. 5).

1. An athlete is contending for a prize.

The verb translated "compete in an athletic contest" is *athleō*, from which our words "athletic" and "athlete" are derived. Athletics were important in Greek life, and must have greatly interested Paul. The prize in such Greek events was the laurel wreath (*stephanos*), and this is the imagery employed by Paul in his reference to crowning (*stephanoutai*). The value of the wreath was not its intrinsic worth but the accomplishment which it commemorated. So every Christian has the privilege of contending for a prize (1 Cor. 9:24, 25; Phil. 3:14), and the goal of Christ's approval should spur each one to greater effort.

2. An athlete must abide by the rules.

To be eligible for the prize, the athlete must contend according to the rule book (*nomimōs*, lawfully). Mere effort is not sufficient. There must be discipline and sacrifice as well as energy. Americans are familiar with the experience of the Indian youth, Jim Thorpe, who won many events at the Olympics in Sweden but was later disqualified when his amateur status was questioned. It is possible to spend much effort in Christian service, and yet be disqualified for the crown (1 Cor. 9:27).

D. *The minister as a farmer* (vv. 6-13).

It is necessary for the laboring farmer first of the fruits to partake (v. 6).

1. The farmer must labor at his task.

The same verb (*kopiaō*) was used of elders in 1 Timothy 5:17, and depicts labor carried to the point of great weariness and exhaustion. This is one of the inescapable accompaniments of farming. The minister of God, who does his work well, also will find that God's service demands great effort. The glamor soon wears off. But the nature of the task is abundant compensation.

2. The farmer receives priority of reward.

The difficulties in translating and interpreting this verse are seen in the variety of explanations which have been offered. Four of the more prominent ones are given here.

Some explain Paul's meaning as demanding a spiritual partaking of the gospel before laboring is possible. God's husbandman must first partake of spiritual fruit himself before he can produce fruit in his hearers, just as a farmer cannot expect others to buy his produce unless he can personally vouch for its worth. However, in this verse the fruit seems to be presented as the result of labor, not the cause.

Another viewpoint emphasizes that laboring must precede partaking. One must labor first and enjoy the fruit afterward. This explanation must rearrange "first" in the sentence without adequate grounds, and therefore cannot be correct.

A third view holds that the farmer gets first choice of the fruit he produces ("first of the fruits"), and explains the verse as an argument for paying preachers. This is certainly a scriptural principle. However, there is some difficulty in understanding the fruit which he produces as salary, although it may be viewed in a general way as reflecting the Pauline principle that those who "preach the gospel should live of the gospel" (1 Cor. 9:14).

The fourth view does not restrict the "first of the fruits" to remuneration, but sees it as a promise of priority in reward provided that the minister has labored faithfully. The context deals with Christian service, and of sacrifice preceding reward. Hence the minister who labors long and hard is given the assurance that God is not unmindful, and that appropriate reward will be given, both in this life and the next. God's farmer labors in order to produce the fruits of faith and Christian graces in the lives of those in his care. As he faithfully performs this function, he himself benefits from the joy of a work well done and from the gratitude of those whose lives he has helped. And in the life to come, such faithful laboring will be rewarded by Christ Himself.

3. Paul's summary.

> Understand what I say: for the Lord will give you understanding in all things. Remember Jesus Christ, raised out of the dead, out of David's seed, in accord with my gospel; in connection with whom I am suffering hardship to the extent of bonds as an evil-doer, but the word of God has not been bound. On account of this I endure all things on account of the elect, in order that they may obtain salvation which is in Christ Jesus with eternal glory. Faithful is the word:
> For if we died with him, we shall also live with him;
> If we are enduring, we shall also reign with him;
> If we shall deny, that one also will deny us;
> If we are faithless, that one remains faithful,
> For he is not able to deny himself (vv. 9-13).

The principle Paul has set forth in the previous verses is that before the crown there must be the cross. Hardship, struggle, discipline, labor—all must precede the enjoyment of reward. He now summarizes by calling upon Timothy to think upon these sobering truths and note two outstanding examples. First, Christ Himself went to a cross and suffered as a man (David's seed) at the hands of men before being raised out from the realm of dead men. This was the very core of Paul's message which he had proclaimed to Timothy and the whole region of Asia.

Paul also suffered affliction in this life in anticipation of the life to come. At present he was imprisoned by the government, but he rejoiced that this was not a calamity for the gospel, for the Word of God was not bound but was free to do its work in the hearts of men. Paul was prepared to remain firm under any sort of circumstance (*hupomenō*), because his purpose was to bring the message of salvation in Christ to those whom God had chosen. In Paul's thinking, salvation was entirely the work of God, both in God's election for salvation and in the means employed to reach them with the gospel. Hence Paul regarded his personal sufferings as part of God's plan to reach lost men, and he did not fret under such difficulties.

This principle of the need for present suffering, to be followed by future glory, is reinforced by a quotation from an early hymn or confession. The rhythmical clauses are introduced by the phrase common in the Pastoral Epistles, "Faithful is the word" (*pistos ho logos*). The use of this phrase seems to indicate a well-known quotation, rather than a statement written here by Paul for the first time. The tenses in these lines are significant, as are the conditional particles used. "If" in each clause is *ei* used with an indicative mood, a construction which assumes the condition to be an actuality. "Died" is an aorist tense, indicating an act in the past. Thus the meaning is, "If we died with Him (and I am assuming that we all did)." These words remind us of other Pauline teaching (Gal. 2:20; Rom. 6:1-11). When Christ died for sin at Calvary, God identified us with Him, and accounts

His death as our death. By faith this identification is appropriated by believers. By this identification with Christ, His resurrection meant new life for us as well. This new life is our present possession and is eternal, eventually to be enjoyed in His presence when He comes again.

The new life in Christ also causes us to endure the afflictions from an unbelieving world, but the prospect is a future reigning with Christ. If we shall deny Him, we may expect Him to deny us (Matt. 10:33). The same particle "if" (ei) is employed, assuming the condition to be true. However, the verb is a future tense, and thus Paul is not stating that which was presently the case. He does not mean, "since we are denying him," but "if we shall deny him in the future (and some may)," the consequence is clear.

In the last contrast, apistoumen is to be translated "faithless" (rather than "believe not") because there is an obvious play on words with pistos (faithful). Though Christians are often faithless, even as Peter was, Christ remains faithful to us, to His promises, and to His own unchanging nature. The closing words, "He is not able to deny himself," have been understood in two opposite ways. One view understands the words as an explanation of Christ's activity in upholding us in our weakness (Luke 22:31-32). Others view it as a stern warning that He is unchanging, and if we are faithless, we must expect Him to remain just and holy. He will not accept as faithful that which is unfaithful. It appears to me that both elements may be included in these words. The faithlessness is not some violent act of heresy or apostasy, whereby one abandons Christian faith, but is a condition assumed as true (ei), even with Paul and Timothy. Therefore, it refers to the faithlessness that characterizes each Christian life so frequently. Yet Christ has promised to give strength, and to complete that which He has begun (Phil. 1:6). He will fulfill all His promises to believers. To do otherwise would be to deny His nature. Of course, He will not be unrighteous in His faithfulness. In all of His words and actions, we have the confidence that He is perfectly consistent. What He has spoken He will do.

E. *The minister as a workman* (vv. 14-19).

> Continue reminding [them] of these things, charging [them] in the presence of God not to be disputing about words—useful for nothing, for subversion of the ones who hear. Be diligent to present yourself approved to God, a workman not needing to be ashamed, cutting straight the word of truth (vv. 14-15).

1. God's workman must encourage others to avoid useless discussions.

The infinitive "to dispute about words" (*logomachein*) appeared in its noun form in 1 Timothy 6:4. Such action was described in that passage as indicative of false teaching. Paul is describing those whose discussions were of no good use whatever (*chrēsimon*), and whose result is the subversion and ruination of those who hear. (*Katastrophē* is the root of our word "catastrophe.") Of course, Paul does not mean we should not study minutely the Word of God (he commands it in the next sentence), but mere controversy and wrangling with those whose motives are questionable and whose influence is factious and destructive must be avoided. God's workman must not allow such persons any opportunity to engage in their disputes.

2. God's workman must enforce his teaching by his own example.

Because of the KJV translation "study," this verse has sometimes been thought to picture a student. However, the figure employed is a laborer or workman (*ergatēn*), usually one who works for hire. In contrast to the useless discussions just warned against, the laborer for God must give diligence to the kind and quality of his work, so that when he meets God's inspection, he will stand the test and be approved (*dokimon*), having no need for shame because of faulty workmanship (*anepaischunton*). This was what motivated Paul (Phil. 1:20). Some Christian workers have no shame, although there seems to be cause for shame in their motives and methods. We must be concerned that there be no reason for shame in our service for Christ.

The work of God's laborer is handling the Word of God, proclaiming it and applying it to men's lives. He is to "cut straight" (*orthotomounta*). The metaphor has been understood of apportioning food, plowing, quarrying, or laying out a road. Since the context does not provide any light as to what type of workman was in Paul's mind, the interpreter dare not dogmatize. Perhaps he was thinking of his own craft, tentmaking, and pictures the artisan trimming the hides precisely so that they will fit together. In some such manner, God's workman must treat with discernment the Word of God. Simpson says it "enjoins on every teacher of the Word straightforward exegesis."[5] There must be discernment between the various subjects taught in Scripture: salvation and service, the Jew and the church. Interpretation and application must be clearly treated. Attention must be paid to dispensing of the Word, the use of wisdom and tact. The Holy Spirit will guide God's workman, but there is latent here much need for precise and earnest labor.

    3. God's workman must shun the corrupting influence of false teaching.

> But the profane empty-talkings continue shunning, for they will progress further in ungodliness, and their word as gangrene will have pasturage, of whom are Hymenaeus and Philetus, who concerning the truth missed the mark, saying resurrection already to have occurred, and they are upsetting the faith of some (vv. 16-18).

The *nature* of this false teaching is a profane babbling (see 1 Tim. 6:20; Titus 3:9). It is empty speech with no sacred character at all. Timothy is to stand aloof (*periista-*

so) from it, giving it a wide berth, going around it rather than being drawn into it.

The *result* of false teaching is the growth of ungodliness. Creed and conduct are inseparable. Ungodly conduct is advanced by an ungodly creed. As Paul wrote this letter, possibly by dictation to Doctor Luke, the medical figure of gangrene (*gaggraina*) came to mind. Perhaps Luke said, "Paul, your description of the spreading influence of wrong teaching is like the growth of gangrene in the human body, once it gains an entrance." Gangrene is a disease in which bacteria enters a wound or injury and destroys the flesh. So if false teachers are allowed to enter, their corrupting doctrine will spread from that opening, finding pasturage among the unspiritual and the unsuspecting in the congregation. The contamination which had infected the teachers would spread to others.

Two examples of false teachers are Hymenaeus and Philetus. Hymenaeus is probably the same man mentioned in 1 Timothy 1:20. Philetus appears only here. They taught that resurrection was already past. They apparently taught that spiritual rebirth (from death to life) is the only resurrection which occurs. This teaching, if allowed to go unchecked, would spread to denial of Christ's physical resurrection and second coming (see 1 Cor. 15, for the pivotal position this doctrine holds in Christian truth). Small wonder that the faith of weaker ones was being upset! The hope of meeting loved ones who have died was being destroyed. The prospect of reigning with Christ was removed. The implication to be drawn was that we should be reigning now, instead of suffering. Paul speaks most clearly in saying that they have missed the mark (*ēstochēsan*) regarding the truth.

4. God's workman must remain true to God's firm foundation.

Nevertheless the solid foundation of God stands, having this seal: the Lord knew the ones who were his;

and, let everyone who names the name of the Lord depart from unrighteousness (v. 19).

Verse 19 is an encouragement to the believer, in contrast to the apostasy previously sketched. That solid entity which God has founded has stood and continues to stand, in spite of false teachers and insincere followers. Although a great many explanations are offered of the identity of this "foundation," it is most clearly a reference to the true church, called elsewhere the "pillar and support of the truth" (1 Tim. 3:15). The seal whereby God has guaranteed the inviolability of His true church is twofold: a divine and a human proof. The first (and basic) guarantee that the true church is solidly founded and secure is the election of God: The Lord knew the ones who were His. In eternity past (egnō, aorist "knew") God knew with favor those who would be His, and His seal was fixed upon them. Scripture calls this "election." From the human standpoint, the outworking of this election is godly living. Hence by looking at the life of the saint, one can see the evidence of his new nature.

F. *The minister as a utensil* (vv. 20-23).

> And in a great house are not only gold and silver utensils, but also wooden and earthenware ones, even some for honor and some for dishonor. If therefore anyone shall cleanse himself from these, he shall be a utensil for honor, sanctified, useful to the master, prepared for every good work (vv. 20-21).

1. There are two general kinds of utensils in the house. *Skeuos* denotes an object used for some purpose, equipment, vessel, jar, dish, instrument, utensil. The great house is a symbol of the professing church in its widest aspect (note the adjective "great"). The figure is of a large household in which can be found all sorts of utensils. In this illustration, they are of two basic types: those of honor and much value (gold and silver), and those of dishonor and little value (wood and pottery). The emphasis in this illustration is not upon the usefulness of the

utensils, for the wood and pottery vessels are probably used much more frequently in a house than the fine silver or gold pieces which are reserved for special occasions. Neither is Paul speaking of the various gifts which believers possess, for here we are encouraged to be vessels for honor, whereas the ones who possess lesser gifts from Christ are not to covet gifts of greater prominence (1 Cor. 12:14-31). Rather, he is depicting the value or quality of the utensil. In a house the wood and pottery vessels eventually chip or break and must be replaced, but the gold and silver ones are never destroyed. So in the church, false teachers arise from time to time, but eventually their worthlessness is recognized, and they are removed.

2. The honored utensil must purge himself from other utensils.

After a large dinner with many guests, the washing of the dishes begins. The wife usually washes the sterling silver and the crystal first, and they are restored to their places of safekeeping in the china cabinet or the silver chest. They are not left with the pots and pans, or piled haphazardly with the kitchen utensils in the drying rack.

Likewise, the contamination that clings to the dishonored vessels must not be allowed to infect the honored ones. Therefore, the true servant of God must purge himself from the company of the valueless ones. By doing so, he will have become separated from evil (*hēgiasmenon*), and thus be of use (*euchrēston*) to the Master of the household.

3. The honored utensil maintains his value by avoiding contamination and following godliness.

But the youthful desires continue fleeing, and continue pursuing righteousness, faith, love, peace with those who are calling upon the Lord out of a pure heart. But the foolish and ignorant questionings be declining, knowing that they produce battles (vv. 22-23).

He must *flee* youthful desires. Those desires include not only bodily appetites, but all temptations which particularly beset the young minister (older men can fall prey to them too). Pride, love of money, sex, contentiousness, display of knowledge—all can ruin the usefulness of God's young servant. The only safe course is to continually flee from them. It is unfair to suspect Timothy of unusual weakness along this line. Paul may properly speak thus to every man.

He must *pursue* the life of godliness. The fruits of the Christian life, produced by the indwelling Spirit, are to be cultivated and developed.

He must *avoid* questionings which result in strife. These discussions are described as foolish (*mōras*) and are the product of untrained, uneducated minds (*apaideutous*). They show failure to understand the points at issue. Such discussion results in only profitless battling, and the minister must decline participation in them (see 1 Tim. 4:7).

G. *The minister as a bond servant* (vv. 24-26).

> And the Lord's bond servant must not be battling but be gentle to all, able to teach, forbearing, in meekness instructing those who are placing themselves in opposition, if perhaps God may give them repentance unto full knowledge of truth, and they may return to soberness out of the snare of the Devil, having been captured alive by him, for the will of that one [i.e., God] (vv. 24-26).

The bond servant or slave (*doulos*) had no will of his own, but was expected to be governed by his master in every respect—surely an apt metaphor for God's ministers.

The activity expected of God's bond servant is shown as instructing men in the ways of God. He is obligated (*dei*) to avoid continual quarreling and battling with false teachers, for wrangling never produces repentance or conversion. (Certainly, however, there are times when being faithful to the truth involves "contending" for it

[Jude 3], but the general principle of gentleness is here emphasized.) The minister must be gentle in his manner to all men, whether friends or opponents. He must be able to teach what is true doctrine, and be willing to hold up under evil treatment (*anexikakon*). He must regard his ministry as involving the continued educating (*paideuonta*) of those who are immature and misinformed, but must remember to carry out this instructing with meekness (*en prautēti*). This is not always easy to do, but the responsibility is clear.

The purpose of this action is twofold. By faithful teaching directed to those who have set themselves in opposition to the truth (the victims as well as their teachers), there is always the possibility that God will use the instruction to produce repentance. When awakened from their drunken stupor (*ananēpsōsin*), they may escape from the devil's trap into which they have fallen (1 Tim. 3:7).

The final clause of verse 26 has been variously interpreted. The problem lies in the antecedents of the pronouns: "having been captured alive by him [*autou*] for the will of that one [*ekeinou*]." The capturing has been viewed as by God in order for the one captured to do God's will. It has also been explained as a capturing by God's bond servant, to do God's will. Others view it as a capturing by Satan for doing his will. To me, the most feasible explanation understands the capturing as by Satan (in his snare of false teaching), but sees the "will of that one" as referring to God. This viewpoint gives proper recognition to the change in pronouns, since the shift to "that one" (*ekeinou*) undoubtedly was meant to indicate a different antecedent (see 3:9 where the same pronouns in the plural, *autōn* and *ekeinōn*, are used in this way). Thus the capturing by Satan is regarded as somewhat parenthetical, and "for the will of That One" refers to the return to soberness rather than the capturing. The meaning is this: "They may return to soberness (out of the snare of the Devil, having been held captive by him) to do the will of That One (God)."

These persons who have been trapped by the devil were not the same type as those described in 2:21 or Titus 3:10. From such, the minister is to remove himself. Those in 2:25-26 are to be dealt with kindly in order to bring about a return to sober thinking. They are captured *alive* by Satan. There is at least an inference that these persons may be true believers who have become ensnared. If they are, the repentance and recovery may be expected, and the offenders may yet be restored to the will of God.

III. CHARGE TO WITHSTAND THE APOSTASY FROM CHRIST (3:1-17).

Verse 14 provides the theme of this section, with its command to Timothy to remain in the doctrine which had been faithfully taught to him.

A. *The coming of the apostasy* (vv. 1-9).

1. The time of the apostasy.

> But know this, that in the last days there will set in difficult seasons . . . (v. 1).

The "last days" (*eschatais hēmerais*) is an expression often used in Scripture to refer to messianic times. This period began with the first coming of Christ and includes the time now present. New Testament writers regard Christians as living in the last days (1 John 2:18; Acts 2:16-17), and Paul indicates that the apostasy of this chapter is to be guarded against in Timothy's day (v. 5).

Within this period of the last days, which has already extended more than nineteen centuries, there will set in shorter seasons (*kairoi*) which will be difficult to endure (*chalepoi*). These will occur from time to time (even during Timothy's lifetime), but conditions will become progressively worse (v. 13). Whereas 1 Timothy 4 told of certain seasons when "some" would be involved, 2 Timothy 3 indicates a general decadence in the professing church (v. 5). The very worst apostasy, which will occur under

Antichrist just before the Lord returns, is described in 2 Thessalonians 2.

2. The nature of the apostasy.

The difficult seasons will be so because of the persons involved. The men and women (*anthrōpoi*, mankind) who promote this apostasy are described in a long series of characteristics.

> For there shall be men [who are] self-lovers, money-lovers, boasters, haughty, blasphemers, disobedient to parents, unthankful, unholy, without natural affection, implacable, slanderers, uncontrolled, untamed, not lovers of good, betrayers, headstrong, puffed up, pleasure-lovers rather than God-lovers, having a semblance of godliness but having denied the power of it. And from these keep turning yourself away (vv. 2-5).

Mankind shall be self-lovers (*philautoi*), instead of God-lovers (v. 4). Modern man may call it humanism, but the Bible pictures it as selfishness and lists it as basic in man's departure from God. Regeneration in Christ was intended to cause men to "not henceforth live unto themselves, but unto him which died for them and rose again" (2 Cor. 5:15). They shall also be money-lovers (*philarguroi*), for those whose chief concern is their own desires will love the money which can supply those desires. Boasters (*alazones*) are those swaggering, bragging persons who glory in making a big display of themselves, whether the realm be in riches (1 John 2:16) or in knowledge. (Cf. the church at Laodicea, Rev. 3:17.)

Haughty ones (*huperēphanoi*) like to appear above others (from *phainō, huper*). Blasphemers (*blasphēmoi*) speak evil, specially of God. Modern examples range from the lowest rebellious sinner to the liberal theologian who denies the deity of Christ. Another example of self-will is found in those who are disobedient to parents (*goneusin apeitheis*). It is not necessary for adulthood to be attained before the apostate spirit of self-will may manifest itself.

The breaking up of our social system is suggested by the phrase.

Those who are unthankful (*acharistoi*) have no feeling of dependence on the assistance of others. Romans 1 sets forth ingratitude as contributing to the condition of the pagan world. It is probably not accidental that the next term is *anosioi*, for ingratitude and unholiness are usually found together. The *anosios* person has no respect for anything sacred. Those without natural affection (*astorgoi*) have allowed their apostasy of doctrine to disrupt even their domestic relations, so that the very foundations of family life are destroyed. This adjective describes the absence of natural attachments based on love. An examination of present-day divorce statistics shows how rapidly we are pursuing this course.

Implacable ones (*aspondoi*) not only refuse to be bound by agreements (KJV, trucebreakers), but will not even enter into any truce (cf. Psalm 2:3). The word is derived from *spondē*, a libation which accompanied the making of a treaty, and the alpha privative which negates it. Their formal assent to a creed in days past means nothing to them. They became slanderers (*diaboloi*), partaking of the character of Satan himself.

Such men are also uncontrolled (*akrateis*), exercising no restraint upon themselves in any way. They become as wild as untamed, savage beasts (*anēmeroi*), considering only their own purposes, and ruthlessly violating the welfare of others. How different from the Spirit of Christ: "Learn of me . . . for I am meek and lowly in heart" (Matt. 11:29). So degraded are these persons that they are not lovers of good (*aphilagathoi*). A great many people who do evil in reality admire the principle of good, and fail to follow it because of weakness and lack of sufficient motivation. But not so with these apostates. Isaiah 5:20 pronounces a woe upon those who call evil good. Romans 1:32 mentions those who do evil and take pleasure in others who do the same.

Betrayers (*prodotai*) display that form of malice which traitorously delivers others to ruin. Christ experienced such treatment from Judas. Headstrong ones (*propeteis*) rush forward in pursuit of their own wills, regardless of the will of God or the welfare and interests of others. Puffed up persons (*tetuphōmenoi*) have become so inflated with a sense of their own knowledge and importance, that they envelop themselves in a cloud of smoke (root is *tuphos*, smoke, mist, cloud) and are unable to recognize the truth.

In the difficult seasons which grip the church from time to time there will be found many who are pleasure-lovers (*philēdonoi*) rather than God-lovers (*philotheoi*). Personal pleasure is paramount in their lives. This describes a time when the church will be characterized by loving entertainment more than loving God. Certainly the church of today, which so often seems to feel the need to "compete" with the world in order to gain a following, needs to beware. It is easy for entertainment, which may have a God-honoring goal, to degenerate into mere pleasure.

Men will be possessors of mere formal religion. They will have the form of godliness (*morphōsin eusebeias*) which will resemble the real essence, but a careful examination will reveal that the power which energizes the Christian life is missing. The power is the gospel (Rom. 1:16) which these persons have denied, even though they wish to remain in the professing church. The same situation was described in Titus 1:16, where the works of these professed believers show that they are not the product of divine energy. Since such persons have always attached themselves to the church in greater or lesser numbers, Timothy is urged to continually turn himself (present tense, middle voice) away from them.

> For out of these are the ones who ingratiate themselves into the houses and take captive silly women heaped with sins, being led by various desires, always

learning and at no time being able to come into full knowledge of truth. But in which manner Jannes and Jambres withstood Moses, so also these withstand the truth, men corrupted in the mind, disapproved concerning the faith (vv. 6-8).

Deceivers of women are among the apostates who afflict the church. Such men furtively gain access (*endunontes*) to the houses of their victims, and succeed in captivating the allegiance of silly women (*gunaikaria*, diminutive form used contemptuously). The women so victimized are heaped with sins (*sesōreumena hamartiais*). This type of woman, perhaps neurotic and depressed by the guilt of sin, is easily led astray by religious quacks who may satisfy the desire for some sort of religion without demanding abandonment of sin. Church history is full of female victims and companions of false religionists, from the tradition of Simon Magus and Helena to the multitudinous wives of Brigham Young. Satan's method in the garden was to insinuate himself into the confidence of Eve.

These women-victims are further described as continually learning, but never arriving at real knowledge (*epignōsin*). They remind us of the Athenian pastime, which in its desire to always find something new prevented concentration on real spiritual truth in order to assimilate it (Acts 17:21). These women never come to the truth because they know not Him who is the Truth (John 14:6).

The final description pictures the apostates as active resisters of the truth. For illustration of this resistance, Paul names Jannes and Jambres who withstood Moses. Since these men are not named elsewhere in Scripture, the source from which Paul derived the names can legitimately be asked. The best answer is that the names were preserved in Jewish tradition (either oral or written), and were thus known to Paul. Some of the data in Stephen's speech (Acts 7) must have come from such sources.

Although much of the material in Jewish traditional literature is legendary and allegorical, the Holy Spirit so guided that only what was true was included in Scripture. Jannes and Jambres are named in the Targum of Jonathan (Exod. 7:11, 22). They are described as counselors of evil in Egypt, who ultimately perished either in the Red Sea or in the slaughter which followed the making of the golden calf.

Jannes and Jambres withstood Moses by imitating his works. So these apostates in Christendom are imitators of true religion. However, they are in a state of corruption (perfect tense of *katephtharmenoi*) in their minds. Their intellectual faculties, having refused the light of the truth, have become unable to receive the truth which cleanses the life and enlightens the understanding. Consequently, when these men are tested by the standard of the Christian faith, they are disapproved (*adokimoi*) as worthless metal.

3. The exposure of the apostasy.

> But they shall not progress further, for their folly shall
> be clearly evident to all, as even that of those men came
> to be (v. 9).

Ultimate defeat is certain, just as occurred with the opposers of Moses. The senselessness (*anoia*) of these men will eventually be unmasked and become clearly evident (*ekdēlos*) to men generally (*pasin*). Even the magicians of Moses, who were successful for a time, came to see their rods swallowed up (Exod. 7:12), and their inability demonstrated (Exod. 8:18-19; 9:11).

This restriction upon the progress of the apostates must refer to their influence and success in gaining followers, rather than personal advance along their evil ways. God will see to it that His faithful remnant is preserved in every difficult season. (This explanation is confirmed in 3:13 since evil men are definitely predicted to "proceed further" in their ungodly ways.)

B. *The withstanding of apostasy* (vv. 10-17).

Paul challenges Timothy with three safeguards as an encouragement to withstand the evil forces arrayed against him and the church.

1. The example of Paul is an encouragement to withstand apostasy.

> But you followed closely my teaching, my conduct, my purpose, my faith, my longsuffering, my love, my patience, my persecutions, my sufferings, such as came to me in Antioch, in Iconium, in Lystra; such persecutions as I bore, and out of all the Lord delivered me. But also all who wish to live godly in Christ Jesus shall be persecuted. And evil men and impostors shall progress to the worse, deceiving and being deceived (vv. 10-13).

Nine aspects are listed in which Paul contrasts himself to the apostate leaders. Paul's teaching (*didaskaliāi*) had the foremost place among his influences on Timothy. Teaching was surely Paul's great gift, preserved for all believers in the epistles of our New Testament. Just as Luke carefully traced all the facts before writing his gospel (Luke 1:3), so Timothy had closely followed (*parēkolouthēsas*, same word used by Luke) the doctrinal instruction of Paul. Furthermore, Paul's teaching was supported by his conduct (*agōgē*), which showed clearly to any careful observer what sound doctrine can do to a man's manner of life (cf. 1 Thess. 1:5-6).

Paul's purpose (*prothesei*) since his conversion was never adulterated. Even when personal danger was involved, Paul had as his aim the carrying out of the commission Christ gave him (Acts 26:19-20), and the winning of His approval. Paul's personal faith (*pistei*) enabled him to triumph in every circumstance. His longsuffering (*makrothumiāi*) caused him to hold out long until the fruit of his labor should appear. He persisted in his efforts to reach and train men in the gospel of Christ. His love (*agapēi*) enabled him to win many for whom others showed no concern, and made him rise above jealousy and strife. Patience (*hupomonēi*) caused Paul to remain firm under the most discouraging circumstances, never capitulating to self-pity or despair.

Persecutions (*diōgmois*) denote those harassing experiences when opposition forced Paul to flee. Often such persecution produced sufferings (*pathēmasin*). Paul speaks of the incidents in Pisidian Antioch, Iconium, and Lystra, towns in Timothy's native region where the young boy had opportunity to see for himself or at least hear others tell of the apostle's physical sufferings (Acts 13–14). In every instance the Lord protected and delivered. Now Paul is persecuted with no hope of release, but his confidence in divine deliverance is still unshaken (cf. 4:18). Deliverance, however, does not always mean escape, and Paul was well aware of this. Of far greater significance is the delivering power of God in preventing eternal harm being done to His children by wicked men.

Paul reminds Timothy that persecution, in some sense at least, is the lot of all Christians who live without compromise. Jesus said: "In the world ye shall have tribulation" (John 16:33). (Consider also Acts 14:22; 1 John 3:13.) Those whose will is (*hoi thelontes*) to live lives of piety in their union with Christ will be objects of the world's displeasure.

Verse 13 completes the paragraph, indicating that persecution is not over. Though the success of their efforts is definitely limited (v. 9), the offenders themselves will become increasingly worse, leading men astray and being duped themselves by the god of this world.

    2. The childhood training of Timothy should inspire him to withstand apostasy.

> But you, keep remaining in the things which you have learned and were assured of, knowing from whom you learned, and that from a babe you know sacred letters, which are able to make you wise unto salvation through faith which is in Christ Jesus (vv. 14-15).

The *nature* of Timothy's training is the imparting of
information such as is acquired by a disciple from his
teacher (*emathes*, "you learned" is the root of *mathētēs*,
disciple). Those who had given this instruction to
Timothy—Lois, Eunice, perhaps Paul also—were bound
to him in love, and their Christian character had borne
out the truth of their teaching. This type of early training,
given competently, fully, and sincerely, is a strong deter-
rent to apostasy.

The *material* used for this training is called *hiera grammata* (sacred letters). The Scriptures as such are never
designated by this expression in the New Testament,
although Josephus and Philo use it for the Old Testament.
Surely the remainder of verse 15 makes it clear that the
reference is to Scripture. However, Lenski's explanation
that *grammata* should be taken in its usual sense of "letters, written characters, script," suggests that Timothy
had been taught the letters of the alphabet from the Old
Testament, and had first learned to read from God's
Word.[6] This occurred when Timothy was very young
(*brephous*, young child, infant, even used sometimes of
unborn child). Thus from his earliest recollections he was
steeped in the sacred writings which God had given to
Israel. What an example for Christian parents to emulate!

The *purpose* of this training was to lead him to salvation. Old Testament knowledge, which Timothy had been
taught in childhood, is not synonymous with salvation,
but it is valuable as a foundation to explain the New
Testament. It should not be neglected today (notice present tense, "are able to make you wise unto salvation"), for
it sheds much light on God's plan of redemption. But
salvation comes only as the knowledge gained from
Scripture causes us to put our faith in Jesus Christ.

    3. The Scriptures are the final safeguard against apos-
tasy.

      All Scripture is God-breathed and profitable for
teaching, for refutation, for correction, for education

which is in righteousness, in order that the man of God
may be equipped, for every good work fully equipped
(vv. 16-17).

Paul does not leave Timothy's faith to rest on family
authority alone, but takes it to the Word of God.

   a. All Scripture is God-breathed.

Graphē is without the article, thus qualitative,
and emphasizes that all that can lay claim to the quality
of divine Scripture is God-breathed. Since only the Old
Testament was complete at this time, Paul's reference
must be primarily to it, but the qualitative emphasis
leaves room for the New Testament to be considered by
later Christians as within the scope of this assertion.
Graphē means that which is written—words, phrases,
sentences (not just ideas).

Theopneustos suggests the method of writing. God
"breathed" Scripture by His breath of Spirit (*pneuma*),
the Holy Spirit. This is corroborated by 2 Peter 1:21.

The KJV and RSV translations are better than ASV,
which renders "every scripture inspired of God is also
profitable." The latter is ambiguous, and while its proponents say it assumes inspiration for Scripture, it is certainly capable of being misunderstood. As Simpson
observes, to say every God-breathed Scripture is profitable presents a "curious specimen of anticlimax."[7] The
omission of the copula "is" finds a parallel in 1 Timothy
4:4, where no one translates "every good creature of God
is also nothing to be thrown away."

   b. All Scripture is profitable.

      Its usefulness is shown in four functions. It is
profitable for teaching (*didaskalian*). All that a man
needs to be taught for salvation is found in Scripture. If
the doctrine is not found in the Bible, we have no reason
to accept it as spiritually significant. Scripture has a use
in refutation (*elegmon*). It is the greatest instrument to use
in counteracting religious falsehood, and in rebuking the
sinning person. It functions in correction (*epanorthōsin*),

setting up straight again those who have stumbled and fallen. The Word provides the means whereby sinners may be restored to God and may be set apart from sin to Him (John 17:17). Scripture is profitable also for education in the realm of righteousness (*paideian tēn en dikaiosunēi*). It not only shows men their faults, and restores them to the right path, but it also helps them to walk in that path.

       c. All Scripture is intended to equip the believer for life.

       Every Christian should wear the title "man of God" humbly but appropriately. Though it was usually reserved for prophets in the Old Testament, it belongs to all Christians. Such a designation places great responsibility upon the believer. To fulfill it, he needs to be equipped (*artios*), yes, fully equipped (*exērtismenos*, same root) for the life before him. Such complete equipment is found in the Word of God. It is our armor and our weapon to meet the declension of evil days.

IV. CHARGE TO PREACH THE WORD AS THE MINISTER OF CHRIST (4:1-8).

    A. *The nature of the charge* (v. 1).

       I solemnly charge in the presence of God and Christ Jesus, who is about to judge living and dead, and by his appearing and his kingdom (v. 1).

This last charge which Paul lays upon Timothy is a most solemn obligation (*diamarturomai*). The witnesses who are called upon to observe this testimony give it particular solemnity and awe. God the Father (*tou theou*), who sent the Son to redeem sinners, is incomparably interested in the proclamation of the gospel. So also is Christ Jesus (*Christou Iēsou*), who not only died for sinners, but is the Judge of all. To Him every man must some day give an account. For Christ's ministers the account will concern their faithfulness in performing this responsibility of proclaiming God's Word. (Wuest concludes that *kai* should be "even" here, thus restricting the reference to Christ, "God even Christ Jesus."[8] This is possible but not mandatory.)

The two accusatives which follow (*epiphaneian*, appearing, and *basileian*, kingdom) are the usual accusatives after verbs of adjuration (Mark 5:7; Acts 19:13; 1 Thess. 5:27). The English idiom is "by His appearing and His kingdom." In view of Christ's coming, when falsehoods will be unmasked, and the kingdom which Christ will establish at His coming, there should be faithful laboring of Christ's servants. His appearing and His kingdom are certain, and are thus incentives to faithfulness on the part of His ministers. At that time faithfulness will be vindicated and rewarded. Opposition to the preaching of the gospel will be dealt with and removed.

B. *The content of the charge* (v. 2).

> Preach the word, stand by in a good season, in no season, refute, rebuke, exhort, with all longsuffering and doctrine (v. 2).

1. Preach the Word (*kēruxon ton logon*).

He must proclaim as a herald (*kēruxon*) the message which has been given to him by his Lord. He must announce it in its completeness (Acts 20:27), without alteration, addition, or subtraction. He must proclaim, not philosophize or argue. This message is the Word of God, which has previously been explained as God-breathed Scripture (3:16-17). To proclaim God's Word involves all the themes of Scripture, not picking out some and ignoring others. The Word of God in its entirety is the basic material of the preacher's message.

2. Stand by (*epistēthi*).

The verb means to be ready, be at hand, stand by. The preacher of God's Word should always be ready to minister it whether the time is opportune (*eukairōs*) or not (*akairōs*). God's Word is always profitable, and is always in season. Since sinners are always in season also, God's servant must show a readiness to minister the Word, even outside of "office hours."

3. Refute (*elegxon*).

By applying the Word of God to sinners, their sin is pointed out as a violation of God's standard and will. The ideas of convict and convince are also to be understood in *elegxon*. This and the following terms are to be used "with all longsuffering and doctrine." Merely denouncing audiences rarely produces conversion or spiritual growth. But the use of godly patience, together with a clear presentation of the teaching of God's Word, is good ministry. There is a tendency today to refer to "doctrine" as dry and academic. Yet doctrine is the teaching which God has revealed. We dare not preach anything else. To do so is to use man's wisdom. We should not let men who are careless with words ruin this good term (the same is true of the term "theology").

4. Rebuke (*epitimēson*).

This carries the thought farther and includes the idea of censure or placing blame. As the Word is proclaimed, the issues must be so clearly drawn that erring Christians and the unconverted can see their own condition.

5. Exhort (*parakalesan*).

Those who have been rebuked need encouragement, comfort, and exhortation. All these ideas form the connotation of *parakaleō*. On the basis of the Word, each person needs to be shown the means whereby sin can be forgiven and spiritual life strengthened.

C. *The reason for the charge* (vv. 3-4).

> For there shall be a season when they shall not endure the healthy teaching, but in accord with their own desires, being tickled in the hearing, they shall heap up for themselves teachers, and from the truth they shall turn away the hearing, and for the myths they shall be turned aside (vv. 3-4).

The reason why this command is given is found in the

attitude of certain hearers in a day future to Paul. These people will not "hold themselves upright" (anexontai) under the healthy teaching of the gospel. The explanation for their action follows: they are motivated solely by their own desires (epithumias). These people reject doctrine which does not satisfy their cravings for aesthetic pleasure. Nor will they have great difficulty in finding preachers who will not preach unpopular doctrines. Their own cravings are substituted for the Word of God.

Since these hearers desire to have their hearing tickled by beautiful sermons and only those messages which they want to hear (notice that knēthomenoi, being tickled, makes it clear that the hearers are being tickled), they will accumulate to themselves teachers who will give them what they want. Perhaps this "heaping up" (episōreusousin) may show itself in a succession of pastors, or in much outward show with many teachers. Or these hearers may become "church tramps," going from one to another in search of something new. Vincent writes:

> In periods of unsettled faith, skepticism, and mere curious speculation in matters of religion, teachers of all kinds swarm like the flies in Egypt. The demand creates the supply. The hearers invite and shape their own preachers. If the people desire a calf to worship, a ministerial calf-maker is readily found.[9]

As a result, these hearers will actively turn away their hearing (apostrepsousin) from the truth. They will refuse to listen. But when God's truth is rejected, the human mind invents a substitute. Paul does not state what types of myths these are (muthous), whether Jewish, Gnostic, or other religious falsehood. "Turned aside" (ektrapēsontai) has a medical usage referring to the dislocation of the limbs, a wrenching out of place. Hence Paul is stating that those who turn away from the truth leave themselves vulnerable to be wrenched out of joint spiritually by satanic influence.

D. *The continuation of the charge* (v. 5).

But you, be sober in all things, suffer hardship, do an evangelist's work, carry out fully your ministry (v. 5).

1. Be sober in all things (*nēphe en pasin*).

From the primary sense of drinking no wine comes the metaphor of being watchful and alert. In view of the tendencies in the church previously mentioned, Timothy is to stay clear of all motives and persons and teachings which might spiritually stupefy.

2. Suffer hardship (*kakopathēson*).

One of the accompaniments of the Christian life is the bearing of burdens which would not otherwise have to be endured. So Timothy is charged to suffer the ills which are the lot of believers in this unbelieving world. Yet Paul was not laying upon Timothy a burden which he himself had not borne. But though previously, he had urged Timothy to "suffer with him" in this matter (2 Tim. 1:8), now Timothy must stand alone, for Paul would soon be gone.

3. Do an evangelist's work (*ergon poiēson euaggelistou*).

The gift of the evangelist (Eph. 4:11) was a special endowment for announcing the good news of salvation. Philip is called "the evangelist" (Acts 21:8). In this charge to Timothy, the absence of an article before "evangelist" indicates the type or quality of work is being stressed, rather than some official position. In his pastoral duties, he is not to forget the unsaved, but must always be concerned with announcing the good news of man's redemption through Christ.

4. Carry out fully your ministry (*tēn diakonian sou plērophorēson*).

All elements of his service to God among the Ephesians—evangelizing, teaching, pastoring—must be conscientiously performed. No halfhearted, professional performance will satisfy the spiritual needs of God's people.

E. *The encouragement toward the charge* (vv. 6-8).
For I already am being poured out, and the season of
my departure is present. I have contended in the good
contest, I have finished the course, I have kept the faith;
as to the rest there is laid up for me the crown of the
righteousness, which the Lord the righteous Judge shall
award me in that day, and not only to me but even to all
who have loved his appearing (vv. 6-8).

1. The experience of Paul.

Encouragement for Timothy to carry out his responsibilities is provided by the example of Paul who now faces
the end of his career. *Spendomai* is a liturgical word and
signifies the pouring out of a religious libation or drink-
offering. The metaphor was supplied by Jewish custom,
in which a libation of wine was added to the sacrifice
proper as the last act (cf. Num. 15:1-10). Paul regarded his
ministry in winning the lost to faith in Christ as an offering to God (Rom. 15:16; Phil. 2:17), and his approaching
death would complete the sacrifice. The series of events
which would culminate in death in a few weeks or
months had already started, and Paul was fully cognizant
of these facts. "Departure" (*analuseōs*) suggests the taking down of a tent, breaking camp by an army, removal of
shackles, or weighing anchor. The term was used in all
these senses, any of which could have provided the
metaphor for Paul. However, it was also commonly used
to mean "death," and perhaps we should not press the
figure.

Paul's testimony that he had contended in the good
contest is not a note of personal pride (not KJV, "have
fought a good fight"), but is a joyful note that he had spent
his labors in the good contest, which is the realm of Christian faith (1 Tim. 6:12). The metaphor is probably an
athletic one as was usual with Paul, but Simpson shows
how it could be military.[10] Every Christian is in the good
contest.

From a general reference to the athletic field, Paul narrows the events to the foot race, and states that he has now completed the course. His service for God was at an end. Paul's ambition was to complete his course with no regrets (Acts 20:24). He wanted to end as well as he had begun, and now he has done so. How great is the tragedy when Christians and particularly ministers become disqualified in old age (1 Cor. 9:25).

In all of Paul's labors he had kept the faith. He had guarded and thus preserved (tetērēka) intact the gospel message entrusted to him. This meant defending it against attacks from Judaizers, pagan philosophers, and unspiritual compromisers. Perhaps Paul continues his metaphor by regarding it as the rule whereby the race is run (2:5). We along with Timothy may be encouraged by the experience of Paul and determine to hold fast the truth of God which constitutes the Christian faith.

2. The prospect for Paul.

At the end of the course there was awaiting the victor's crown (stephanos). In the games this crown was a laurel wreath placed upon the head of the winner. Other uses of stephanos show it could signify a crown worn by a ruler, but the connotation of victory was probably always present (Rev. 4:4). The crown Paul awaited was the crown which belonged to "the righteousness." Probably this was a reward to be given for pursuing the practical righteousness which pleases God. It is suggested by some, however, that it refers to imputed righteousness which is even now possessed by believers, but in "that day" of Christ's appearing will shine forth as a crown.

The reward for a life of righteousness will be awarded by the righteous Judge. There will be no favoritism nor unfair decision. But the reward for righteous living is certain. Since salvation is the free gift of God wholly unmerited by men, He will reward men for any righteous acts they do lest they be misunderstood as producing salvation.

3. The encouragement for Timothy.

Paul names the greatest incentive for living righteously: the coming of Christ (1 John 3:2-3). One who loves Christ's coming is one who is living righteously, but he whose life is sinful will dread that day. The crown Paul anticipated will be granted also to Timothy and to others who have run the course successfully (1 Cor. 9:25). The coming of Christ, when He shall gloriously be vindicated (*epiphaneian*) and put down His foes, should be longed for and loved by every believer.

Concluding References (4:9-22)

A. *Timothy is instructed to come to Paul quickly (vv. 9-13, 21a).*

Be diligent to come to me quickly; for Demas abandoned me, having loved the present age, and went to Thessalonica, Crescens to Galatia, Titus to Dalmatia; Luke is alone with me. Having picked up Mark, bring with yourself, for he is useful to me for ministering. And Tychicus I have sent to Ephesus. The cloak which I left in Troas with Carpus, bring when you come, and the books, especially the parchments . . . be diligent to come before winter (vv. 9-13, 21a).

1. The reason for this urgent call was that Paul was practically alone.

   a. Demas had abandoned Paul.

"Abandoned" is from *en* (in), *kata* (down), *leipō* (leave), and suggests our expression, "left in the lurch." It depicts one who has left his companion down in the clutch of circumstances. Demas had previously been a valued fellow laborer (Col. 4:14; Philemon 24), just a few years before. Now he has fallen victim to loving this present age (*ton nun aiōna*). What a contrast to that which God expects, that we should love the appearing of His Son (v. 8)!

The "age" is "all that mass of thoughts, opinions, maxims, speculations, hopes, impulses, aims, aspirations, at any time current in the world, which it may be impossible to seize and accurately define, but which constitute a most real and effective power, being the moral, or immoral, atmosphere which at every moment of our lives we inhale, again inevitably to exhale—all this is included in *aiōn.* . . ."[11] Such a statement does not necessarily imply that Demas had completely forsaken Christ, but he had surely forsaken Paul. Furthermore, his interest in the present life to the neglect of the hereafter is a most dangerous course to follow. Some infer that his trip to Thessalonica was a return to his home, especially since in Philemon 24 he is listed with Aristarchus, a Thessalonican (Acts 20:4).

      b. Crescens had gone to Galatia.

      Since he and Titus are not given any sort of blame, as was Demas, there is not sufficient warrant to suspect their motives. They went out in the Lord's service, perhaps at Paul's direction. (The reason why Paul uses "I sent" with Tychicus only, and not with Crescens and Titus, is explained by its function as an epistolary aorist.) Crescens is named in the New Testament only in this instance.

      c. Titus had gone to Dalmatia.

      Dalmatia lay directly east across the Adriatic Sea from Italy. Doubtless we are to infer that Titus was engaged in Christian ministry also.

      d. Luke was Paul's only companion as he wrote.

      This note portrays the heroism of Luke, as well as the loneliness of Paul.

   2. Timothy is instructed to bring Mark with him.

Here is encouragement for servants of God who at some time have known the bitterness of failure. Since his initial lapse (Acts 13:13; 15:36-41), Mark had proved himself a worthy Christian leader, recognized as such by Paul (Col. 4:10; Philemon 24). Now Paul clearly states that there is a good use (*euchrēstos*) for him in the service of Christ.

   3. Timothy's place at Ephesus will be supplied by Tychicus.

The aorist "I sent" (*apesteila*) is epistolary, and thus may well indicate that Tychicus would be the bearer of this letter. When Timothy would receive the letter at the hand of Tychicus, he would be informed in it by Paul, "Tychicus I have sent to Ephesus." Tychicus was from the province of Asia, and was one of Paul's trusted associates (Acts 20:4; Eph. 6:21; Col. 4:7; Titus 3:12). He is given high praise (Col. 4:7).

4. Timothy is instructed to bring Paul's cloak, books, and parchments.

These items Paul had left with Carpus, an otherwise unknown Christian at Troas, at a visit during his freedom between imprisonments (see pages 21 and 50). The cloak (*phailonēn*) was a long cape of extremely heavy material, not needed in summer traveling, but most important for the winter ahead. "The books" (*ta biblia*) are probably the papyrus sheets or rolls, and the parchments (*tas membranas*) are better quality rolls or books made from skins. The parchments may have been Old Testament portions. Some suggest that the papyrus was for writing, and the parchments for reading. However, I think both were reading matter, for writing materials could probably be obtained without this special trip.

It should be remarked that even with approaching death, Paul never lost interest in studies. Even the inspired apostle did not discount reading. Every preacher should take notice. Books are tools. The quality of some sermons heard today makes one suspicious that some preachers have not read a serious book since they graduated from seminary.

5. Timothy is urged to come before winter (v. 21a).

Paul knew the rigors and dangers of winter traveling (Acts 27). He needed the cloak for cold days in the dungeon. He also craved Christian fellowship with his younger friend. Did Timothy get to Rome in time? Christian hearts sincerely hope he did. (Heb. 13:23 calls

Timothy an ex-prisoner, which circumstances might have occurred in Rome, but nothing certain is known.)

B. *Timothy is warned against Alexander the coppersmith* (vv. 14-15).

Alexander the coppersmith showed me many evils. The Lord will repay him in accord with his works. Whom also you continue guarding yourself against, for he greatly withstood our words (vv. 14-15).

Since the name "Alexander" was so common, there must be more evidence than the name to identify this antagonist with the Alexander of 1 Timothy 1:20, or the enigmatic figure of Acts 19:33. The fact that he is called a coppersmith (*chalkeus* may also refer to a worker in other metals) does not relate him to Acts 19, for there Demetrius was the silversmith (a different word used), and Alexander is not said to be a metal worker at all. Rather, the description "coppersmith" serves to distinguish this man from other Alexanders in the New Testament.

The occasion when Alexander opposed Paul can only be conjectured. In view of the following verses, one is tempted to explain the opposition as occurring at Paul's hearing before the courts. However, Alexander seems to have been at Ephesus, not Rome, for Timothy is warned to be on guard against him. We must infer, therefore, that he was an opponent of the gospel and of Paul personally on many previous occasions.

Though Paul suffered from the opposition of Alexander, he knew that God would render him his due reward for those malicious acts. This was not an imprecation but a statement of fact (*apodōsei* is future indicative, not optative). As long as personal vindictiveness does not enter, this remark of Paul should not be deplored, for it is not wrong to trust in God's final victory over the forces of evil. If we rejoice in a God of justice, then we should also rejoice in His putting down of injustice.

C. *Timothy is informed of Paul's first defense* (vv. 16-18).

In my first defense no one supported me, but all abandoned me. May it not be put to their account. But the Lord stood by me and empowered me, in order that through me the proclamation might be fully carried out and all the gentiles might hear, and I was delivered out of the lion's mouth. The Lord will deliver me from every evil work and will save for his heavenly kingdom. To whom be the glory forever and ever, Amen (vv. 16-18).

1. Human aids who should have supported Paul forsook him.

The first defense (*prōtēi apologiāi*) was apparently a preliminary hearing at which the charge was read and Paul had opportunity to make an initial statement. No one came to be beside Paul to vouch for his statements (classical usage of *paraginomai* was "to second"), or act as his helper and advocate. We know too few facts to allow a full understanding here. The reference may mean that men of influence whose testimony would have strengthened his case could not be found. It may mean that none of his friends at all were there. (Luke may not have arrived in Rome in time.) Whatever the reason, Paul felt abandoned but not vengeful, and prayed that their failure would not be held against them by the Lord.

2. The Lord stood by him and delivered from immediate danger.

But in contrast to the insufficiency of human aid, the Lord took His stand beside Paul (*parestē*) and infused him with power (*enedunamōsen*). The purpose (*hina*) of this divine enabling was that the proclamation of the gospel (*kērugma*) might be fully made to this significant Roman audience. The Roman officials who heard Paul's defense were also made the recipients of an inspired recital of the gospel.

The presence and power of the Lord also rescued Paul from the lion's mouth. This well-known metaphor is found also in Psalm 22:21. Various attempts to identify the lion as Nero, the devil, or wild beasts seem inadequate if not completely wrong. Paul's Roman citizenship would have secured him from being thrown to the wild beasts. To refer the "lion" to Nero would indicate acquittal, and this was not the case. Rather, it seems to be a figure of extreme and immediate danger, and from this he was spared at that time. He was not executed immediately, but his case was deferred. However, Paul had no doubts about the outcome (4:6).

Towering above the immediate dreary circumstances was Paul's unshaken faith in the preserving power of his Lord. Just as Christ had stood by him and delivered from immediate death, so He would continue to deliver him from every evil work. The absence of the article in the phrase, plus the use of "every" (*pantos*) prevents undue restriction upon the "evil work." Hence we may view it passively as the evil deeds plotted against him by others, and actively as evil works which Paul himself might do. From all these possibilities, the Lord will provide protection and deliverance. Nothing would prevent Paul's participation in the joys of Christ's heavenly kingdom, a kingdom which at His coming will be established upon the earth. Small wonder that Paul can exult in this doxology!

D. *Greetings are sent to Paul's friends* (v. 19).

> Greet Prisca and Aquila, and the house of Onesiphorus (v. 19).

Prisca (called by the less formal "Priscilla" in Acts) and Aquila were close friends of the apostle since his second missionary journey (Acts 18:2). They had lived in Rome for a time, although Aquila was a native of Pontus in Asia Minor. After a residence of some length in Corinth, they traveled as far as Ephesus with Paul (Acts 18:19). There they were used of God in leading Apollos into full Christian faith. Now as Paul writes, we find them still at Ephesus.

Onesiphorus was mentioned in 2 Timothy 1:16-18 (see

discussion on those vv.). Paul evidently knew that One-siphorus had not returned to his household at Ephesus, and thus he does not specifically include him in the greeting. The notion that he was dead is unfounded.

E. *Paul's fellow workers are indicated* (v. 20).

> Erastus remained in Corinth; and Trophimus being sick I left behind in Miletus (v. 20).

Two men named Erastus appear elsewhere in the New Testament. One was the city treasurer, apparently of Corinth (Rom. 16:33). The mention of Corinth makes the identification of the Erastus in 4:20 with the city treasurer appealing, but it seems unlikely that this official would have been an itinerant missionary. The other Erastus was an associate of Paul (Acts 19:22) and is most likely to be understood here.

Trophimus, the Ephesian who had been a traveling companion of Paul on the third journey and provided the occasion for the uproar in the Temple at Jerusalem (Acts 21:29), was left behind at Miletus as Paul had journeyed to Rome for the final time (see page 22). The reason was illness which made traveling impossible. Evidently Paul did not practice divine healing on all, not even upon his close associates.

F. *Greetings are sent from Paul's companions* (v. 21b).

> Eubulus greets you, and Pudens and Linus and Claudia and all the brethren (v. 21b).

These persons are not otherwise known by name in the New Testament. They belong to the group of Roman believers known mutually to Timothy and Paul. Irenaeus, writing in the second century, states that Peter and Paul appointed Linus as the first bishop of the church at Rome.[12] However, he also claims that Peter and Paul founded the church at Rome, a note which conflicts with every scriptural indication. Thus the whole statement of Irenaeus must be viewed with suspicion.

G. Benediction (v. 22).

The Lord [be] with thy spirit. The grace [be] with you (v. 22).

The best manuscript evidence omits "Jesus Christ" from the designation. One should notice in this closing benediction the change in pronouns from the singular "thy" (sou), referring to Timothy alone, to the plural "you" (humōn), which widens the scope to include all readers of this letter. Even though this letter was intimately personal in many places, it had also a wider audience in view, and thus it is properly regarded by the church as one of her sacred treasures, in which the Lord of the church has made known His will to believers through the pen of His intrepid apostle.

With these three letters Paul's literary life was ended. How provident was our all-wise God in preserving His apostle, through the vicissitudes of a most exhausting career, until these remarkable letters were penned! Without them the Christian church would be much the poorer. In them the Christian has found instruction for his local congregation. He is warned of religious charlatans who have employed many of the same principles for nineteen centuries. He has received encouragement to remain faithful in adversity. And he has been given in Paul and his younger colleagues an example of the true apostolic succession—the committal of the sacred message by one generation to the next. It was Paul's attitude toward the gospel that explains his career. Who can doubt the divine nature of a gospel which can change a blasphemer into an apostle, and though it brought incredible sufferings in its wake, still was glorious to contemplate and was a comfort in the face of execution? Millions of Christians along with Paul have found it so.

NOTES

[1]Guy H. King, *To My Son* (London: Marshall, Morgan and Scott, Ltd., 1944), pp. 17-18.

[2]William F. Arndt and F. Wilbur Gingrich, *A Greek-English Lexicon of the New Testament* (Chicago: U. of Chicago, 1957), p. 645. Copyright 1957 by the University of Chicago.

[3]Alford, p. 558.

[4]William F. Arndt and F. Wilbur Gingrich, *A Greek-English Lexicon of the New Testament* (Chicago: U. of Chicago, 1957), p. 256. Copyright 1957 by the University of Chicago.

[5]Simpson, p. 137.

[6]Lenski, 839.

[7]Simpson, p. 150.

[8]Wuest, p. 152.

[9]Vincent, p. 321.

[10]Simpson, pp. 155-56.

[11]Trench, pp. 217-18.

[12]Irenaeus, p. 416.

APPENDIX A

NEW WORDS IN 1 TIMOTHY

1. Proper Names (3):

    Ἀλέξανδρος   Ὑμέναιος
    Πόντιος

2. Words used by Paul in Acts (11):

ἀντιλαμβάνω	περιποιέω
εὐσεβέω	Πιλάτος
ἱματισμός	πρεσβυτέριον
νεότης	προσέχω
παραδέχομαι	σωφρωσύνη
παραιτέομαι	

3. Cognates used by Paul in the epistles or Acts (55).
   Here are listed the words in 1 Timothy, after which
   is placed in parenthesis the cognate form found in the
   epistles or Acts:

    ἀγαθοεργέω (ἀγαθουργέω—Acts)
    ἀδηλότης (ἀδήλως—Ep.)
    αἰσχροκερδής (prefix αἰσχρο- — Ep.)

299

ἄλλως (ἄλλος—Fp.)
ἀνόσιος (ὅσιος—Acts; Heb.)
ἀπέραντος (πέρας—Ep.)
ἀπόβλητος (ἀποβολή—Ep., Acts)
ἀπόδεκτος (ἀποδέχομαι—Acts)
ἀποδοχή (ἀποδέχομαι—Acts)
ἀποθησαυρίζω (θησαυρίζω—Ep.)
ἀποπλανάω (πλανάω—Ep.)
ἀργός (καταργέω—Ep.)
ἄσπιλος (σπίλος—Ep.)
βίος (βίωσις—Acts, βιωτικός—Ep.)
βλάσφημος (βλασφημία—Ep.)
βυθίζω (βυθός—Ep.)
δέον (δεῖ—Ep.)
διαβεβαιόομαι (βεβαιόω—Ep.)
διατροφή (τροφή—Acts)
διδακτικός (διδακτός—Ep.)
διώκτης (διωγμός, διώκω—Ep.)
ἑδραίωμα (ἑδραῖος—a Pauline word)
ἐκζήτησις (ἐκζητέω—Ep.)
ἔντευξις (ἐντυγχάνω—Ep.)
ἐπισκοπή (ἐπίσκοπος—Ep.)
εὐμετάδοτος (μεταδίδωμι—Ep.)
εὐσέβεια (εὐσεβέω—Acts)
ἡσύχιος (ἡσυχία, ἡσυχάζω—Ep.)
κατηγορία (κατηγορέω—Ep.)
κενοφωνία (prefix κενο- — Ep.)
κήρυξ (κήρυγμα—Ep.)
κοινωνικός (κοινός, κοινωνέω, κοινωνία, κοινωνός—Ep.)
κτίσμα (κτίζω, κτίσις—Ep.)
λοιδορία (λοιδορέω, λοίδορος—Ep.)
μαρτυρία (μαρτυρέω, μαρτύριον, μαρτύρομαι, μάρτυς—Ep.)
ματαιολογία (μάταιος, ματαιότης, ματαιόομαι—Ep.)
μελετάω (μέλει—Ep.)
μετάληψις (μεταλαμβάνω—Acts)
μονόω (μόνος—Ep.)

νηφάλιος (νήφω—Ep.)
νομίμως (νόμος—Ep.)
ὁμολογουμένως (ὁμολογέω—Ep.)
παραθήκη (παρατίθημι—Ep.)
σεμνότης (σεμνός—Ep.)
σωματικός (σωματικῶς—Ep.)
σώφρων (σωφρονέω—Ep.)
ὑπερπλεονάζω (πλεονάζω—Ep.)
ὑπόνοια (ὑπονοέω—Acts)
ὑποτύπωσις (τύπος—Ep.)
ὕστερος (ὑστερέω, ὑστέρημα—Ep.)
φιλαργυρία (prefix φιλα- — Ep.)
φιλόξενος (φιλοξενία—Ep.)
ψευδολόγος (prefix ψευδο- — Ep.)
ψευδώνυμος (prefix ψευδο- — Ep.)
ὠφέλιμος (ὠφελέω—Ep.)

4. Words used in Hebrews (23):
ἀμελέω
ἀνυπότακτος
ἀπόλαυσις
ἀρνέομαι
ἀφιλάργυρος
βέβηλος
γυμνάζω
εἰσφέρω
ἐκτρέπω
ἐκφέρω
ἐμπίπτω
ἐπίθεσις
ἐπιλαμβάνω
ἐπίσταμαι
ὀρέγω
ὅσιος
περιέρχομαι
πρεσβύτερος

προάγω
πρόδηλος
προσέρχομαι
τάχιον
χείρων

5. Words or cognates used by Luke (29).
In the following listing, if a cognate appears, it is given in parenthesis:

ἁγνεία (ἁγνίζω)
αἰδώς (ἀναιδία)
ἄμαχος (θεομάχος)
βαθμός (ἀναβαθμός)
βλαβερός (βλάπτω)
βραδύνω (βραδυπλοέω)
δεσπότης
δυνάστης (in Luke and Acts only)
ἐντρέφω (τρέφω)
ἐπιμελέομαι (in Luke only)
ἐπιτίθημι
εὐεργεσία (in Acts only, cognates are Lukan only)
ζήτησις
ζῳογονέω (in Luke and Acts only)
θνήσκω
κατασιολή (καταστέλλω)
κοσμέω
κόσμιος (κοσμέω)
λογομαχία (θεομάχος)
νομοδιδάσκαλος (in Luke and Acts only)
νοσέω (νόσος)
οἰκοδεσποτέω (οἰκοδεσπότης)
παρακολουθέω
περίεργος
πορισμός (εὐπορία, εὐπορέω)
πρόσκλησις (προσκλίνω)
προσμένω

πυκνός
ὑγιαίνω

6. Words without other Pauline or Lukan usage (54):
ἀμοιβή
ἀνδραποδιστής
ἀνδροφόνος
ἀνεπίλημπτος
ἀντίθεσις
ἀντίλυτρον
ἀπρόσιτος
ἀστοχέω
αὐθεντέω
γενεαλογία
γυμνασία
γραώδης
διάγω
ἀνδραποδιστής
δίλογος
διπλόος
ἔκγονος
ἐξήκοντα
ἐπακολουθέω
ἐπαρκέω
ἐπίορκος
ἐπιπλήσσω
ἑτεροδιδασκαλέω
ἤρεμος
θεοσέβεια
καταλέγομαι
καταστρηνιάω
καυστηριάζω
μαργαρίτης
μητρολῴας
μῦθος
νεόφυτος
νίπτω

ξενοδοχέω
πάροινος
πατρολῴας
περιπείρω
πλέγμα
πλήκτης
πολυτελής
προϋπάθια
πρόγονος
πρόκριμα
ῥητῶς
σκέπασμα
σπαταλάω
στόμαχος
τεκνογονέω
τεκνογονία
τεκνοτροφέω
τυφόω
ὑδροποτέω
ὑψηλοφρονέω
φλύαρος

APPENDIX B

STRICTLY PAULINE WORDS IN 1 TIMOTHY

In the following list of thirty-two words, if the other Pauline usage is in Acts or Hebrews, it is so noted:

ἀγών
ἀθανασία
ἀλοάω
ἀνέγκλητος
ἀόρατος
ἀρσενοκοίτης
αὐτάρκεια
γνήσιος
ἐνδείκνυμι
ἐνδυναμόω (by Paul in Acts)
ἐξαπατάω
ἐπιταγή
ἐπιφάνεια
ἔρις
μεσίτης (Heb.)
ναυαγέω

ὀδύνη
οἰκεῖος
οἰκέω
ὄλεθρος
ὁμολογία   (Heb.)
ὀνειδισμός
παράβασις   (Heb.)
προΐστημι
προκοπή
προνοέω
σεμνός
στρατεία
ὑβριστής
ὑπεροχή
ὑποταγή
ὑποτίθημι

BIBLIOGRAPHY

Alford, Henry. *The New Testament for English Readers.* Vol. 2. London: Rivingtons, 1872.

Arndt, William F., and Gingrich, F. Wilbur. *A Greek-English Lexicon of the New Testament.* Chicago: U. of Chicago, 1957.

Barnes, Albert. "The First Epistle of Paul to Timothy." In *Notes On the Old and New Testaments.* 27 vols. Reprint. Grand Rapids: Baker, 1949.

Barrett, C. K. *The Pastoral Epistles.* Oxford, Clarendon, 1963.

Baxter, J. Sidlow. *Explore the Book.* Vol. 6. London: Marshall, Morgan & Scott, 1955.

Bruce, F. F. *Commentary on the Book of the Acts.* New International Commentary on the New Testament. Grand Rapids: Eerdmans, 1954.

Calvin, John. *Commentaries on the Epistles to Timothy, Titus, and Philemon.* Translated by William Pringle. Grand Rapids: Eerdmans, 1948.

Canfield, Leon Hardy. *The Early Persecutions of the Christians.* New York: Columbia U., 1913.

Clement. *First Epistle to the Corinthians.* The Ante-Nicene Fathers: Translations of the Writings of the Fathers Down to A.D. 35. Edited by Alexander Roberts and James Donaldson, revised by A. Cleveland Coxe, vol. 1. Reprint. Grand Rapids: Eerdmans, 1950.

Clement of Alexandria. *The Stromata.* Translated by William Wilson. The Ante-Nicene Fathers: Translations of the Writings of the Fathers Down to A.D. 35. Edited by Alexander Roberts and James Donaldson, revised by A. Cleveland Coxe, vol. 2. Reprint. Grand Rapids: Eerdmans, 1951.

Constitutions of the Holy Apostles. Translated by William Whiston. The Ante-Nicene Fathers: Translations of the Writings of the Fathers Down to A.D. 35. Edited by Alexander Roberts and James Donaldson, revised by A. Cleveland Coxe, vol. 7. Reprint. Grand Rapids: Eerdmans, 1951.

Conybeare, W. J., and Howson, J. S. *The Life and Epistles of St. Paul.* 1949. Reprint. Grand Rapids: Eerdmans, 1951.

Dana, H. E., and Mantey, Julius R. *A Manual Grammar of the Greek New Testament.* New York: Macmillan, 1946.

Earle, Ralph. "First Timothy." In *The Expositor's Bible Commentary.* Edited by Frank E. Gaebelein, vol. 11. Grand Rapids: Zondervan, 1978.

Ellicott, Charles J. *The Pastoral Epistles of St. Paul.* 5th ed. London: Longmans, Green, and Co., 1883.

Erdman, Charles R. *The Pastoral Epistles of Paul.* Philadelphia: Westminster, 1923.

Eusebius. *The Ecclesiastical History and The Martyrs of Palestine.* Translated by Hugh Jackson Lawlor and John Ernest Leonard Oulton. 2 vols. London: SPCK, 1927.

Fairbairn, Patrick. *The Pastoral Epistles.* Edinburgh: T. & T. Clark, 1874.

Foh, Susan T. *Women and the Word of God.* Philadelphia: Presbyterian and Reformed, 1980.

Foley, Leo P. "The Pastoral Epistles." In *A Commentary on the New Testament.* Edited by E. H. Donze, et al. Kansas City, Mo.: Catholic Biblical Association, 1942.

Gealy, Fred D. Introduction to "The First and Second Epistles to Timothy and the Epistle to Titus." In *The Interpreter's Bible*. Edited by Noland B. Harmon. New York: Abingdon, 1955.

Gundry, Patricia. *Woman Be Free!* Grand Rapids: Zondervan, 1977.

Gurney, T. A. *The First Epistle to Timothy*. 2nd ed. London: Religious Tract Society, 1908.

Guthrie, Donald. *The Pastoral Epistles*. The Tyndale New Testament Commentaries. Grand Rapids: Eerdmans, 1957.

Harrison, P.N. *The Problem of the Pastoral Epistles*. London: Oxford U., 1921.

Hegesippus. *Commentaries on the Acts of the Church*. Translated by B. P. Pratten. The Ante-Nicene Fathers: Translations of the Writings of the Fathers Down to A.D. 35. Edited by Alexander Roberts and James Donaldson, revised by A. Cleveland Coxe, vol. 8. Reprint. Grand Rapids: Eerdmans, 1951.

Hendriksen, William. *Exposition of the Pastoral Epistles*. New Testament Commentary series. Grand Rapids: Baker, 1957.

Hestenes, Roberta, and Curley, Lois, eds. *Women and the Ministries of Christ*. Pasadena, Calif.: Fuller Theological Seminary, 1979.

Hiebert, D. Edmund. *First Timothy*. Chicago: Moody, 1957.

Hohenstein, Lewis C. "She Shall Be Saved Through the Childbearing." Monograph. Winona Lake, Ind.: Grace Theological Seminary, 1949.

Hoyt, Herman A. *All Things Whatsoever I Have Commanded You*. Winona Lake, Ind.: Herman A. Hoyt, 1948.

————. "The Pastoral Epistles." Mimeographed. Winona Lake, Ind.: Grace Theological Seminary, n.d.

————. *This Do in Remembrance of Me*. Winona Lake, Ind.: Herman A. Hoyt, 1947.

Hurlbut, Jesse Lyman. *A Bible Atlas*. New York: Rand McNally, 1938.

Irenaeus. *Against Heresies*. Translated by Alexander Roberts. The Ante-Nicene Fathers: Translations of the Writings of the Fathers Down to A.D. 35. Edited by Alexander Roberts and

James Donaldson, revised by A. Cleveland Coxe, vol. 1. Reprint. Grand Rapids: Eerdmans, 1950.

Ironside, H. A. *Addresses on the First and Second Epistles of Timothy.* New York: Loizeaux Brothers, 1947.

Jerome. *Prolegomena ad Titum.* Translated by J. E. Ryland. The Ante-Nicene Fathers: Translations of the Writings of the Fathers Down to A.D. 35. Edited by Alexander Roberts and James Donaldson, revised by A. Cleveland Coxe, vol. 2. Reprint. Grand Rapids: Eerdmans, 1951.

Jewett, Paul K. *Man as Male and Female.* Grand Rapids: Eerdmans, 1975.

Kelly, J. N. D. *The Pastoral Epistles.* Black's New Testament Commentaries. London: Adam & Charles Black, 1963.

Kelly, William. *An Exposition of the Two Epistles to Timothy.* 3rd ed. London: C. A. Hammond, 1948.

King, Guy H. *A Leader Led.* London: Marshall, Morgan & Scott, 1951.

————. *To My Son.* London: Marshall, Morgan & Scott, 1944.

Lenski, R. C. H. *The Interpretation of the Acts of the Apostles.* Columbus, Ohio: Wartburg, 1944.

————.*The Interpretation of St. Paul's Epistles to the Colossians, to the Thessalonians, to Timothy, to Titus, and to Philemon.* Columbus, Ohio: Wartburg, 1937.

Liddell, Henry George, and Scott, Robert. *A Greek-English Lexicon.* New ed. Revised by Henry Stuart Jones. 2 vols. Oxford: Clarendon, 1940.

Lidden, H. P. *Explanatory Analysis of St. Paul's First Epistle to Timothy.* Minneapolis, Minn.: Klock & Klock, 1897.

Lightfoot, J. B. *The Apostolic Fathers.* 3 vols. London: Macmillan, 1889.

————. *The Epistles of S. Clement of Rome.* London: Macmillan, 1869.

Lock, Walter. *A Critical and Exegetical Commentary on the Pastoral Epistles.* The International Critical Commentary. New York: Scribner's, 1924.

Makrakis, Apostolos. *Interpretation of the Entire New Testa-

ment. Translated by Albert George Alexander. Vol. 2. Chicago: Orthodox Christian Educational Society, 1950.

Moffatt, James. *Encyclopaedia Brittanica.* 1946 ed., s.v. "Pastoral Epistles."

Mollenkott, Virginia Ramey. *Women, Men and the Bible.* Nashville: Abingdon, 1977.

Moulton, James Hope. *A Grammar of New Testament Greek.*
Vol. 1, 3rd ed. Edinburgh: T. & T. Clark, 1908.

Moulton, James Hope, and Milligan, George. *The Vocabulary of
the Greek Testament.* Grand Rapids: Eerdmans, 1949.

Nestle, Eberhard, ed. *Greek New Testament.* Revised by Erwin
Nestle. Stuttgart: Privileg. Wurtt. Bibelanstalt, 1936.

Newman, Albert Henry. *A Manual of Church History.* Vol. 1,
rev. ed. Philadelphia: American Baptist Publication Society,
1933.

Plummer, Alfred. "The Pastoral Epistles." In *The Expositor's
Bible.* Edited by W. Robertson Nicoll, vol. 6. Reprint. Grand
Rapids: Eerdmans, 1943.

Purdy, Warren E. "The Meaning of the Phrase 'Saviour of All
Men' in First Timothy 4:10." Monograph. Winona Lake, Ind.:
Grace Theological Seminary, 1954.

Rackham, Richard Belward. *The Acts of the Apostles.* London:
Methuen, 1901.

Ramsay, W. M. *The Church in the Roman Empire.* Reprint.
Grand Rapids: Baker, 1954.

————. *The Cities of St. Paul.* 1949. Reprint. Grand Rapids:
Baker, 1960.

————. *St. Paul the Traveller and the Roman Citizen.* Reprint. Grand Rapids: Baker, 1949.

Raymond, Irvin Woodworth. *The Teaching of the Early Church
on the Use of Wine and Strong Drink.* New York: Columbia
U., 1927.

Reynolds, H. R. "The Pastoral Epistles." In *The Expositor,* vol.
1. London: Hodder and Stoughton, 1875.

Robertson, A. T. *A Grammar of the Greek New Testament in the
Light of Historical Research.* Nashville: Broadman, 1934.

————. *Word Pictures in the New Testament*, vol. 4. New York: Harper, 1931.

Rutherford, John. "Pastoral Epistles." In *The International Standard Bible Encyclopaedia*, 5 vols., edited by James Orr. Grand Rapids: Eerdmans, 1955.

Scanzoni, Letha, and Hardesty, Nancy. *All We're Meant to Be*. Waco, Tex.: Word, 1974.

Schaff, Philip. *History of the Christian Church*. 8 vols. 1930. Reprint. Grand Rapids: Eerdmans, 1960. Vol. 1, *Apostolic Christianity*.

Shepard, J. W. *The Life and Letters of St. Paul*. Grand Rapids: Eerdmans, 1950.

Simpson, E. K. *The Pastoral Epistles*. Grand Rapids: Eerdmans, 1950.

Sitzinger, Michael F. "The Function and Authority of Women in the Church: Biblical Hierarchy versus Feminine Egalitarianism." Master's thesis, Grace Theological Seminary, 1980.

Snyder, Howard A. "Woman's Place." *Light and Life* 114, no. 2 (February 1981)

Spence, H. D. M. *The Epistles to Timothy and Titus*. Ellicott's Commentary on the Whole Bible. Edited by Charles John Ellicott, vol. 8. Grand Rapids: Zondervan, n.d.

Stirling, John. *An Atlas Illustrating the Acts of the Apostles and the Epistles*. London: George Philip and Son, 1954.

Tertullian. *Against Marcion*. Translated by Peter Holmes. The Ante-Nicene Fathers: Translations of the Writings of the Fathers Down to A.D. 35. Edited by Alexander Roberts and James Donaldson, revised by A. Cleveland Coxe, vol. 3. Reprint. Grand Rapids: Eerdmans, 1951.

————. *On Prescription Against Heretics*. Translated by Peter Holmes. The Ante-Nicene Fathers: Translations of the Writings of the Fathers Down to A.D. 35. Edited by Alexander Roberts and James Donaldson, revised by A. Cleveland Coxe, vol. 3. Reprint. Grand Rapids: Eerdmans, 1951.

Thayer, Joseph Henry. *A Greek-English Lexicon of the New Testament*. Rev. ed. New York: American Book Co., 1889.

Thiessen, Henry Clarence. *Introduction to the New Testament.* 3rd ed. Grand Rapids: Eerdmans, 1943.

Trench, Richard Chenevix. *Synonyms of the New Testament.* 1948. Reprint. Grand Rapids: Eerdmans, 1950.

Van Oosterzee, J. J. "The Two Epistles of Paul to Timothy." Translated by E. A. Washburn and E. Harwood. In *A Commentary on the Holy Scriptures.* Edited by John Peter Lange and Philip Schaff, vol. 8. New York: Scribner's, 1915.

Vincent, Marvin R. *Word Studies in the New Testament.* Vol. 4. Reprint. Grand Rapids: Eerdmans, 1946.

Westcott, Brooke Foss, and Hort, Fenton John Anthony, eds. *The New Testament in the Original Greek.* New York: Macmillan, 1947.

White, Newport J. D. *The First and Second Epistles to Timothy and the Epistle to Titus.* The Expositor's Greek Testament. Edited by E. Robertson Nicoll, vol. 4. Grand Rapids: Eerdmans, n.d.

Wright, George Ernest, and Filson, Floyd Vivian, eds. *Westminster Historical Atlas to the Bible.* Philadelphia: Westminster, 1945.

Wuest, Kenneth S. *The Pastoral Epistles in the Greek New Testament.* Grand Rapids: Eerdmans, 1953.

Zahn, Theodor. *Introduction to the New Testament.* Translated by John Moore Trout, et al. Vol. 2. Reprint. Grand Rapids: Kregel, 1953.